Suburban Motel

George F. Walker

Talonbooks
1997

Published with the assistance of the Canada Council.

Talonbooks
#104—3100 Production Way
Burnaby, British Columbia, Canada V5A 4R4

Typeset in New Baskerville and printed and bound in Canada by Hignell
Printing Ltd.

First Printing: September 1997

Talonbooks are distributed in Canada by General Distribution Services,
30 Lesmill Road, Don Mills, Ontario, Canada, M3B 2T6; Tel: (416) 445-3333;
Fax: (416) 445-5967.

Talonbooks are distributed in the U. S. A. by General Distribution Services
Inc., 85 Rock River Drive, Suite 202, Buffalo, New York, U.S.A., 14207-2170;
Tel.: 1-800-805-1083; Fax: 1-800-481-6207.

Canadian Cataloguing in Publication Data

Walker, George F., 1947-
  Suburban Motel

  Plays
  ISBN 0-88922-379-3

  I. Title.
PS8595.A557S92 1997   C812'.54   C97-910726-1
PR9199.3.W342S92 1997

Contents

Introduction *by Daniel De Raey*.............................4

Problem Child 7

Adult Entertainment...50

Criminal Genius 105

Featuring Loretta 157

The End of Civilization.....................................213

Risk Everything...264

Suburban Motel is a group of plays, all set in the same slightly rundown motel room, each play made to stand on its own.

Chords: Lost and Vocal
An Introduction

I had the idea that the world's so full of pain
it must sometimes make a kind of singing
Robert Hass

With *Suburban Motel*, George F. Walker adds significantly to an already impressive body of work. These new plays, each of which can stand alone (or be done in combination with any other[s]), live in even richer, darker, funnier, sadder, more tender places than any of his previous work. He once again brings characters who are usually presented by writers marginally, if at all, to the full light of center stage. On the fringes, these characters are barely visible, never audible, seem vaguely cloddish and are certainly easy to miss. In Walker's center stage light, however, they are seen to be vivid, articulate, perceptive and never to be forgotten.

The six plays all take place in the same motel room, a stopover between yesterday and tomorrow, assuming (and don't assume too glibly) that today can be survived, and through this room pass the hurt and the confused, the haunted and the lost, the desperate, the dumb and the depressed. Ever been there? Come on. Somewhere in your past is one of those plastic motel key rings and a story. I got the very unsettling impression reading these plays that, if they kept coming, eventually I would run into several acquaintances and relatives, and ultimately, no doubt, find myself in that room as well.

In this deceptively unremarkable place, a drab, camouflaged circle of hell with an ice machine, we meet people, blue collar people, standing toe-to-toe with life; groping it, throttling it, pulling it closer or fending it off, and in the process coming to some greater self-awareness that usually scalds as it enlightens. Can any of this be funny? Yes, very. However, as in all of Walker's work, the heartier the laugh, the more likely it is to be keeping company with a tear or a shudder. This is work in which, to take a line of Seamus Heaney's, wit confronts hurt and holds a balance that deserves to be called wisdom.

Walker is a master of humor without attitude, of laughter honestly earned from situations and never at the expense of the characters. This is not the clubby "aren't we better than they are" comedy of superiority. These plays will not give you a platform from which to sneer—indeed, the high moral ground here often seems like a sinkhole—nor will they put these characters on pedestals for you to admire—pedestals in sinkholes are precarious at best. You will, instead, have to encounter these characters at eye level. You may discover in these people a certain bare-knuckled integrity that makes them both very accessible and very difficult to pass judgment on. Walker's moral compass sometimes seems to have no needle, but it always makes a sound suspiciously like a human heartbeat. This is work that will allow you to nod sagely only with a quizzical expression on your face, and even that only after you have caught your breath. It is versatile comedy that is in the very sinews of the work itself, operating the muscles that can as easily tweak your nose as give you a rabbit punch to the heart or a good, swift kick in the ass. What do you wear to an evening like that?

It has been more than 12 years now since I first became aware of Walker's work, and in that time I have acted in three of his plays, been involved in the production of two more, and directed six others (including the first productions of three of the plays in this volume). I've also become a friend of the man and a real fan of the work. It is no exaggeration to say that I have learned more about theatre by doing the plays of George Walker than from any other single source.

I always enjoy and grow from working with actors, but working with actors on a Walker play is always a very special experience. I think this is mostly because actors immediately recognize text that cries out to be inhabited by complete, complex human beings—beings who make their way through the world not just with their brains and a little bag of tricks, but with a heart and age-old wise blood, as well as other vital organs and fluids too numerous and indelicate to mention here. Men respond to the opportunity to take off the gloves with this work, and women, even in auditions, revel in shedding the cutesy touches they frequently have to trot out, to deal from their smarter, darker, wilder places. A lot of the fare actors usually get to work on is really watery, and actually needs to be carried by the actors. These plays are water that actors can walk on.

Actors intuit that, in the playing, Walker is more akin to basketball than chess. It's a verbal workout. These characters don't talk for talk's entertainment value. They're far too busy for that. With serious decisions hanging in the balance, they are desperately trying to make sense to each other or to themselves. Even their emotional states are largely dependent on the success or failure of these attempts at sense-making. This involves in-the-moment, intense dealing from the hip and the heart, from which emotions will surely follow.

The human condition is a damnedly complex, messy thing apparently, and Walker will not be caught attempting to wrap it up in neatly tied parcels. The stakes are high, usually life or death, and his respect for these stakes is serious. No one is safe, and almost everyone is sorry, and, as for endings, Walker's stories don't really end, and his characters don't ever lie down—unless, of course, they die. And even then we know that the room will be cleaned up, new people will check in, and life will go on.

Daniel De Raey
New York City, July, 1997

PROBLEM CHILD

PERSONS
R.J.
DENISE
PHILLIE
HELEN

PLACE
A slightly run-down motel on the outskirts of a large city.

Problem Child was first produced by Rattlestick Productions at Theatre Off Park in New York City on May 13, 1997 with the following cast:

R.J. ....Christopner Burns*
DENISE ....Tasha Lawrence*
PHILLIE ....Mark Hammer* / Alan Benson
HELEN...Kathleen Goldpaugh*

Director ....Daniel De Raey
Set Design...Van Santvoord
Lighting Design ....Chad McArver
Costume Design...Rachel Gruer
Sound Design...Laura Grace Brown
Production Manager ....Vicoletta Arlia
Casting...Liz Woodman Casting
Stage Manager...Genia Domico

* *Member of Actors Equity Association*

Scene One

R.J. REYNOLDS is watching TV. DENISE is in the washroom taking a shower. There are two old suitcases on the floor and a small baby crib up against the wall beside the bed.

R.J.: Ah man, will you look at that. That guy is too ugly for that woman. When they bring that woman out she's gonna pass out. You can't do stuff like that. Bring in some good looking woman and tell her she's got a secret admirer then bring her out in front of millions of people to see some ugly guy with pimples on his ears just smiling at her. She's gonna freak out when she sees him. She's gonna be embarrassed. The studio audience is gonna be embarrassed. It's a weak concept for a show so it's gotta be handled just right. Oprah never does this shit.

DENISE comes out of the bathroom. Drying her hair. Wearing a large man's shirt.

DENISE: Can't you do anything besides watch those things.

R.J.: This is life, Denise. Don't be a snob. Just because it's on TV doesn't mean it's not real.

DENISE: Gimme a break.... Mothers who confront their cross-dressing sons. That's your idea of real, eh.

R.J.: What? You think that doesn't happen. When was that anyway.

DENISE: Yesterday.

R.J.: Which one. Jerry Springer? Montel?

DENISE is putting on a pair of jeans.

DENISE: How the hell should I know.... There was that guy in a black garter belt and fish-net stockings and his mother wailing, "I don't mind that he dresses like a woman, but does he have to dress like a slut!"

R.J.: Garter belt, yeah. Sitting next to his mother in a garter belt. Sad. Kind of touching. But too extreme for daytime. What a cool thing for her to say though.

DENISE: *(shaking her head)* Yeah, cool, sure. Man, you are losing your perspective. Turn that thing off. Take a shower. Let's get out of here. Get a meal.

R.J.: Can't leave. She might call.

DENISE: It's been a week, R.J. I'm beginning to lose—

R.J.: A week isn't long. She could still call.

DENISE: We could get the guy in the office to take a message. Whatsisname.

R.J.: Philips. Phillie Philips. Yeah right. I really want to put our future in the hands of a brain-damaged drunk.

DENISE: But I'm going a bit nuts. Maybe I'll go out for a—

R.J.: You gotta stay. She told us to stay put. She was specific. We're on...you know...probation or something. We gotta obey. We'll order in. Something different.... We'll order Siamese.

DENISE: Siamese? What's that.

R.J.: Not Siamese. The other one.

DENISE: What? Szechuan?

R.J.: No.... Indian.

DENISE: Indian? How do you get Indian confused with Siamese?

R.J. is pointing at the TV.

R.J.: Shush. They're bringing her out. This is gonna be awful. The audience knows. Look at their faces.... It's gonna be really embarrassing.... Man, when she sees that guy.... I hate it when it's this embarrassing.... No I can't watch...

R.J. pulls his sweater over his head.
DENISE is in front of a wall mirror. Brushing her hair.

DENISE: What is Siamese food anyway.... I mean is there such a thing.... I guess there must be.... They gotta eat, don't they...the Siamese, I mean.

R.J. pulls down his sweater.

R.J.: Oh man. She's laughing. She's pointing. She's laughing. She's putting her fingers in her mouth. She's making the puking sound. Oh.... oh that's just cruel. Look at the guy. He's devastated. He's ruined for life. Fuck you. Fuck you. Ricky Lake. Enough is enough.

R.J. turns the TV off.

R.J.: I'm disgusted. Did you see that.

DENISE: No.

R.J.: I think I'll write a letter. Yeah. Right now. We got any paper?

DENISE: We don't have anything, R.J.... A change of clothes. That's it.

R.J.: Yeah but.... I have to write that letter!

DENISE: Why are you getting so worked up.

R.J.: Because I'm disgusted.... Life is disgusting.

DENISE: That wasn't life, R.J. It was a TV talk show.

R.J.: Hey that's no more disgusting than life, that show. Life is disgusting like that. Life is the place where dopes like that guy get to be humiliated.... Life is the place that fucks people like you and me up. Life is just like that show.

DENISE: No it's not.

R.J.: Yes it is.... Okay no it's not. It's worse. But I can't do anything about life. I can write that show a letter.

DENISE: Look. Calm down.

R.J.: Forget the letter. I'll call.

DENISE: Who you gonna call? You gonna call Ricky Lake?

R.J.: The network.... Hey I've done this before.

R.J. walks over to the phone.

DENISE: You have?

R.J.: Once. I called Geraldo. When they had that KKK guy on with his grand-child. The old prick had the little kid—eight months old—in a Klan costume. That really disgusted me.

DENISE: I remember that one. That was bad. You called, eh. Why didn't you tell me.

R.J.: Well I didn't get through.... So there was nothing to tell.... But maybe this time I'll—shit!

He has the phone to his ear.

DENISE: What's wrong.

R.J.: It's not working. It's dead.

DENISE: No way. Jesus.

She scrambles over the bed. Grabs the phone. Listens.

DENISE: Ah no. No.... When was the last time you used the phone.

R.J.: I can't...remember.

R.J. is pacing.

R.J.: What is this. Is this fate. Is this a kick in the face from fate. What is it. What.

DENISE: Calm down. We'll get it fixed. We can't do anything except get it fixed. Maybe Phillie will fix it.

R.J.: If he can. If he's even around.

DENISE heads for the windows.

DENISE: I can see if he's in the office from here.

She throws back the drapes. And screams because PHILLIE PHILIPS' unshaven face is pressed against the window.
DENISE is backing up in horror.

DENISE: Jesus. Holy shit. Look at him. Look at him. What's he doin'.

PHILLIE: *(yelling)* Your phone is broken! Your phone is broken!

R.J. runs to the door. Opens it.

R.J.: Why are you on the window, man! What are you doin'!

R.J. goes to PHILLIE. We can see through the window as R.J. pushes PHILLIE.

R.J.: I asked you what the hell you're—

PHILLIE falls over.

R.J.: Shit!

R.J. bends over. DENISE is straining to see. But trying not to get too close. When R.J. straightens he has PHILLIE under his arms and is dragging him towards the door.

DENISE: R.J.? R.J. What are you doing.

R.J.: He's unconscious.

DENISE: Why are you bringing him in here.

R.J.: So he can fix the phone.

DENISE: Like that?

R.J.: Well first we have to revive him.

R.J. manages to get PHILLIE in a chair.

DENISE: God. Look at him. He's so.... Whatya think is wrong with him.

PHILLIE: *(eyes closed)* Drunk! He's drunk.

DENISE and R.J. look at each other

PHILLIE: *(opens eyes)* Yeah he's drunk. He's so drunk he just passed out against our window. Smells too. *(stands unsteadily)* Smells bad. Well why shouldn't he? Do you think he bathes. Not often. Look at him he's so.... he's so. Well what I think is fuck it, wastin' all our time tryin' to figure out what brought him to this sorry state. Let's just shoot him. Bring him out back under the billboard, near the trash in the place where rats live. Fuck it.... *(focuses on DENISE)* Oh yeah, a lady called.... Your phone's busted. Couldn't put her through. Bitch got all...unpleasant.... What did she want. Oh yeah. Something about...something...

DENISE: A baby?

PHILLIE: A what?

DENISE: A baby!?

PHILLIE: What about a baby!? Oh yeah, baby.... She was callin' about a baby!! *(grabs his head)* Shit. All this excitement has made me nauseous.

He rushes into the washroom. Wretching sounds.
R.J. goes to DENISE. Puts his arms around her.

DENISE: This is not good. You told me everything would be all right.... This is not all right.

DENISE moves away from R.J. Another loud wretching sound. R.J. goes toward DENISE.

DENISE: No. Just stay away from me. Suppose she doesn't call back...I said stay the fuck away from me.

R.J.: I was gonna...comfort you. You know?

DENISE: You wanna comfort me? Get the phone fixed.

A wretching sound.
R.J. gestures toward the bathroom.

R.J.: It'll probably be a minute or two more.... I dunno.

DENISE continues to pace. PHILLIE continues to wretch. R.J. continues to look helpless. Blackout.

Scene Two

HELEN MACKIE stands just inside the open door. Wearing a business suit. Carrying a briefcase. DENISE and R.J. are standing. Staring at her.

HELEN: Can I...sit down.

DENISE: Where's the baby...

HELEN: I'm sorry?

DENISE: Didn't you bring the baby.

HELEN: We're a long way from that yet.... Can I sit down.

R.J.: Sure. There.

He points to a chair.

HELEN: Actually over at the table would be better. I've got some paper work.

She sits at the small table in the corner.
DENISE has started to pace.

DENISE: What's she mean we're a long way from that.... Ask her what she means.

HELEN: Did you think this would be easy, Denise.

DENISE: Look I.... I just want to know what she meant.

HELEN: *(to R.J.)* What's wrong with her.

R.J.: Nothing. She's just—

HELEN: She looks pretty...edgy. *(to DENISE)* Are you on any...medication, Denise.

R.J.: No she's—Well we thought you'd be bringing—Look we've been cooped up in here for a week.

HELEN is opening her briefcase. Putting papers on the table. A pad.

HELEN: Why.

DENISE: Why? Waiting for you.

R.J.: Yeah. And we didn't go anywhere. We never left.

HELEN: Never left? I don't get it.

R.J.: You told us to stay put. We stayed put.

HELEN: I never meant you couldn't go out. I just said I'd need a week to get things moving. So you should just—

DENISE: Where's the baby!

HELEN: Denise…. Denise come over here. Sit down.

DENISE: No.

R.J.: Denise.

DENISE: No. I'm not sitting. I'm not doing anything until she tells me where the baby is.

HELEN stands. Goes to DENISE.

HELEN: She's in the same place she's been in for the last six months. She's in a loving foster home. And we can't just take her from a place where she's secure and loved and give her back to you unless we're sure she's going to be okay…. And making sure she's going to be okay takes time. Do you understand. Time and consideration. And…some questions.

R.J.: We'll answer questions. I've already told you that. Any questions.

HELEN: Good…. Now Denise, are you on any medication…. Lift your head. Look at me.

(DENISE obeys)

HELEN: Denise, what's that expression on your face supposed to mean. All that…attitude. You think that's helpful? I'm just doing my job

DENISE: I just…I just thought you were bringing the baby…. I guess I got that wrong.

R.J.: *(to HELEN)* That's my fault. I heard you wrong. Or I misunderstood…. We both got pretty worked up…. The phone was broken…. We were cooped up…. Things…things…

DENISE: I'm not on anything. I haven't been on anything for a long time. We've got doctors' papers. *(to R.J.)* Show her.

R.J.: Where are they.

DENISE: In my suitcase.

(R.J. gets the suitcase)

R.J.: Yeah we've got doctors' papers. We've got a social worker's letter. We've got a letter from our landlord.

DENISE: He's got a job.

R.J.: Yeah. I've got a job…. It's…good…. It's—

DENISE: Okay. It's an okay job. He works for a builder. He does drywall.

R.J.: It's almost a trade…. I've got a letter from my boss.

He hands HELEN a large envelope.

R.J.: They're all in there. All the letters.

HELEN: What about you, Denise.

DENISE: I've been looking. I had a part-time waitress thing. A small restaurant…

R.J.: Well you know, it's a small town. There's not a lot of places where—She put in some applications…but…

HELEN: You like life in a small town?

R.J.: Yeah. It's cool.

HELEN: Denise?

DENISE: It's okay. It takes getting used to. I'll be okay. Look what are you asking. Do you wanna know if I turn tricks. Do I put stuff in my veins.

R.J.: That's not happening, Miss…Miss…

HELEN: Helen. Just Helen is okay…

R.J.: Okay, Helen…. Look. Look at the letter. The letter will tell you we've got a new life in that town. It was hard at first. You know? But we did it. We went away from everyone we knew. Everything we…did. And we started…. I mean it was hard. Denise was great. What she did was so hard. It was—

DENISE: We need our baby back. It's not gonna work if we don't get Christine back. I won't make it.

HELEN: What do you mean by that, Denise. Do you think you'll start back on drugs, Denise. Do you feel that's a possibility.

DENISE: Of course it's a possibility. Everything is a possibility. I'm not a new person. They didn't throw out the old Denise and make a new one. It's a repair job. I'm just…repaired…*(to R.J.)* She doesn't get it.

R.J.: *(to HELEN)* She needs the baby. Everything she's done these past few months she's done for the baby.

HELEN's cell phone rings. She answers it.

HELEN: *(into phone)* Yeah?…. Yeah. Okay…. Okay sure. About a half hour. *(She puts the cell phone back in her briefcase.)* Look I'm needed somewhere. Why don't I just take these letters away. Look them over. Call you. Set something up.

R.J.: Set something up like what?

HELEN: A meeting. We'll talk some more.

R.J.: We thought it was set. The court said it was okay…. I mean here we are in this dump. We've come back and—

HELEN: Look the court needs our approval. If we say it's—

DENISE: We?

HELEN: Me…. If things look okay to me then the court is just a rubber stamp. Listen, I'm sorry if I gave you the wrong impression but we can't rush this. We're going to have to…get to know each other a bit better. We'll have to reveal a few things. Rehash a few things probably. Do you understand what I'm saying, Denise.

DENISE shrugs. Turns away.
HELEN picks up her briefcase.

R.J.: We'll…just wait then.

HELEN: I'll call you.

HELEN looks for a moment at both of them. Leaves.
R.J. looks at DENISE. Goes to the open door. Yells after HELEN.

R.J.: Goodbye…. *(to DENISE)* She waved…. She turned and waved.

DENISE: This is not going to happen.

R.J.: Ah don't—

DENISE: Nah, we've got a judgement against us. We've been found guilty. And no one, especially her, is going to all of a sudden find us not guilty, throw that judgement away and say here, here's your kid, start over, make a family…. Ah aren't you cute—We thought you were the scum of the earth but really you're cute. We're sorry…

R.J. is moving toward her.

R.J.: Listen, are you tired. You're probably hungry and tired so—

DENISE: Ah please stay away from me. I can't do this. I can't let you get my spirits up. I'm not up to getting positive. It's hard. Sometimes it's just like—I don't know.... bullshit. Can't you just let me feel like it's all bull-shit and leave it at that.

R.J.: No.... I can't.... Because then it all falls apart, Denise.

DENISE: I'm going out. *(grabs a jacket)* If I don't get out of here for awhile I'll go—

R.J.: It's okay. You go out. I'll stay. I'll be here if she calls. There was some-thing in the way she waved goodbye. I think she'll call soon. Maybe she felt sorry or something but...she'll call. Don't worry.... I'll be here.

He sits on the couch.

DENISE: Yeah.... I know you will.... You're a rock or something. How'd that happen. I mean you used to be as messed up as me and now...now you're some kind of solid thing.

She leaves. R.J. is just staring ahead.

R.J.: Bullshit...

He lowers his head. Blackout.

Scene Three

PHILLIE is vacuuming the room. R.J. is watching the TV.

PHILLIE: *(shouting)* This bothering you?

R.J. gestures that it's okay.

PHILLIE: 'Cause I could turn it off. Come back later.

R.J. gestures again.
PHILLIE turns off the vacuum.

PHILLIE: Are you sure.

R.J.: Definitely. Just do your job, man. It's okay.

PHILLIE: I appreciate that.

R.J.: Yeah.... By the way, it's good to see you sober.

PHILLIE: It's Wednesday. I clean the rooms on Wednesdays. It's almost impossible to do that under the influence.

R.J.: I bet...

PHILLIE: I mean it can be done.... But I gotta tell you, cleaning toilet bowls when you're smashed...is kind of...unnatural.

R.J.: Yeah.

PHILLIE turns on the machine. Vacuums awhile. Something on the TV grabs his attention. Turns off the machine.

PHILLIE: Why are those three chubby women crying.

R.J.: They're sisters.... See the skinny guy with the skimpy beard next to them? He's been having sex with all of them. And today they've finally confronted him.

PHILLIE: Yeah? Confronted? So how come they're crying. And he looks...

R.J.: Kinda pleased with himself?....Because there's no justice in the world, man. None. He thinks he's the cock of the walk. He's on national TV and he's a winner and the women are...fools. Crying fools. There is definitely hardly any justice in the world.

PHILLIE: You think I don't know that? I know that.... The thing about me is I don't give a shit.

R.J.: I give a shit. I think justice is the only thing. Fair behaviour for fair behaviour. You know? Even breaks for everyone.

PHILLIE: No no.... Don't take me there, man. I can't get into that. Next thing I'll just get upset. I'm capable of some pretty self-destructive behaviour. I gotta concentrate on doing my job. I'm lucky to have this job. If it wasn't for my cousin Edward.... No.... No I can't get into that justice shit. The lucky and the unlucky. The haves and the have-nots. The fuckers, the fuckees—oh man. Let me just suck up some dirt. Let me just do what I can do, and suck up what little dirt I can here.

PHILLIE turns on the machine. Vacuums for awhile. PHILLIE turns off the machine.

PHILLIE: Whose the guy in the suit.

R.J.: The expert. They always have an expert.

PHILLIE: What? A social worker.

R.J.: Sometimes. Or a doctor. Or someone who's written a book.

PHILLIE: So. Yeah? Is he supposed to solve this. Is he supposed to bring justice to this situation.... I really don't think so!

PHILLIE is unplugging the vacuum. Gathering his cleaning supplies.

PHILLIE: Look. Here's the truth. I can't do anymore. It's that...justice thing. Once it's in your head you can't ignore it. You just can't.... It colours everything.... It makes all work futile.

He is leaving.

R.J.: Sorry.... It looks pretty clean though.

PHILLIE: There's a stain on the carpet. It's permanent. Other than that yeah it's pretty clean.... The bathroom is spotless...not that I give a shit!

He gets choked up and leaves, not closing the door.
R.J. turns back to the TV.

R.J.: ...Oh yeah right. Take it out on her. Like it's her fault. Look at him. Look at that grin. Get serious, man.... No no it's not about sibling rivalry you twit, it's about the guy and his dick. It's about the dick.... Go ahead ask him. Ask him about the dick! The truth is in the dick!

DENISE appears in the doorway. Doesn't come in. Just leans against the frame. Watching R.J. She looks a little messed up.

R.J.: Ah man.... Enough. Look she's crying. She's really crying. Okay—Host intervention! Host intervention! Come on! Come on! Fair is fair. Come on, for chrissake. Intervene!

DENISE: Hey!

R.J. turns to DENISE.

DENISE: Calm down! It's just a fucking TV show!

R.J. looks at DENISE. At TV. At DENISE.

R.J.: Yeah.

He turns off the TV. Stands.

R.J.: Hi.

DENISE: I mean don't we have enough problems of our own. Real ones? You have to go looking for something to get upset about on a...a fucking TV show!?

R.J.: Where you been?

DENISE: Downtown.

R.J.: How far downtown?

DENISE: All the way.

R.J.: You see your mother?

DENISE: She wasn't there…. I went over to your place. Your mother wasn't there either. Hey, there's a show idea you can send in: "Mothers Who Aren't There When you Need Them."

R.J.: You on something?

DENISE: Ah you're gonna wanna talk about that, aren't you. I wanna talk about where our mothers are when our life is going down the toilet but you'll have to get into that "let me see your eyes" bullshit.

R.J.: I'm not gonna look in your eyes. I don't have to look in your eyes. You can't even stand up.

DENISE: Says who.

She stands. Falls back against the door frame.
R.J. sits on the bed. Hangs his head between his legs.

DENISE: Ah don't go falling apart on me. Hanging your head like that. It's just booze. Six beers. Nothing. I needed to feel better than I felt.

She is staggering a bit as she moves toward him.

DENISE: I was feeling so bad…. I was afraid I wouldn't be able to…you know…make good choices…because the way I was feeling was—fuck it…. So I thought—hey, feel better. Make better choices so…

She sits next to him. Rubs his head.

DENISE: So really it's okay…. I'm not falling. I'm really not falling…. I'm still…. hopeful. Look there's still hope in me…. Look at me. Look at me. Come on.

She lifts his head.

DENISE: Now is this the face of an…optimistic person…a basically optimistic person…or…isn't it. I say it is.

R.J.: Well you must know…. Why'd you go see your mother.

DENISE: Ah…. 'Cause it's hard not to go see your mother when you think… "God I sure could use a little mother talk!" Even when you remember your mother's kind of written you off. Even when you remember it was your mother who called in "the government" and had them take away your kid…so…so I went to talk…. But…well…

R.J.: She wasn't there. Big surprise. When was she ever.

DENISE: Hey don't get uppity. Neither was yours.

R.J.: Yeah but mine has an excuse. She's dead.

DENISE: Holy shit. You're right.

R.J.: Just six beers?

DENISE: Or more.... Holy shit. That's right. She died just after I got pregnant.... I forgot. How could I forget that.... I walked over to your building. Took the elevator to the twelfth floor. Went down the hall to 1209. Knocked. Waited. Left.... I just forgot.

R.J.: It's been a rough year.

DENISE: Ah look who's trying to cheer me up. Doesn't it ever just wear you down.... Trying to make sure I'm...okay? *(kisses his face)* Really. How could I forget your mother is dead. Do you think I've got permanent brain damage. Memory loss?

R.J.: Maybe you were just...drunk.

DENISE: That's my man. Always got the right answer. Always looking to let me off the hook. Always looking for...a reason.... Why?

R.J.: I don't know. I love you. I...love you.

He kisses her. He puts his hand under her sweater. She kisses him back.

DENISE: Are we gonna have sex now?

R.J.: It's better than...you know...

DENISE: What.

R.J.: Thinking...about the baby.... About mothers. I mean your mother. Of all the hypocritical bullshit in the world.... Your mother gets us busted.... your mother, the biggest screw-up in the universe gets to play Miss Citizen and—

DENISE: I did that. *(she kisses him)* Shush. I did that.

R.J.: What.

DENISE: That "my mother's gotta go to hell" thing. After the six beers...

R.J.: Or more.

DENISE: Yeah. Anyway it's been done. She's in hell. I sent her in my mind to hell. You know maybe I didn't go to see her to talk.... Maybe I went to kill her. Yeah. I think I actually went to kill her.

R.J.: Yeah. Sure.

DENISE: No really. I mean why else would I buy a gun.

R.J.: What? Get real.

DENISE: No…No. I bought it off…Billy Richards. Remember him? I ran into him and he says "Hey…. So? What's new"…All that shit. And I find myself asking if he's got any weapons I can purchase…

R.J.: Denise…. What is this—

DENISE: It's in my bag. Over by the door.

> *R.J. walks over to the door. Bends. DENISE's canvas bag is on the floor. He empties the contents onto the table. A few things. No gun.*

R.J.: So?

DENISE: No gun? I guess I musta made it up.

R.J.: And why would you do something like that, Denise.

DENISE: Your worst fear, dear. What is it. Something like that? Denise gets a gun. Goes on a rampage. Takes revenge on her mother. Then…what? Turns the gun on herself. Well whatever…. Your worst fear…. I was just putting it out where we could both see it…. I don't know…. I don't know…

R.J.: Maybe I should go get us some coffee.

DENISE: I guess…

R.J.: How about food…

DENISE: Food…. No…. Look…. I'm just going to crash…. You go out. Eat.

R.J.: No I'll—

DENISE: No I went out. You go out. It's probably good…. I mean you are talking to the TV. So…

R.J.: Yeah…Yeah maybe I'll just go get a—

DENISE: Take your time. I'm just going to sleep.

R.J.: She didn't call by the way. Helen. The social worker? She didn't call.

DENISE: No?

R.J.: But…you didn't ask me if she called. Why not.

DENISE: I don't know.

R.J.: Sure you do…. You're preparing for the worst.

DENISE: Maybe.

R.J.: You are…. What's the good of that…Denise?

She shrugs. Turns away. He leaves.
She takes off her jacket. Reaches inside her pocket. Takes out a small gun.
Puts it under the mattress. Lies down on the bed. Takes the bed spread.
Pulls it over herself. Rolls in it until she is wrapped.
Blackout.

Scene Four

HELEN is standing over the bed. Watching DENISE sleep.... She begins
to look casually around the room. Poking at a pile of newspapers. Looking
in one of the dresser drawers. Eventually she goes into the bathroom. We
hear glass objects being shifted. DENISE stirs. A glass crashes in the
bathroom. DENISE sits up quickly.

DENISE: R.J.?

HELEN: *(coming out of the bathroom)* No...it's just me.... I broke a glass....
Hi.... I was just...just...

HELEN is wrapping her hand in a towel. DENISE is up.

DENISE: Searching?

HELEN: Searching?.... No I was thirsty. So I—

DENISE: Is that a bad cut.

HELEN: I don't know.

DENISE: You're bleeding.

HELEN: A little.... Yes. There's glass all over the floor. Do you want me to...

DENISE: I'll get it later.

HELEN: I can do it.

DENISE: I said I'll get it later! I'll do it! *(smiles)* It'll get done. Honest.

HELEN: Sure. Fine. Thanks.... So.... Can I sit down.

DENISE: Yeah, sit down.... I'll sit down too. We'll both sit down.

DENISE sits at the table.

HELEN: What's wrong.

DENISE: Nothing. Sit down.

HELEN: *(sitting)* You look tired, Denise.

DENISE: Do I?.... You look fine.... You look just fine. Well you've got a bad cut on your hand. And you're bleeding all over the table but other than that—

HELEN: Oh dear I better—

HELEN starts to stand. DENISE grabs her wrist.

DENISE: Where you going.

HELEN: I don't...well to the bathroom. I'm bleeding.

DENISE: Stay put. Just for a minute.

HELEN: But I'm bleeding on the table.

DENISE: Hey it's okay. Stay put. Can you just stay put. I need to talk to you.

HELEN: Well I need to talk to you too. But—

DENISE: So good. Let's talk. It's just that I've been worried you know. Worried that you were out there doing your investigation without having all the—

HELEN: It's not really an investigation.

DENISE: Yes it is. We're suspects. And you're investigating us.

HELEN: I'm doing my job. I'm just trying to determine if you're capable of caring for your child. You're not a suspect. It's not a criminal—

DENISE: Hey, we're suspected of being inadequate. Let's not argue over the fucking word here. Look I'm sorry. But I was just worried you were out there "doing your job" without knowing something essential about me. And that is...I need my baby. I need her.

HELEN: I know that.

DENISE: No you don't.

HELEN: Yes—

DENISE: No you don't! I didn't tell you. I should have told you how much I need her. And how much I love her. And that I never would do anything to hurt her.... And how what happened before wasn't really what they said happened. My mother...you know, we were fighting and to get back at me she made it look like I was neglecting the baby and called you people.

HELEN: Look all that's on record.

DENISE: Some of it. Not all of it.

HELEN: The point is, it doesn't matter how we got involved. We're involved.

DENISE: Yeah but listen—

HELEN: No you listen. We were called. We got involved. We saw things we didn't like. We took action.

DENISE: Pretty drastic though...I mean the action you took was...pretty fucking drastic.

HELEN: Were you or were you not a drug addict.

DENISE: Hey Helen that sounded pretty...you know "legal." Like a lawyer, that "were you or were you not" stuff.

HELEN: Were you or were you not a prostitute.

DENISE: I turned a few tricks. It happened. Hey I thought I should pay the rent.

HELEN: Please.

DENISE: Please? What's that mean. Did that sound feeble to you. I mean as an excuse.

HELEN: I didn't want to go backwards here, Denise. We have enough to deal with in the present.

DENISE: I just want to make sure you...got it clear. I mean maybe you don't. Maybe you don't know R.J. was in jail. I was alone. Did you know that.

HELEN: Yes.

DENISE: So I was alone. I'd had this baby. My husband was in prison. I was broke.

HELEN: You were receiving welfare.

DENISE: It wasn't enough,

HELEN: Look I've told you I don't want to rehash—

DENISE: It wasn't enough. I wasn't making it.

HELEN: Others do.

DENISE: I wasn't. It wasn't enough. The rent was too high. I couldn't get them to lower it. I had expenses.

HELEN: Drugs.... Crack, speed, what else.

DENISE: No!.... No, you see, this is what makes me think you don't really know everything you should. I'd been clean since I got pregnant.

HELEN: Not according to your mother.

DENISE: My mother yeah. See? I told you. We've got to investigate my mother's part in this. I think if you were to examine her in more detail you'd see—

HELEN: Your mother isn't an issue.

DENISE: Sure she is.

HELEN: No. No you're the issue. You're a drug addict and a prostitute who wants her daughter back and that makes you the only issue...

DENISE is up. Moving around.

DENISE: I was never a prostitute. I turned a few tricks and even if I was a prostitute, who says a prostitute can't raise a child.

HELEN: I do.

DENISE: You do?

HELEN: Yes I do.

DENISE: Is that an official position there Helen.

HELEN: More or less. Yes.

DENISE: And one you agree with.

HELEN: Oh, yes.

DENISE: Is this getting personal here, Helen. It sounds like you take this personally.

HELEN: I want to talk about your new life, Denise. I've read the letters you've given me. I've made a few calls.

DENISE: I was a drug addict though. You were right about that. I mean I kind of messed around with drugs all through my teens. I stopped when I got pregnant. But when you took my baby away I became a drug addict. That's when I became a drug addict! For the record! Okay!?

HELEN: So. What strikes me about your new life in this small town is that it's really not your life. It's R.J.'s. I mean all the reference letters are about him. He seems to have become a real member of that community. But there's no reference to you at all. What do you do up there, Denise.

DENISE: I stay at home and take drugs. Sometimes I go out and fuck people for money. The guy who runs the hardware store. The mayor. The Scoutmaster. I fuck them all!

HELEN: Do you think that smart-ass mouth is going to help you out here, Denise. Do you think you're going to impress me into giving you back your baby with that smart-ass talk? Sit down.

DENISE: I feel better up.

HELEN: Sit down!

DENISE sits.

DENISE: Okay?

HELEN: So?.... What do you do. Look for work? Watch TV?

DENISE: I look for work.

HELEN: What kind. Waitressing?

DENISE: Yeah.

HELEN: What about at home. Do you cook?

DENISE: Cook?

HELEN: Meals. Do you cook meals for R.J. Do you cook his dinner when he comes home from work.

DENISE: Ah.... no.

HELEN: No? Why not.

DENISE: He doesn't like my cooking. It's not very good. He cooks better.

HELEN: So he comes home, cooks his own dinner.

DENISE: And mine. He cooks for me too, Helen. I mean he doesn't just cook for himself. That would be cruel.

HELEN: Do you clean.

DENISE: Clean. You mean vacuum? I vacuum.

HELEN: How often.

DENISE: What? What is this crap.

HELEN: I notice R.J. joined a church last month. I guess he did that to impress us.

DENISE: Probably…. But with R.J. you never know. It's possible he found God. Prison changed him. He discovered the TV talk shows in prison. Maybe he discovered God there too.

HELEN: I'm assuming he did it to impress us. That's okay. It's still a good thing no matter how you come to it.

DENISE: You think so? You think church is a big deal.

HELEN: It can be. You don't think so, though. I mean you wouldn't even make the effort to impress us, I mean let alone actually sincerely looking for some true religious experience—

DENISE: I'm getting a really uneasy feeling about you Helen.

HELEN: Oh really. Why? Do you think I might be questioning your values, Denise. Do you have values Denise. Do you know what values are Denise.

DENISE: This is personal isn't it, Helen.

HELEN: You want me to give you back the baby so you can hang out with her, Denise? Maybe take her to the mall? Train her to give you a hug when you're feeling low…. Is that why you want the baby, Denise. You need a "friend"?

DENISE: I want her because she's…mine!

HELEN: Well frankly I think she's better off where she is. She's in a real family.

DENISE: I want her!

HELEN: *(standing)* Well I don't think you're going to get her. I really don't.

DENISE leans over the table. Grabbing HELEN's injured hand. HELEN yells.

DENISE: I want her! I want her!

HELEN: Let…. go of my hand. You're hurting me.

DENISE: You shouldn't have made it personal.

HELEN: Let go!

DENISE lets go.

HELEN: Ah. It's really bleeding now.

HELEN goes into the bathroom.

DENISE: What gave you the right to make it personal.

DENISE goes to the bed. Takes the gun from under the mattress.

HELEN: *(from bathroom)* Ah, damn. It's bleeding pretty badly.

DENISE: I mean what kind of position does that put me in? You think I should go to church and become a better cook or I'll never see my kid again. What kind of shit is that.

HELEN: *(from bathroom)* Look. You better help me. I'm feeling a…little…light-headed…

DENISE is staring at the gun.
PHILLIE comes in. Carrying a pile of towels.

PHILLIE: Oh. Sorry. Should have knocked. *(hits himself on the head)* Moron. Learn. Why can't you learn! You wanna lose this job? Do you? *(hits himself again, looks at DENISE, smiles)* I brought some fresh towels.

HELEN groans loudly in the bathroom. Passes out with much noise and spilling of things. PHILLIE looks toward the bathroom. DENISE stands. Puts the gun in her waistband. Walks over to PHILLIE. Takes the towels.

DENISE: Thanks.

DENISE and PHILLIE both look into the bathroom. DENISE looks at PHILLIE intently.

DENISE: What's your name again?

Blackout.

Scene Five

R.J. is on the phone and he is very upset.

R.J.: No I won't calm down. No…No. I've had it. It's gross, man. It's fucking pathetic and gross. Are you watching this shit. Are you watching that big prick scream at his mother. You let some big piece of garbage come on national television and humiliate a helpless pensioner. Are you nuts. Are you people insane. No! Bullshit…No! Fuck you. It's gotta be…stopped…. Oh really…. Oh right…. No! No! Mothers Who Never Visited Their Sons in Prison is a fucking stupid idea for a show. Ah look at that. What's he gonna do? Hit her? Do you just let him hit her? Well it looks like he's gonna hit her…. I want the producer. Get me the producer! Get me the producer. I need to tell him something.... Get him. Get him! Get him! Get him!!

PHILLIE and DENISE come in. They are both a bit messed up. R.J. sees them.

R.J.: I'll call you back.

He hangs up.

DENISE: Who was that.

R.J.: No one.

DENISE: You're losing it, right? You're flipping out.

R.J.: Come here. *(points to TV)* Look at that. Piece of shit! Piece of shit won't stop!! It's not her fucking fault he was doing eight to ten. *(to TV)* I mean a fucking reality check might be in order here, son. I didn't blame MY mother when I was inside. I mean I didn't even know anyone who blamed their mother. *(to DENISE)* I mean where did they dig this guy up.... Look at her face. Look at that poor woman's hurt and confused face. It's a crime. I can't believe they syndicate this shit.

DENISE: Do you mind if I turn it off.

R.J.: No. Please. Turn it off. I want you to turn it off. Do you think I like watching this stuff. It's fucking infuriating.

DENISE turns off the TV.

PHILLIE: It's the injustice that gets to him.

R.J.: Yeah...yeah.... Hi Phillie.

DENISE has taken HELEN's briefcase from under the bed.

PHILLIE: Hi.

R.J.: You're both covered in mud...or something.

DENISE: I'll explain later.... I've got to give Phillie something...

R.J.: Whose briefcase is that. Is that whatshername's.

DENISE: In a minute, okay?

DENISE has taken an address book from the briefcase. Looks through it. Tears out a page. Hands it to PHILLIE.

DENISE: It's the one on top.... Do you know where that is.

PHILLIE: Yeah.

DENISE: Do you think you can do this.

PHILLIE: Do you.

DENISE: Yeah I think you can. But you have to be sure you want to…

PHILLIE: I want to…

DENISE: Okay then…. Go.

PHILLIE: Yeah. Okay…. I'm going.

He starts off. Stops.

PHILLIE: I feel good.

DENISE: I'm glad.

PHILLIE nods. Leaves.

R.J.: What's going on. Where you been. Where's he going…. What's going on.

DENISE: Things got a bit weird when you were out before. I'm trying to think of how to explain this to you. Trying to think if maybe there's some TV show I can compare it to for you.

R.J.: Gimme a break.

DENISE: I don't know, man. Life is just crawling all over us here and you're putting all your energy into that crap you watch on that stupid box. So I'm wondering maybe you're not really capable of understanding what I have to tell you unless…. I don't know maybe I should go on TV and sit on one of those stupid chairs. Cry. And then you'll see me and hear my story and your heart will go out to me and you'll understand. But if I just tell you how it happened and I'm just me and you're just you…I don't know if you'll…

R.J.: Ah…this is gonna be bad, isn't it.

DENISE: She's dead.

R.J.: Who's dead.

DENISE: Helen.

R.J.: Helen? Helen the social worker?

DENISE: Yeah…. She's dead…. She fell down and hit her head against the toilet.

R.J.: The toilet…. Our toilet?

DENISE: Yeah...the bowl...you know.

R.J. walks into the bathroom. Walks out.

R.J.: She's not in there.

DENISE: No. She's...gone.

R.J.: I was afraid to look. I had my eyes closed. But when I opened them she wasn't there.

DENISE: Yeah.

R.J.: A lot of blood though.

DENISE: Yeah. Some of that's from her head. Some of it from when she cut her hand.

R.J.: She cut her hand?

DENISE: On a glass. I had nothing to do with that.

R.J.: Oh. Did you have anything to do with her hitting her head.

DENISE: Not directly. I think I sped-up the flow of blood from her hand when I squeezed it and that might have made her woozy. I think that's what happened...

R.J.: Why were you squeezing her hand.

DENISE: Look we gotta skip all that and get to the important thing. I didn't shoot her. I wanted to shoot her. I didn't. She told me we weren't getting our child back. She told me to basically forget it and I thought okay, I'll forget it. I'll put a bullet in you and then one in myself and it'll be forgotten. But I didn't. Of course maybe she made the decision for me by falling and hitting her head on the toilet bowl. But I don't think so. I think I'd already decided not to use the gun. To remain hopeful. I mean I can't be sure because the timing was...tight. But I think I'd already decided. And then Phillie was standing there with the towels and my mind started to race. You know how it races sometimes when I'm upset. Like that. But different. Because this time it was clear. My mind. It had purpose. So I knew the first thing I had to do. And I did it.

R.J.: You got rid of the body.

DENISE: No. I got Phillie on my side.... I mean I had to.... He was right there so I had to get him on my side. It wasn't hard really. Because really he's one of us...

R.J.: What's that mean, "one of us?"

DENISE: Scum of the earth. So he knows. He knows about getting screwed…. Because it's just so easy to screw us, people can do it without even trying really.

R.J.: Justice.

DENISE: What.

R.J.: He's got a thing about justice. He think it's like, candy. No not candy exactly. But something…good…that's…forbidden or something.

DENISE: No. He knew her. He knew her type, that's all. I told him what she said to me. That I won't be getting the baby cause I don't go to church and I don't cook.

R.J.: She said that?

DENISE: Yeah she said that.

R.J.: She said "I'm sorry Denise but you can't have your child back because we've found out you're a lousy cook?"

DENISE: Yes! She said that! Exactly!

R.J.: And so you killed her!?

DENISE: I didn't kill her.

R.J.: No you didn't kill her. You thought about killing her with the gun you told me you didn't have but you didn't really kill her. Oh you squeezed her hand a little. But that was it. Come on, Denise. There's a lot of blood in that bathroom. A lot!

DENISE: I didn't kill her. I didn't kill her, I'm telling you!

R.J.: Good thing I didn't go in there unprepared. If I'd gone in there not knowing…. All that blood. Good thing I went right for the TV. I mean you're down on me watching television but it's a damn good thing I wanted to watch television instead of taking a piss, or I might be really fucked up now! Because I would've thought that was your blood. Your blood. And I would've thought you'd hurt yourself. Really bad…. And I would have freaked…. Okay. But that didn't happen. Something else happened. Let's try and stay with what really happened.

DENISE: Good idea…

R.J.: She died?

DENISE: Yeah.

R.J.: Accidentally.

DENISE: Ah…. Yeah…

R.J.: You got Phillie on your side and he helped you get rid of the body.

DENISE: Yeah.

R.J.: Because you had to…. because you couldn't call the goddamn police or a goddamn ambulance like most people…even though it was a fucking accident you had to get rid of the body. Sure. That makes sense! Oh my God. Oh my God what have you done. We could have appealed. She wasn't the only social worker in this city. We could have appealed. *(he grabs DENISE)* You didn't have to kill her. Killing her was not the right thing to do.

DENISE: Listen to me!

R.J.: It was a bad idea! Bad bad bad—

DENISE: Listen to me. Listen!

R.J.: Bad!

DENISE: Listen! Listen it was over before she fell. We were finished as parents. Our life. Our future. Everything we wanted to do was over. She was going to make sure it wasn't going to happen. I didn't kill her. But…it would've maybe looked like I had…so we buried her…

R.J.: Where.

DENISE: Out back.

R.J.: We could've gotten a lawyer. We're trying to be the kind of people who get lawyers in circumstances like this, Denise.

DENISE: Please. No. No lawyers. No law. No official investigation. We're not going that route. It's not our route. Listen to me. We're doing it our way. The only way we've got…really.

R.J.: Where'd you send Phillie.

DENISE: She had their names in her address book. The foster parents…

R.J.: Ah no—

DENISE: He can do it.

R.J.: Ah. No he can't.

DENISE: I gave him the gun.

R.J.: You sent him to get our baby. And you gave him a gun?

DENISE: No bullets. Just the gun. Something to...produce if he meets resistance. I think it'll be okay. They don't know him. He'll just ring the door bell. They'd recognize me probably. She's probably described me to them. Thought I might pull something.... So I couldn't do it myself.... Because she prepared them.

R.J.: Are you nuts.

DENISE: What.

He grabs her.

R.J.: Are you fucking nuts!?

DENISE: Yes! Yes I am. I'm out of my fucking mind. I want my baby. I can't sleep, I can't eat, without her. I can't live without her. And I want her now! I want her. That's all I want. Just let me have her and it will be okay. I promise. Let this happen and it will be okay. Just...please let this happen!

She buries her head in his chest.

DENISE: Please...

R.J. is staring off. Rubbing DENISE's back.
Blackout.

Scene Six

R.J. and DENISE are waiting for the phone to ring. He paces. She sits on the bed staring at the phone.

R.J.: He said he'd call? You're sure?

DENISE: Yeah.

R.J.: And you think he...understood.

DENISE: Yeah.... Understood what?

R.J.: To call.

DENISE: I said "Call when you've got her."

R.J.: There could've been a problem.

DENISE: Yes.... Lots of them.

R.J.: The chances are slim he got her out of there.

DENISE: I thought he could do it. I mean they're just a nice suburban couple. They're not the mob or anything. They're not protected. He shows up. Shows the gun if he has to.... Says, "give me the kid".... They should cooperate.... It's human nature to cooperate.

R.J.: Yeah? Would you give her over to someone.

DENISE: I did. Remember? People came into our apartment and I gave her to them. And they didn't have a fucking gun. They just had a piece of paper.

R.J.: Well we'll see...we'll see how reckless you've been. Why doesn't he call.... Why.... It's been enough time.

DENISE: Shit.... Oh shit.

She stands and heads for the door.

DENISE: There's no one in the office to put the call through.

R.J.: Is that how it works.

DENISE: Yes. That's how it fucking works.

She leaves. Slamming the door behind her.

R.J. paces awhile. Looks at TV. Paces. Goes to TV. Turns it on. Flips the channels. Flips. Flips.
A knock on the door.
R.J. goes to the door. opens it. PHILLIE is standing there.

PHILLIE: I saw Denise leave. I've been waiting. Can I come in.

R.J.: Yeah come in. *(he pulls PHILLIE in)* Have you got her?'

PHILLIE: The baby?

R.J.: Yeah, the baby!

PHILLIE: No...no. I didn't do it. I mean I thought about doing it. But I couldn't. It was a wild idea. It was like an idea from my youth. In my youth I could've done it. I had guts then. But not now. I tried though. Got in the car. Headed in the right direction. Five or six blocks. But then I stopped. Reality stopped me. I mean what am I. I'm a drunk. I'm not a kidnapper. There's a difference.

R.J.: Yeah.

PHILLIE: You understand?

R.J.: Yeah.

PHILLIE: I mean I couldn't say this to Denise.... She was wild. Intense and wild. You got anything to drink?

R.J.: No.

PHILLIE: Because I need a little something.

R.J.: I'm sorry.

PHILLIE: That's okay. Don't feel bad. I was telling you about Denise.... She was wild. She was intense. *(hits himself)* Well which was it. Wild or intense? She couldn't be both.... She was intense. Yeah. Focused. "Why are we burying this body?" I asked her. I mean she fell. I heard her. It was an accident. *(shrugs)* You use hair tonic? I could go in the bathroom and you wouldn't have to watch me drink or anything. I'd just go in there if that's where it is. Anyway I was telling you about Denise. What Denise said about the body was "I can't take any chances".... So what about that hair tonic.... Aftershave...

R.J.: There's nothing like that in there. You want me to go get you a bottle?

PHILLIE: You might have to.... I mean I have to face Denise. I've let her down.

R.J.: It's okay.

PHILLIE: I don't think so. I don't think it's okay.

R.J.: Denise isn't.... She's not thinking clearly.

PHILLIE: Yes. She is. She's trying to survive. Look, nothing I've said should be taken as criticism of Denise. She's just trying to...what's the word I'm looking for. Survive?

R.J.: Yeah but she's.... Look we've got to go dig up that body.... Call the police. Get it straight.

PHILLIE: Dig up the body?

R.J.: Yeah.

PHILLIE: Tell the police?

R.J.: Yeah.

PHILLIE: Tell the police what? We buried a body. But now we think that was unwise.

R.J.: Well it was unwise. It was really really...unwise. Why didn't you call the police.

PHILLIE: Denise couldn't take a chance. That's what she said. They come in. They see the situation. They find out the social worker was going to make a bad report about her. They make Denise a suspect. She couldn't let that happen. She couldn't. Don't you know that, man. God are you her husband or not. Can't you see she's right! Denise was doing it right, man. She's gotta get that baby. And the two of you gotta take that baby and disappear. And make a great life. That's the only way for justice to be served. Okay I'm goin'. I'm going this time for sure.

R.J.: Where.

PHILLIE: To get the baby.

R.J.: No, no. No!

He grabs PHILLIE.

PHILLIE: No listen. It's okay. I can do it. I'm worked up. I can do it.

R.J.: No I don't want you to do it.

PHILLIE: But if I do it, I'll feel better about myself. I think it's something I could take pride in.

R.J.: Someone could get hurt.

PHILLIE: It'll be all right. I'll get her. Don't you want her. She's your baby too. Don't you want her.

R.J.: Yes. Yes I want her. But not like this. I want her in a way that'll be okay…

PHILLIE: That can't happen. Nothing is ever going to be truly okay again. Everything is wrong. Everything in the world is wrong. There is no justice. Not really. There's only grab and run!…. Everyone for themselves. I gotta do this.

R.J.: I can't let you.

PHILLIE: Look. I gotta.

He pulls the gun from his pocket.

PHILLIE: I'm sorry. But I'm doing this so stay back.

R.J.: That isn't loaded.

PHILLIE fires a shot into the floor.

PHILLIE: What gave you that idea.

PHILLIE runs out of the room.

R.J. is about to follow when the phone rings. He runs over. Answers it.

R.J.: *(into phone)* Yeah.... yeah speaking.... Yeah. Really. How'd you get my number.... I did? Oh yeah, right—Yeah...yeah well it was about that Mothers Who Didn't Visit Their Sons In Prison show. I mean don't you think you went a bit too far with that one. There was real pain on that woman's face. She didn't need.... Well sure she has free will but do you think she expected to be treated like that by her own son. I mean—

DENISE bursts through the door.

DENISE: Jesus Christ! What is wrong with you!?

She rushes over. Grabs the phone. Hangs up.

DENISE: I mean you left your number with the network? I put the call through because at first I thought...then I thought what the hell was that. Is that all you've got on your mind considering the circumstances of our life right now.

R.J.: I made the call earlier. Things were okay when I made the call.

DENISE: You made the call six months ago? Cause that's the last time I remember things being okay.

R.J.: No I made the call before you killed the social worker.

DENISE: Look for the last time. I didn't kill the social worker. I just buried the social worker.

R.J.: You know what though.... It's gonna turn out to be the same thing. I think it's gonna have basically the same impact on our lives as if you'd killed her. So let's just say you did. Okay!?

DENISE: Why? Because it'll sound better on TV? You thinking ahead 'til when we're invited on one of those shows. Look I can't talk to you anymore. I'm waiting for Phillie's call.

R.J.: He's not calling.

DENISE: He'll call. Have faith.

R.J.: He was here.

DENISE: When.

R.J.: Just now.

DENISE: Did he have Christine.

R.J.: No he couldn't do it.

DENISE: Shit…. Shit…. Okay okay, we'll have to do it…. We'll go get her ourselves. Come on.

R.J.: No he's doing it.

DENISE: You just said he wasn't doing it.

R.J.: He changed his mind. He went to do it. He's….doing it.

DENISE: He changed his mind?

R.J.: He convinced himself. It's something he has to do. He says it'll make him feel better.

DENISE: It will…. It'll be an accomplishment.

R.J.: He's got a gun.

DENISE: I know.

R.J.: It's loaded.

DENISE: So?

R.J.: You told me it wasn't.

DENISE: I did?

R.J.: Suppose he hurts someone.

DENISE: It's a risk worth taking. Hey R.J. it's our life we're talking about here.

R.J. goes to the phone.

DENISE: What are you doing.

R.J.: I have to call that TV guy back.

DENISE: You're kidding.

R.J.: You hung up on him. He took the time to call me and you hung up on him…. He might never take the time to call anyone again. That would be a shame. Because improvements can be made in how things are done and he's in a position to make them…. Probably all he needs is encouragement…and, you know…input.

DENISE: You're too much.

R.J.: So are you, Denise. So are you.

He dials the phone. Blackout.

Scene Seven

R.J. and DENISE are near the bathroom door. Looking tense. The door is closed and someone is having a shower. DENISE becomes exasperated, throws her arms in the air and begins to pace. R.J. puts his head against the bathroom door. Listens. The water stops running. R.J. gestures to DENISE. She stops pacing. They wait. Suddenly the bathroom door is opened. Steam pours into the room.
They wait.
HELEN comes out of the bathroom. Wet hair. Wearing one of R.J.'s shirts.

HELEN: That feels better…. A lot better. *(to R.J.)* Thanks for the shirt.

R.J. nods.
HELEN looks at herself in the wall mirror. Touches her forehead.

HELEN: Nasty little bump. *(to DENISE)* Do you have a brush I could borrow.

DENISE gets a brush from the bedside table. Takes it to HELEN.

HELEN: Thanks…. I said thanks.

DENISE: You're…welcome.

HELEN sits at the table. Begins to brush her hair.

HELEN: *(brushing)* It's important to be polite…. Politeness is a cornerstone of civilized behaviour. I guess no one ever taught you that…. That's just one of the things you weren't taught…. Politeness. Moderation…. Reasonable behaviour. I don't think people know these things intuitively. They have to be taught. So as I was lying in that mud under that pile of leaves and debris under that billboard out back afraid to move, not knowing if I were paralyzed, how seriously injured I was—I thought about your lack of education. Why didn't Denise call for help. Why has she taken the criminal route in this. Why hasn't she taken the reasonable moderate—yes, even polite approach and called an ambulance. And then of course I remembered all my training and everything I've been taught about people like you and I decided you just don't know any better.

R.J.: Are you going to call the police.

HELEN: *(brushing)* I don't know yet. Probably. I mean it is the reasonable thing to do. I was just buried alive.

R.J.: You see, what happened was, she panicked.

HELEN: I was buried alive! I had to claw my way up through garbage and leafy smelly muddy things because I was buried alive in a deep hole.

DENISE: *(to herself)* Not deep enough.

HELEN: I heard that.

R.J.: She didn't mean it.

HELEN: Oh she meant it.

R.J.: *(to DENISE)* Tell her you didn't mean it.

DENISE: *(to HELEN)* I didn't mean it.

HELEN: Yes you did! You meant it. What's wrong with you. Don't you have any civilized instincts left in you. Have they all been dulled or killed by your senseless self-indulgent life style.

DENISE: Look I'm sorry. Don't start…with that judgement crap. I can't take it.

HELEN: Well look who's going on the offensive. I mean talk about inappropriate responses. I mean who buried who alive.

DENISE: It wasn't personal. Why are you always making it personal. I didn't do it to punish you. I thought you were dead. I was just—

R.J.: She panicked.

DENISE: I didn't panic. I thought it through. I was taking precautions. I did what I thought I had to do…so we could get on with our life.

HELEN: *(standing)* You're a bad girl, Denise. That's all you are. Someone should have just told you this a long time ago. You're a very bad girl.

DENISE: Ah shut up.

HELEN: I won't shut up! *(rubs her head)* I have a job here. I'm a representative of our government. And what government represents to me is the people's will to have a civilized society. And what that means is dealing with people like you and getting you back in line. You're out of line, Denise. Way out of line!

HELEN rubs her head. Wobbles.

HELEN: Oooh. I have to sit down.

She sits.

R.J.: Are you all right.

HELEN: No. I have a serious concussion. And I was buried alive. I'm not all right…. Did you call a doctor as I asked, Denise.

DENISE: Yes.

HELEN: Did you.

DENISE: Yes!

HELEN: Did you really!?

DENISE: No! No I didn't!

HELEN: No you didn't! Couldn't you see I was maybe giving you a second chance to do the right thing. Why didn't you call a doctor, Denise. It would have been the right thing for you to do.... So why didn't you do it?

DENISE: Because!.... I needed to know if you were going to tell the police.

HELEN: Protecting yourself.

DENISE: Yes.

HELEN: At any cost.

DENISE: Yes.

HELEN: Bad bad girl! Bad girl! Wicked girl!

DENISE: Oh please shut up. *(to R.J.)* Make her shut up.

R.J.: How.

DENISE: Any way you can.

HELEN: Don't get him to do your dirty work. Maybe it's time you stopped dragging him down, Denise. He's trying to do better things with his life. Why don't you let him do them...these better things.

DENISE: *(to R.J.)* She's impressed with you because you joined the church.

HELEN: Or maybe I'm impressed because he doesn't bury people alive!

R.J.: *(to HELEN)* The church thing. I just did it to make points with you people.... It's not real.

HELEN: It could be, R.J. Just open up your heart. I know you want to. I know you've got the...right things in you.

DENISE: *(to R.J.)* I told her you could cook. She thought that was great. Well she thought it was sad you had to cook your own supper after working hard all day. She thought I was some demon bitch for making you do that. But the fact that you could cook, she thought that was cool.

R.J.: *(to HELEN)* I like to cook.

HELEN: I'm sure you do. The desire to cook. To serve. To nurture. These are good things. The things civilized people feel.

R.J.: Denise has been sick. Really sick. Sick about losing the baby.

HELEN: That's not an excuse.

R.J.: Yes it is.

HELEN: Not enough of an excuse.

R.J.: Yes it is. Losing the baby made her life…made her feel her life was…didn't have any value. And she hated herself…. She'd cry all night. Night after night for weeks and months.

DENISE: No, no I don't want you telling her this stuff.

R.J.: She should know. She thinks you're just some punk kid who—

DENISE: *(to R.J.)* No no listen. I don't want to…it's not what I'm worried about, what she thinks of me. *(to HELEN)* I just want to know if you're going to tell the police.

HELEN: I…don't know.

DENISE: When will you know.

HELEN: I don't know when I'll know! I mean I'm trained, you know. Trained to think things through…. Act in the best interests of people. The people in this instance are your child, R.J. here and even yourself. I have to weigh intent with possibility. And possibility with harsh reality.

DENISE: I don't know what you're talking about.

HELEN: *(standing)* Is it better if I just let this pass. Or is it better for everyone if you're put away! I have to think about these things…. And then of course there's the issue of…compassion…I am a Christian. I believe in Christian things.

R.J.: That's…good…. I don't know much about it…. I mean I just started to learn and I wasn't paying a lot of attention. But I got the general feeling it was a good thing to be…a Christian.

DENISE: Oh please…. I just want to know what she's going to do…. Maybe you can ask her. Christian to Christian. I'm tired.

DENISE sits on the bed.

HELEN: *(to R.J.)* Can you get my briefcase. All my muddy clothes are on the bathroom floor. Can you stuff them all in my briefcase. Can you take a twenty dollar bill out of my wallet. And put it in my hand. Can you take me and my possessions to the street and hail a cab for me. Can you get started on those things now.

R.J.: Yeah...yeah.

He goes about his tasks.

HELEN: Good...because I think I need to have an x-ray. I feel that would be the best thing for me to do right now. Go to the hospital and get an x-ray.

R.J.: *(from bathroom)* I'm coming. I'm coming.

HELEN: Good.... Denise?

DENISE: What.

HELEN: Stay put.... I'll let you know what I decide.

DENISE: Sure.

HELEN: I mean the chances of you getting your child back now are slim. Very slim.

DENISE: Right.

HELEN: I mean you have really messed up.... But we'll see.... I've reclaimed worse people than you.... I have.... I'm trained.... And it's...possible.... We'll have to meet...and meet again.

DENISE: Here?

HELEN: Here or in prison.... Wherever. We'll see...

R.J. comes out of the bathroom.

R.J.: Okay.... Ready?

HELEN: I need a hand.

R.J.: Okay.

He helps her up. They start off. HELEN holding R.J. for support. They are leaving.

HELEN: Denise?

DENISE: What.

HELEN: Remember. Stay put.

DENISE: Sure...

They are gone.

DENISE goes into the bathroom. Runs water. Comes out drying her face vigorously. There is a knock at the small window on the wall opposite the door. PHILLIE is in the window. Gesturing.
DENISE goes to the window. Opens it.

PHILLIE: Is she gone.

DENISE: Yeah…. How did you—

PHILLIE: Wow. That was weird. Good thing I looked through the window before coming in. So…. she's alive. Well I guess that's better in the long run.

DENISE: I don't know. How did you get on.

PHILLIE: Did you talk to R.J…. You know I didn't go the first time?

DENISE: Yeah…. But you went back…. So?

PHILLIE: I got up to the front porch…. I looked in the window. I saw her.

DENISE: You saw her? Really?

PHILLIE: Yeah. She looks like you. She's cute. She was playing with blocks. Blue and red and orange blocks. She looked…happy…I couldn't go in. I would've scared her.

DENISE: Yeah.

PHILLIE: We've got to think of a way that won't scare her.

DENISE: Yeah…

PHILLIE: I'll be in touch…ah…Wednesday…. Wednesdays are my best days…. So…we'll talk…. I mean I'm committed to this project. I think it's good…. I feel good about it.

DENISE: I'm glad.

PHILLIE: See ya.

DENISE: Yeah.

She closes the window. PHILLIE disappears.
R.J. comes back in.
DENISE just leans against a wall.

R.J.: I think she's bleeding internally.

DENISE: Really.

R.J.: I mean her eyes are bloodshot…. If that's a sign…. I don't know for sure.

DENISE: Me neither.

R.J.: So...what do you think's gonna happen.

DENISE: I don't know.

R.J.: I mean should we stay here. Should we go back home. Should we go on the run.

DENISE shrugs.

R.J.: I mean if Phillie grabs Christine we can just take off like you said.... I'm up for that if we have to...

DENISE: I wouldn't count on that happening.

R.J.: No?

DENISE: No.

R.J.: You know something I don't?

DENISE: Yeah.

R.J.: You wanna tell me what it is?

DENISE: No. Not really.... No point.... Later maybe...

R.J.: So......*(shrugs)* so...

The phone rings. R.J. looks at DENISE but she seems far away So he goes to the phone. Picks it up.

R.J.: Hello.... Yeah hi Phillie.... Oh.... wait a sec. (covers the receiver) It's that guy from the television network. Can I talk to him. Will it piss you off.

DENISE looks at R.J. for a long time.

DENISE: *(shaking her head)* Go ahead.

R.J.: Thanks.... (into phone) Put him through, Phillie.

R.J. smiles at DENISE. DENISE smiles sadly at R.J.
There is a lighting change.
DENISE is alone in a light. Everything else is in darkness or shadow.
And DENISE is talking to us.

DENISE: We stayed in that motel room for six months. We hardly left. R.J. watched his shows and took a lot of calls from network executives. They seemed to think he had some special understanding of what their shows were trying to do and they called him to ask for his advice. He'd suggest ideas and plead with them for a more human handling of their guests.

He spent a lot of time explaining to these shows how it wasn't necessary to treat people like shit just to boost their ratings. And he told me he had a feeling that gradually they were coming around to his way of thinking. Phillie made a few more feeble attempts to grab Christine.... Once he made it as far as her bedroom. But she was asleep. And he didn't want to wake her up.... Anyway he was crying so hard he could barely see. Because the book she had open on her sleeping body was the same book his Aunt Jennie used to read to him when he was about Christine's age. And his Aunt Jennie was the only person other than his cousin Edward who ever treated him with justice and a fair heart.... Helen spent seven weeks in the hospital recovering from a...subdural hematoma.... She called me from the hospital daily.... And continues to do so. Asking me questions and counselling me about moderate civilized behaviour. And I have learned to listen patiently and sigh pleasantly like I agree and like I am truly trying to change.... But I'm not agreeing with her or even thinking about what she's saying anymore than I'm listening to R.J. on the phone with his TV people or even when I'm watching those shows with R.J. and listening to those sad, desperate people and all those experts telling them how to live better and everything else and blah, blah blah.... I'm not really listening.... Because I'm not really there. I'm in hell. I'm more desperate than anybody I ever hear on those shows and I'm trapped in a sadness and an anger so deep I know I'll never get out. Because I'm just slipping deeper into the sadness. And deeper into the anger.... I have horrible thoughts about doing horrible things to people. If I were on one of those shows and I told people how I really felt and what I really wanted to do.... they wouldn't be able to give me any advice...they wouldn't even be able to talk.... Maybe they'd just cancel the show.... If I leaned over in bed and told R.J. what I felt about everything...about life...about our life and everyone else's life and how really useless and stupid it all is...he'd die probably. He'd give up and die.... So I don't tell him. I tell him I'm waiting. I'm being a good girl. Seeing if things work out. I tell him maybe there's still a chance we'll get Christine.... But I know...things don't work out.... Not for people Like us. They just get worse.... Until...well you can't take it anymore.... Then you really do get bad.... Helen thinks she knows how bad I am. She probably thinks she knows how sad I am and how angry I am too. She's wrong.... She hasn't got a clue.... She might find out though.... Maybe I'll just...come up with a way of letting her know...

DENISE shrugs.
Lights up on R.J. watching TV. Smiling.
DENISE shakes her head sadly.

DENISE: You okay, R.J.?

R.J.: Yeah. How about you. Still with me? Still hangin' in?

DENISE: Yeah.

R.J.: Thata girl.

DENISE smiles.
Blackout.

The End

ADULT ENTERTAINMENT

PERSONS
JAYNE
MAX
DONNY
PAM

PLACE
A slightly run-down motel on the outskirts of a large city.

Scene One

We are in a motel room. Traffic goes by outside. Occasionally someone walks by the door. JAYNE JOHNSON and MAX MALONE are having sex. They are both pretty vocal and active. A phone rings.

MAX: Ah...Jesus.

JAYNE: That mine?

MAX: What...

The phone is still ringing.
MAX is reaching for the phone on the bedside table.

JAYNE: That's my cell phone. It's on the floor.

MAX: No it's—

JAYNE: On the floor near my skirt, I think.

MAX: No it's—

JAYNE: Answer it.

MAX: It's the...room phone.... I'm trying to reach it...

JAYNE: The room phone? Who knows we're here.

MAX: Ah...

JAYNE: Don't answer it.

MAX: I have to...ah I'm.... Can you move a little.

JAYNE: Whatya mean you have to...

MAX: There.... Got it.

He drops it on the floor.

MAX: Damn...Ah...

JAYNE: Who is it.

MAX: Wait a second. I dropped it. I can't find the.... Okay. Got it....
Hello?... Hello?... Is that you, Donny. Is that you laughing, Donny....
Well screw you. You got nothing better to do?.... Gimme a break here....
What?... Sure sure.... Goodbye.

Pause.

MAX: What.... Why are you staring at me like that.

JAYNE: Why do you think.

MAX: Hey it was just his idea of a joke. You know... "You doing it?" "Did I interrupt?" "What were you doing when I interrupted." He's a jerk. You know he's a jerk.

JAYNE: Yeah. So how come the jerk knows we're here in this motel room.

MAX: I had to tell him.

JAYNE: Really.

MAX: He's my partner. It's our deal. We gotta know where.... I mean each guy has to know where the other guy is at all times.

JAYNE: Really. I didn't know that.

MAX: I never told you that?

JAYNE: No. You didn't.

MAX: I thought I did.... Because it's important. So I thought.... Anyway we gotta know where we are...so we can reach each other. Because once we couldn't and something happened because I went somewhere alone and I almost got hurt.... So...

JAYNE: So it's a cop thing.

MAX: Yeah.... Well it's a detective thing. Anyway forget him. He just called because he thought it was funny we're in a motel.

JAYNE: Yeah. Funny we're here in a motel instead of my place. Because that's where his wife and kid are. Does he think that's funny too.

MAX: What.

JAYNE: That his family left him? Does he think that's funny. I mean what does he think about that anyway, Max.

MAX: I don't know what he thinks about that. Look let's just forget he called.... I thought we were doing pretty good there for awhile. I mean I was nervous because it's been a while but I thought I was doing...okay.

JAYNE: Yeah you were doing fine.

MAX: So let's get back to it...the thing...here.

He is kissing her.

JAYNE: No.... I'm not...

MAX: Come on.... Ah...there...just put your hand...

JAYNE: No.... I don't think I'm in...the mood.

MAX: Come on.

JAYNE: No.

MAX: Really?

JAYNE: Yeah...I'm definitely out of the mood.

MAX: Shit. Come on. I'm worked up. Look at me. I'm still worked up here.

He has lifted the covers so she can see.

JAYNE: Hey. Is that my problem. Go home. Tell your wife. Maybe she'll help you out.

MAX: Oh here we go.

JAYNE: We going somewhere?

MAX: Look I...just put your hand...let me put my...

JAYNE: No.

MAX: Yeah but I really need...I really need to—

JAYNE: Ah shut up.... Don't beg. It's not sexy believe me.

MAX: Okay. Let's start again. We'll—

JAYNE: No.... I'm getting up.

She gets up. She is only partially dressed, in a slip. She adjusts it.

JAYNE: This was a mistake. It was better when it was over. A thing in my past. I felt better about you. I even started to have fond memories.... But looking at you now I'm remembering how much I hate your guts.

MAX: A few minutes ago you liked me well enough.

JAYNE: That was the mistake part. Get it? This is the part where I treat you with the contempt you deserve.

MAX: *(sighs)* You want a cigarette?

JAYNE: I quit.

MAX: Sure you did.

JAYNE: I quit.... You're supposed to say "Good for you." Only an asshole would say "Sure you did."

MAX: You really quit?

JAYNE: Yes.

MAX: Good for you…. Is it okay if I smoke.

JAYNE: Yes…

MAX: Can you throw them to me? My cigarettes? They're on the bureau there.

JAYNE: Yeah. Sure…Here.

She tosses him the cigarettes.

MAX: Thanks…

JAYNE: Look…. Look it's…

MAX: What…

He lights up. Inhales.

JAYNE: It's not you…. No that's stupid…. Of course it's you. It's both of us…. When we're together it just makes it clear.

MAX: What…. What's clear.

JAYNE: We've given up. We're both people who've given up.

MAX: What's that mean? Given up….

JAYNE: Whatya think it means.

MAX: I don't know. Give me an example.

JAYNE: I've given up…on my work…. Yeah. I used to fight like hell for the scum of the earth I defend. But now most of the time I secretly hope they're found guilty and thrown behind bars 'til the end of time.

MAX: Yeah? So you're just feeling like everybody else feels about them. Come on, Jayne. We're talking about rapists and murderers here.

JAYNE: I've given up! I used to be a defence lawyer. Now I'm…not. I'm just someone who used to care…. And you're the same. You don't care either.

MAX: I still care about you if that's what this is really about.

JAYNE: No, that's not what it's really about. It's about what I said it was about…. And no, you don't care about me. But that's not what I was saying.

MAX: Come back to bed.

JAYNE: No…. I need a glass of water.

She goes into the bathroom.

Water running.

JAYNE: *(from bathroom)* You've given up on...things.

MAX: Things? What things?

JAYNE: *(returning)* Your family. You've given up on your family.

MAX: No I haven't.

JAYNE: Yes you have.

MAX: I still care about my family. My kids.

JAYNE: Yeah. You love your kids. But you've given up on your family. That's why you're here. You're not a family man.

MAX: Yeah. I am. I still am—

JAYNE: No, asshole. You're not! You're here. With me. Get it?

MAX: Come on, that doesn't mean I'm not—

JAYNE: Yes it does. The truth is it does. It means you want something else. You're not all there. When you're at home you're only partly there. You had a dream about being a family man but you can't pull it off.

MAX: What is this anyway.

JAYNE: The truth.

MAX: But why are you— What's the purpose—

JAYNE: The purpose of the truth?.... Well I don't know, I guess the truth is the only reliable alternative to bullshit.

MAX: I mean why now. Why all of a sudden do you start—

JAYNE: Hey it's a powerful thing, the truth...once it gets close to you. It's got a powerful...smell. I mean I got a whiff of it a moment ago. You know, how you sometimes get a kind of sense about...a feeling about something that might be true and then to understand it...you need to expand it.... That must happen to you on the job.

MAX: I guess. Yeah...

JAYNE: Well it's happening to me. That's what I'm doing. I'm expanding that feeling. You know, filling in the details so we'll know.

MAX: Know what.

JAYNE: Why we're here.

MAX: Here, here? Or...you know.... Here!

JAYNE: Here in a motel room. Six months after we agreed never to see each other again.

MAX: I'm here because I saw you today in court and I got turned on.

JAYNE: Sorry. It's that truth thing again. You're here because you've given up. Just like me. We sensed that about each other. When we first met we sensed it, and we sensed it even stronger today. We're both finished. Two people of a certain age both done like dinner. Done being useful citizens and lawyers and cops and husbands.

MAX: Hey, I'm still a good cop.

JAYNE: Nah. You're a piece of shit cop. You're a hollow man with a badge.... The way you treated that kid today...

MAX: What kid.

JAYNE: Outside the courtroom. In the hallway. That kid. My client's husband. Sneering at him. Threatening him. Just like a mean hollow bully with a badge.

MAX: That kid is sewage. Crack dealing, pimping sewage. I've got a history with that kid. He's the worst of the worst. How come you're upset about that kid. He's the reason his "wife," your client, is being sent to prison, Jayne.

JAYNE: Yeah. But I'm not talking about the kid. I'm talking about you. The hollow man with the badge who sneers at messed up teenage criminal offenders like they're not even human. Who's lost all sense of fairness and just wants to get on with it.

MAX: That kid is going to kill people. He's probably already killed people. Fairness? What's that kid know or care about fairness. Jesus.

JAYNE: I'm not talking about the kid!...Look the deal was you were sup- posed to care.... About something. The job wasn't supposed to be just about...putting in the hours.

MAX: You know I thought we were just going to have sex. A good healthy humping sweating time here.... And I get—

JAYNE: The truth? Come on. Listen, I know what you're doing out there, Detective. I'm doing it too. That girl today. She's got a problem with drugs. A bad one. But I'm not going to deal with it. I'm going to get her a year's probation and hope I never have to see her sad face again. Anyway, who am I to feel sorry for her. She seems as happy as I do. At least she's young. Good stuff could still happen to her. Who am I to

even worry about her.... I'm forty-one. I hate my job. I've got no life....
At least she's got a husband.

MAX: Do you want a husband.

JAYNE: Did I say that. I said at least she's got a husband. Its like saying at
least she's got a can opener. Or a wallet. It's something. A husband
is...something she's got.

MAX: Come on. A husband who's low-life garbage.

JAYNE: Hey. Maybe they have a real love between them. An abiding fondness
and mutual respect that transcends their unfortunate circumstances.

MAX: Yeah, right. You really think that?

JAYNE: No, asshole. I don't...But the thing is we wouldn't know if they did.
We're dead to that kind of feeling. That's the thing we recognize in
each other. And that's the truth...The thing that brought us together
again...the thing that turns you on.

MAX: What thing.

JAYNE: That kind of deadness. It turns you on because...Because why, Max.

MAX: Because...it means...Yeah it means you don't care that much. And
that...makes it easier to just...What?...Leave I guess.

JAYNE: Yeah...And that feels good...Just doing it...then leaving.

MAX: Yeah...So...Okay we're both sad pathetic bitter people. But does that
mean we can't have sex.

The phone rings.

JAYNE: Is that my cell phone.

MAX: No it's the—

JAYNE: Donny? Is it Donny.

MAX: Must be.... Unless you told someone we were coming here.

JAYNE: Oh yeah sure. I posted it on the office message board.... No, it's
good old Donny. I'll get it.

Picks up the phone.

JAYNE: Okay, Donny, here's what's happened so far. We were doing it. You
called. We stopped doing it. We may do it some more. We may not. We
may...just kill ourselves instead.... Okay? Satisfied?.... Yeah, same to you.
Listen, maybe if you weren't such a dipshit you'd be off doing it yourself

instead of bothering us. Maybe you could even be doing it with your wife.... No no I won't leave your wife out of it.... Yes, she is my business...She's living in my house, that's why. And she's living in my house because you're such a big bloated stupid dipshit.... Where are you anyway.... Why? Because I might wanna come over and kick you in the groin.... Same to you. So where are you. In some porno theatre? Some hooker hotel?.... Same to you.... So where are you. Tell me where you are you cowardly dipshit.

MAX: Open the curtain.

JAYNE: What.

MAX: Open the curtain a little. Look out the window.

She walks over the window. Taking the phone. Opens the curtain. Peeks out.

JAYNE: Oh my.... Is that you Donny. Is that you in the Plymouth Horizon. Are you sitting in an unmarked police car in a motel parking lot waiting for your partner to get a piece of ass, Donny? Is that what you're doing, detective, you pathetic fat balding smelly dipshit.

She bangs the phone down.

MAX: He musta followed me.

JAYNE: He didn't drop you off? You're gonna go with the "he musta followed me" story. Remember who you're talking to now. I deal with liars all day.

MAX: Okay he dropped me off.... But only because...it was convenient.

JAYNE: And you knew he was out there all the time.

MAX: Not for sure.

JAYNE: Come on.

MAX: I had my suspicions.... Okay yeah I knew.... So what.... I mean really. What's it matter.

JAYNE: You see that's what I mean. That's truly low-life amoral I don't give a shit behaviour. Not only are you cheating on your wife, you let your partner wait in your police car in the parking lot while you do it.... You've reached bottom. This is it. Bottom. Look around. Touch it. How's it feel.

MAX: I think you're making too much of this. It's just...convenient. In case we have to go...somewhere.... Because of the job.... In a hurry I mean.

JAYNE: Whatever's happening to you is happening fast. You wouldn't have done this six months ago.... Even then you had a bit of class. You're deteriorating at an amazingly fast rate. Look even as we speak you're deteriorating. Your eyebrows...are growing together.... Your skin is turning yellowish.... You're becoming a kind of jaundiced neanderthal right in front of my eyes.

MAX: *(chuckles)* You're funny.

JAYNE: You think that's funny.

MAX: I forgot how funny you are.... When I've thought about you...when I missed you I thought about your...you know...ass.... But I guess I should've missed your sense of humour too.

JAYNE: Yeah, really. It's better to miss the whole person. It shows you're actually a human being. Not a morphing neanderthal.

MAX: Morphing? That's a word my kids use....

JAYNE: Oh great.... Reflect openly on your children's habits now.... How sensitive.

MAX: I meant it's odd to hear you use it.

JAYNE: I picked it up from Emma.

MAX: Emma?

JAYNE: Yeah, Emma. Your partner Donny's daughter? The one who is living with her mother in my house because her father doesn't care about her.

MAX: He cares.

JAYNE: No he doesn't.

MAX: Yeah I think he does. But he's got problems. It's the job.... The job has made him a...a...

JAYNE: An asshole?

MAX: Yeah...well...yeah. It's those three years he spent on the morality squad. He was never the same. He's got this thing about hookers.... He can't leave them alone. He says he likes their company. He thinks they're.... Well I don't know what he thinks.... He just likes having sex with hookers...a lot.

JAYNE: Yeah but he still cares about his kid.

MAX: He does.

JAYNE: And his wife too.

MAX: Yeah. In his own way.

JAYNE: Is that similar to the way you care about your wife.

MAX: I love my wife.

JAYNE: I love that you love your wife.

MAX: Yeah…

JAYNE: Yeah. Except of course you don't. You don't really love anyone.

MAX: Ah, man. Can't we just—

JAYNE: No we can't.

MAX: You want a cigarette?

JAYNE: I quit. I just told you that.

MAX: You did?

JAYNE: You don't listen. You don't love. You don't care…. You're just…putting in time…getting laid when you can…whatever…blah blah blah…

MAX: You've put on a few pounds….

JAYNE: You're looking at my body.

MAX: Yeah.

JAYNE: You're just lying there idly staring and you're thinking, "She's heavier."

MAX: A little…

JAYNE: You thinking anything else?

MAX: No…

JAYNE: No? Your brain is entirely empty except for that one thought about a few extra pounds?

MAX: Look you know me. I think what I'm thinking when I'm thinking it…. Nothing else. You're standing there…. I'm looking at you…. I notice a few extra pounds. I think about that.

JAYNE: Listen something just came to me here. A way to redeem yourself. A way to stop your slide into meaningless hell…. My client…needs some— But before I get into that I'd just like to say you've put on a few pounds yourself. And I think my pounds are nicer than yours.

MAX: You do?

JAYNE: Yeah. Because mine aren't all around my stomach.

MAX: My stomach? Come on there's nothing extra around my stomach. It's just the way I'm lying. If I sit up then—no if I lie back more then it's—

JAYNE: Anyway about my client. I'm worried she's going to have to do some time.

MAX: I thought you said you didn't care.

JAYNE: That's right I don't.... But I do. Get it?

MAX: No.

JAYNE: I don't want to care. I know it doesn't matter if I care. But sometimes I can't help myself. Get it now?

MAX: I guess.... So what about her.

JAYNE: The only thing she's got going for her is that her husband is one of the world's biggest hosebags.

MAX: I thought you said he might be okay.

JAYNE: Hey are we gonna try and exist in the present tense here or what. What I said before has only passing relevance to what I'm saying now. Whether he's an okay guy to her is not the point. The point is to the court he's someone who...what I mean is if I can switch the responsibility for the illegal actions she's charged with, from her to him—That would be...good. I'd like that. I'd be indebted to someone who could help me do that.

MAX: Do you have an idea of how that could be done.

JAYNE: We'd have to show she was coerced.

MAX: She can't say she was coerced?

JAYNE: No. No she can't say that.

MAX: Why not.

JAYNE: Well for one thing she wasn't coerced. And second even if she was, she loves the guy and she's not going to put him in the shit to save herself. No way. She's not like that. She's loyal. Tough and loyal. I admire her.

MAX: You like her?

JAYNE: Yeah I like her.

MAX: And you care about her.

JAYNE: Okay. I like her. I care about her. But she's the last one. I'm never gonna care about any of them anymore. Because I'm hollow. Just like you.

MAX: Yeah. But in the meantime. You've got a problem and I think there's really only one solution to this problem.

JAYNE: I think that too. I think her husband has to say he coerced her.

MAX: He has to confess.

JAYNE: He has to make a statement. A clear statement of his guilt in this matter. Voluntarily.

MAX: Voluntarily. Agreed.

JAYNE: Because he feels guilty and wants to prevent his wife from suffering because of his actions.

MAX: Exactly. Because he loves her.

JAYNE: She's his life. She means more to him than anything. She even means more to him than all that money he makes selling crack.... So...can you ask him if he'll write that statement for me.

MAX: It'll be a pleasure.

JAYNE: Can you do that soon.

MAX: Donny and I will visit him tonight.

JAYNE: You know where he lives?

MAX: Oh yeah...we know everywhere he lives....

JAYNE: Great.

MAX: Come here.

JAYNE: Why.

MAX: Come here. Sit down on the bed.

JAYNE: Why.

MAX: Come on. Please.

JAYNE: You said please. That's nice.

MAX: Come on.

JAYNE: (moving closer) Only because you said please.

　　She sits.

JAYNE: Well here I am. Whatya got in mind. You got lots of naughty ideas in your head?

MAX: You know me, Jayne. I only get one idea at a time…. So when did you get your idea.

JAYNE: Which idea.

MAX: The one about me leaning on your client's husband.

JAYNE: I told you it just came to me.

MAX: I think you got it this afternoon when you saw me giving him a hard time outside the courtroom.

JAYNE: You do? You really think that.

MAX: Yeah.

JAYNE: Well that would mean I only agreed to come to this motel with you to use you in a selfish manner.

MAX: I guess it would.

JAYNE: How do you feel about that.

MAX: Your client has a sister. This sister has a boyfriend I've been looking for for a month. He's in hiding. The sister knows where. I'm wondering if you could casually get your client to…casually find out from her sister where this bad young man is hiding…. I mean I was just wondering.

JAYNE: You started wondering that when…. When I asked you to arrange for that guy to confess.

MAX: I guess….

JAYNE: Or earlier.

MAX: Could have been earlier. Could have been when I saw your client and her sister today in court. That could have been when I got the idea. I don't know.

JAYNE: You don't know because you had the idea of having sex with me in your mind already. And there was no room for another idea?

MAX: Or maybe I got the idea for sex after I got the idea for asking you for a favour. It's confusing when I got which idea first. I mean I'm a simple guy, Jayne.

JAYNE: Yeah…. So this bad man you want to find….

MAX: Just want to…. No big deal.

JAYNE: It's not important to you. You're not doing it to help society or anything.

MAX: Like you said, I'm putting in the hours.... I need to find this guy. It's a job. I was assigned a task.

JAYNE: Like...a dog.

MAX: Exactly like a dog.

JAYNE: Man we are both sad pathetic shadow people.

MAX: Do you really think my stomach's bigger.

JAYNE: When you're this pathetic you don't even feel guilt when you use people like this.... You feel any guilt?

MAX: No.... Touch my stomach. It's still pretty hard.

JAYNE: Yeah.... Yeah it is.

MAX: So.... Can we have...sex now. Touch me. Here.

JAYNE: There?

MAX: Yeah...ah...yeah.

JAYNE: Let's take our time, okay.

MAX: Yeah sure....

They kiss.

JAYNE: I mean it would be nice to take a really long time doing this....

MAX: Ah...sure.

JAYNE: You know why?

They kiss.

MAX: Sure I know why....

JAYNE: I...bet you don't....

MAX: Because you like the idea...*(they kiss)* of Donny sitting and waiting out in that parking lot...getting steamed.

JAYNE: (laughs) Yeah.... I want that fat dipshit out there for a minimum three hours....

MAX: Three?

JAYNE: Minimum.... Can you manage that.

MAX: What's in it for me.

JAYNE: "What's in it for me?" …This…this is in it for you.

> *She puts her head under the covers. MAX groans.*
> *Blackout*

Scene Two

> *DONNY and PAM. DONNY is a large man in a crumpled sports jacket.*
> *PAM is very blonde and wears tight clothes.*
> *There is an over night bag on the bed. PAM stands a bit nervously*
> *watching DONNY as he looks around the room.*

DONNY: Why here…. *(gestures to PAM)* Why…here.

PAM: You don't like it?

DONNY: Hey what's not to like…. Why this room is all I'm asking.

PAM: This room? Whatya mean this room, Donny.

DONNY: Well, this room. As opposed to some other room.

PAM: You don't like this room?

DONNY: Did you choose it, Pam.

PAM: I don't see what you're getting at.

DONNY: Did Jayne choose this room.

PAM: What's Jayne got to do with it.

DONNY: That's what I'm asking…. So?

PAM: Yeah…

DONNY: Yeah…. What?

PAM: I…It was my idea…. Getting together. But…she got the room.

DONNY: Bitch.

PAM: Bitch? Who's a bitch.

DONNY: She's a bitch. Jayne.

PAM: Why.

DONNY: Never mind.

PAM: All she did was do me a favour.

DONNY: I said never mind. It's okay…. It's just…a joke or something. I guess she thought it was funny.

PAM: I don't understand.

DONNY: Never mind. Maybe it is funny.

He opens the drapes. Looks out the window.

DONNY: She's not in the parking lot.

PAM: Who. Jayne?

DONNY: Yeah. Maybe she's coming later.

PAM: Why would she be in the parking lot. Why would she be coming later.

DONNY: Never mind…. It's okay.

PAM: The thing is…. She did me a favour. I couldn't think of a way for us…for you and me to…. I told her I thought we could work it out if we spent some time together. Next thing I know she's handing me this key…. The thing is…she's been a good friend to me.

DONNY: Yeah.

PAM: I mean we've been at her apartment for two months now, me and Emma and—

DONNY: Yeah yeah I know.

PAM: So…

DONNY: What…. Come on, what.

PAM: So don't call her a bitch. She's my friend. And she's a good person.

DONNY: Yeah…she's a saint.

PAM: Yeah. To me she's been like a saint. That's right.

DONNY: Ah please for chrissake! No look I'm sorry.

PAM: You're ruining the mood.

DONNY: I know I know.

PAM: I mean we just got here and the mood is ruined. I didn't even get a chance to unpack my shampoo and stuff.

DONNY: I'm sorry…. Maybe…Maybe I'm nervous.

PAM: You're nervous? Really?

DONNY: Maybe…. You mind if I drink?

PAM: You brought alcohol?

DONNY: A coupla samplers.

He takes two airline vodkas out of his pocket.

PAM: I thought you were…off that.

DONNY: I am. This is a little something that's all. Just because…. You know, one for each of us.

PAM: I don't want one.

DONNY: So two for me. No big deal. I'll just get a glass.

He goes into the bathroom. Water running.
PAM looks around. Opens her overnight bag. Just stares at the contents.

DONNY comes out. With a glass. Drinking.

DONNY: I mixed it. It's mostly water. Just something to take the edge off.

PAM: Yeah.

DONNY: So…Pam…. You look good.

PAM: Thanks.

DONNY: Yeah…. Why are you wearing…. Why are your clothes so tight.

PAM: Just… *(shrugs)* You don't like them?

DONNY: You kinda…look like a hooker. No offence.

PAM: Why would I take offence, Donny. You like hookers.

DONNY: Yeah…. So…is that the point.

PAM: What…

DONNY: You rubbing something in my face here?

PAM: I just…. Forget it.

DONNY: I thought you wanted to work something out here. But if you're just gonna try to—

PAM: I thought you'd like it. That's all.

DONNY: You're sure?

PAM: Yeah…. I think.

DONNY: You're not sure?

PAM: I'm not sure about anything, Donny. I'm just trying my best here. Maybe I wore the clothes to turn you on. Maybe I wore them to remind you what you've done to me. I don't know. I'm really messed up these days.

DONNY: You want a drink or...something?

PAM: I told you no.

DONNY: I meant a Coke or something. There's a machine down by the office.

PAM: No. I'm okay.

DONNY: Yeah? Well...okay.... So...

PAM: Jesus. *(shakes her head)*

DONNY: What.

PAM: Jesus.... Look at us, Donny. This is pathetic. Look. You're sweating like a nervous kid. Look at me in this dumb tart's halter. Is this some kind of sad fucking joke or what.

DONNY: Well it's been a rough time for both of—

PAM: I mean we were never the world's two smartest people but how did we get here.

DONNY: It's not so bad.

PAM: Look at us. "It's not so bad." It's worse.

DONNY: I...thought you meant the room.

PAM: I didn't mean the room.

DONNY: I know that now.... But.... Well anyway we're here. Trying to...be here...together and that's—

PAM: We've lost our house. We've lost all our savings. We've lost our friends.... I can't look anyone from either of our families in the eye.... Our daughter doesn't talk anymore.

DONNY: Whatya mean she doesn't talk.

PAM: She doesn't talk. Not much anyway...Well what's she gonna say, "Hey Mom, what the fuck's happened to our life here."

DONNY: You never told me she wasn't talking.... That's not good.

PAM: No it's not good. But—

DONNY: Have you done anything about it.

PAM: What?

DONNY: Have you looked for…I don't know, professional help for her.

PAM: No I haven't.

DONNY: Why not.

PAM: I don't know. I just haven't. Maybe I'm hoping she'll come through it.

DONNY: Hoping? Hoping is stupid.

PAM: What.

DONNY: You've got to take action. Hoping won't help her. I think you should look into—

PAM: No no. Don't give me advice here. I don't think you're in any position to give me any advice about this subject.

DONNY: Come on. She's still my daughter.

PAM: She's still your daughter like you're still my husband. Barely.

DONNY: Hey we gotta separate things here. No matter what goes on between us. We gotta keep Emma neutral.

PAM: Neutral? Neutral…. Like not involved?

DONNY: Sort of.

PAM: Sorry. She's involved. What happens to us matters to her. It has…It has…effect.

DONNY: Your job is to protect her.

PAM: My job.

DONNY: Well she's…with you.

PAM: Yeah she's with me in a friend's apartment in a single bed in a guest room. So my job, I guess is to make her feel okay about that. Somehow. And that's job enough. That's plenty. So don't start…I gotta…Excuse me…I gotta…

She goes in the bathroom crying. Closes door.
DONNY just hangs his head

DONNY: What are we doing here…. I mean really…I'm missing some-thing…. It can't be to…get together. It just doesn't have that "getting together" feel about it.... It's gotta be something else.... Can you hear me?

The bathroom door opens a little.

DONNY: I think maybe it's...Maybe I'm supposed to repent...or something.... Offer my apology or a reason...a reason for...I know I blew it. I went through all that money...I...gambled...stuff like that.... I feel like...I've been living in hell so I know I should be trying to get out...Get out of hell.... Become a good guy again. Stop hanging out with low-lifes. Stop fucking whores. Maybe get some counselling. Shit like that. But...I don't know.... The thing is, Pam. It's shit. The world is shit. It truly is.... And somehow I feel better when I'm not pretending it isn't. When I'm with you and Emma and I'm pretending everything is more or less fine...it's like bullshit in the extreme.

The bathroom door opens.
PAM comes out. She has washed some of her makeup off.

PAM: Really?

DONNY: Yeah.

PAM: That's how you feel. That's really how you feel about things.

DONNY: Sometimes.

PAM: Oh, Donny.

She is close to him now.

DONNY: Maybe it's the job...

PAM: It's not the job.

She is very close to him.

DONNY: You don't know—

PAM: Yes I do. I know.... It's not the job. It's...loneliness.... Being all by yourself.... Having these weird dark thoughts and nobody to...share them with....

DONNY: Loneliness?

PAM: Yeah.

She kisses him.

DONNY: Maybe.

He kisses her. Grabs her. They begin to grope each other. DONNY pushes her back against a wall. Kisses her.

PAM: Careful. You're so...

DONNY: Big...Heavy. You always said...you liked it that I'm heavy.

PAM: Just be...

DONNY turns her around. She is face to the wall. He is pulling down her tights. They are both breathing heavily.

PAM: This how you want it?

DONNY: Yeah.

PAM: This way? Not in bed.

DONNY: No...

PAM: This how you take your hookers? Is it.

DONNY: Yeah.

DONNY is undoing his pants.

PAM: From behind like this? Rough like this?

DONNY: Yeah.

PAM: This some of your dark thoughts at work? What? Taking me like this.... Showing me how rough life is. Sharing it with me. Because it's being alone that makes you think the worst. Do things that—

DONNY: Yeah.

PAM: You know what I think it really is.... It's being a coward. It's giving in to it. Saying the hell with it. Ah...Donny...Donny.... Are you just a coward.... You are aren't you.

She turns. Hugs him. Quickly pulls his revolver from his holster.

DONNY: What are you doing.

PAM: Okay then. The hell with it. Let's just get it over with for both of us. Both of us. Me first. *(puts the gun to her head)* You get to watch.

DONNY: Pam...Pam!

PAM: Don't want to watch? ...Okay.

She switches off the lights on the wall.

Blackout.

Gunshot.
Lights back up.
JAYNE and MAX are standing over the crumpled bodies of DONNY and PAM.
JAYNE is in her slip. MAX is in his boxer shorts.

JAYNE: Oh my God. Oh my God.... Look at them. It's— Why am I dressed like this.... Why are we in our underwear.

MAX is leading her back to bed, sleepily.

MAX: Because it's a dream.

JAYNE: A dream...Oh well that explains it.

They are getting into bed.

MAX: It also explains why there are two bodies and there was only one gun shot.

JAYNE: Oh...right.

They pull up the covers.
Blackout.

Scene Three

JAYNE yells. Lights.
JAYNE is sitting on the edge of the bed. MAX is sitting up.

MAX: What...What is it.

JAYNE: A dream. A...bad dream.... Weird too.... I think it was the do-gooder in me working overtime.... You know?.... I went to sleep thinking about ways to help Pam and Emma and next thing I've got Pam in this room. With Donny. Trying to make a reconciliation.... Except it goes bad. Very bad.

MAX: Yeah. Well it would, wouldn't it.

JAYNE: They killed themselves.... During sex. It was weird. Man. What's wrong with me. What part of my subconscious would think it was a good idea to get Pam back with Donny.

MAX: The part that wants your guest room back. Did they really kill them- selves while they were doing it. What was that like. Was it strange. Or was it kind of exciting.

JAYNE: *(just looks at him)* I need a smoke.

MAX: They're on the table.

JAYNE: What's wrong with you. You know I've quit. When I say I need a smoke you're supposed to say "No you don't. Have a glass of water."

MAX: Have a glass of water.

JAYNE: I need a smoke!

MAX: They're on the table.

JAYNE: Have a glass of water!

MAX: Have a glass of fucking water!

JAYNE: Thank you! *(gets out of bed)* You were in my dream too by the way. Wearing those boxer shorts. You looked stupid.

She goes to bathroom. Closes door. Water runs.
A knock at the motel door.
JAYNE sticks her head out of the bathroom.

JAYNE: Tell me, there's no way that could be your wife.

MAX: That's right, no way. I'm working nights. What, you think she has me followed when I'm working. It's probably Donny.

JAYNE: Get rid of him.

MAX: That's what I intend to do…. You thought I was gonna invite him in?

JAYNE: God. I need a smoke.

She slams bathroom door.
MAX opens motel door.
DONNY is standing there. Hands in pockets.

DONNY: Hi.

MAX: Hi.

DONNY: I've got him.

MAX: Who.

DONNY: That kid. Jayne's client's husband. The crack prince. He's in the car.

MAX: Our car?…Why.

DONNY: You called me. Told me to get him.

MAX: I told you to locate him.

DONNY: Locate him. Get him. What's the fucking difference.

MAX: Why'd you bring him here.

DONNY: Had to bring him somewhere. Not going to work on him in public, are we. What's wrong with here.

MAX: Jayne's still here.

DONNY: I thought she'd be gone.

MAX: She's not.

DONNY: Yeah. Well. Usually they're gone by now.

MAX: They?

DONNY: Babes. Women you bring to motels. They usually don't spend the night. Two hours max.

MAX: You're an expert. That's right. I forgot.... Anyway she's here.

DONNY: For how long.... I mean if she leaves soon that's still okay. Where is she.

MAX: Washroom.

DONNY: Can I come in by the way.

MAX: No.

DONNY: Why not. I gotta use the toilet.

MAX: She's in there. What's wrong with you. Are you drunk.

DONNY: I've been drinking.... I wouldn't say I was drunk.

MAX: You've been driving around the city with a prisoner while you're drunk...

DONNY: Okay. If you say so. But really.... He's not officially a prisoner. He's more like...a hostage. Listen I gotta piss really bad.

MAX: Do it out back.

DONNY: Out back? *(shrugs)* Okay...Then what.

MAX: Give me five minutes. I'll get rid of Jayne.

DONNY: Hey I don't want to spoil your party, partner. I'll take the slimeball somewhere else.

MAX: No way. No more driving. You're staying put...Five minutes.

MAX begins to close the door. DONNY stops him.

DONNY: Max?

MAX: What.

DONNY inhales deeply through his nose.

DONNY: Sex has taken place in here hasn't it. Great sweating sex. I can smell it....

MAX: Asshole.

He closes the door firmly.
JAYNE comes out of the bathroom. Already getting dressed.

MAX: How much of that did you hear.

JAYNE: All of it.... I have to get out of here. I can't have anything to do with this. I'll get disbarred.... Jesus. I mean, come on, Max.

MAX: It wasn't my idea.

JAYNE: How drunk is that idiot.

MAX: Drunk enough.

JAYNE is getting her things.

JAYNE: Oh this is great. This is just the way I hoped you'd handle it. Kidnap the guy and bring him to my motel room. Donny can't just be drunk. He must be insane. What do you think. Do you think maybe he's maybe...maybe...

MAX: Yeah, maybe.

JAYNE: Are you worried. I mean can you handle him.

MAX: Yeah it's okay. I'll chill him out.... Then we'll just...talk to the kid. Like you suggested.

JAYNE: I didn't suggest anything. Get into the habit right now of saying "Jayne? She had nothing to do with it." ...Say it.

MAX: Come on.

JAYNE: Say "Jayne? She had nothing to do with it." I want to hear how it sounds.

MAX shrugs.

MAX: *(convincingly)* Jayne?... No. She had nothing to do with it.

JAYNE nods in admiration.

JAYNE: I keep forgetting how good a liar you are. That little "no" you threw in. "Jayne?... No." You're an artist.

MAX: Yeah, right. Anyway don't worry about it. I'll take care of it.

JAYNE: Well if you don't, I'm screwed. I've got almost nothing in pension. No savings. Disbarred and disgraced at my age? No thank you. I'll take death.... Where are my shoes.

MAX: Ah...Shoes.... Were you wearing shoes.

JAYNE: What the fuck's wrong with you. Are you stupid. Of course I was wearing shoes.

MAX: I meant into the room. Maybe you kicked them off in your car. You know, when we started to go at it.... You got pretty hot. I got you pretty hot sister.

JAYNE: Yeah. Right. You were that good. For a moment I even forgot how to breathe.... Inhale, then what.... Gimme a break. Find my shoes.

MAX: There. Under my jacket.

JAYNE: Thanks.

She grabs them.

JAYNE: This was supposed to be a professional thing. An exchange of...favours. Between professionals.

MAX: That's how I think of it. The kid will cooperate. Your client will get off. I'll handle it.

She goes to him.

JAYNE: You keep saying that. But I think you're worried. You're worried Donny's outta control.

They are facing each other. Close.

MAX: You should be going.

JAYNE: Yeah.... Say it...Say it again.

MAX: *(shrugs)* Jayne? No. She had nothing to do with it.

JAYNE: Amazing. You're a genius liar, Max. You're a hollow man, a failure as a husband, a lover and a policeman. But you're a world class liar.

MAX: I love you, Jayne.

JAYNE: *(smiles)* Amazing.

She is leaving. Her arms full of things. Coat, briefcase.

JAYNE: *(to herself)* "I love you, Jayne." ...Amazing.

She is gone.

MAX: Ah man...what a...

He rubs his face vigorously. Goes into the bathroom.
Water running.
DONNY comes to the door.

DONNY: Hey. Max. Is it cool.... I saw her leave.... Can I bring in the kid.

MAX comes out of the bathroom. Drying his face with a towel.

MAX: Come in for a second, Donny. Close the door.

DONNY closes the door.

DONNY: What?

MAX turns on the TV.

DONNY: What.... We gonna watch some TV here? Is there a game on or something. I thought you wanted to deal with this kid.

MAX is changing channels. Stops on one with a loud Latin band
playing something up tempo.

DONNY: Hey.... Direct from Mexico City.... I love this shit.

MAX smiles. Walks to DONNY. Punches him hard in the stomach.
DONNY folds. MAX kicks his feet out from under him. DONNY is down.
MAX twists an arm behind him. Throws DONNY on the bed. Gets on
him with a knee in his back. And puts his face close to DONNY's ear.

MAX: You're fucking up Donny. You're fucking up really badly here. You got that!? ...I said have you got that!!

DONNY: Yeah...

MAX: It's gotta stop. You're putting me in jeopardy. Have you got that!?

DONNY: Yeah...Yeah.... Listen can I get up.... You're hurting my back.... My back isn't in great shape.

MAX: Yeah...I know...

MAX stands.

MAX: I forgot...I forgot about your back.... I'm sorry.

DONNY: No...it's okay.

DONNY is sitting on the bed. MAX turns off the TV.

DONNY: That mean we're finished making noise?

MAX: Yeah.

DONNY: I'm glad...

MAX: Listen, Donny. I don't—

DONNY: No, hey, no apology necessary.

MAX: What?

DONNY: It's okay. You lost it. It happens. Look...I'm okay. Everything is fine between us.

MAX: No. Wrong.

DONNY: What's wrong.

MAX: Everything you just said. I wasn't going to apologize. You're not okay. Everything's not fine between us. You're about as fucking wrong as a person can get. Man, how drunk are you.

DONNY: How drunk? I dunno. How do you measure these things.... I'm not as drunk as you got that night after you shot that old man. I'm nowhere near that drunk. You were barely alive that night, Maxie.... Hey speaking of serious drinking.

He reaches into a pocket. Takes out a paper bag. Empties it on to the bed. Several small airplane size bottles of vodka.

DONNY: Just checking to make sure they survived the landing.... One, two...five...Okay. They're all fine. Check the kid will ya. I don't think he's going anywhere but give him a peek through the curtains just in case.

MAX parts the curtain a bit. Looks.

MAX: He's just sitting there.

DONNY: Yeah. He's scared shitless. No telling what's goin through his head. I bet he thinks we're outta control. I bet he thinks we're rogue cops on some personal vendetta mission.

MAX: What you tell him?

DONNY: That's what I told him. That's why I bet he's thinking that.... No. Just kidding. I told him we needed a favour.... I told him if he cooperated it would be good for him in the long run.

MAX: You didn't tell him he'd have to do five years in prison.

DONNY: No. Hey. Am I stupid…. But even when we tell him he'll still cooperate. Hey. Come on. Five years. If you're thinking positively about your life, that's short term. You could still have a perfectly fine criminal career after that.

MAX: So…what happened.

DONNY: What happened when. So much has happened to me recently I'm not sure I know—

MAX: What happened!? Why is he sitting in the back seat of our car!?

DONNY: Well…I was watching him. He saw me. He ran. I figured where he was going. Got there first…. Looking back, I had no choice. I had to grab him or he'd have gone into hiding.

MAX: But why bring him here.

DONNY: You know, I've been wondering about that myself. I mean I could have taken him to a quiet place. Called you. Very discreet.

MAX: So?… Why didn't you.

DONNY: You're in here. In this much used but still somehow cosy room. You're in here for hours with good ole Jayne. Getting…what? Blown five or six times?!

MAX: Hey man, come on.

DONNY: Why. Is that rude. Or is the number too high. Six blow jobs. Is that just me being a romantic fool.

MAX: Okay, so…you what? Get annoyed I'm having sex with someone and you decided to ruin my night? Is that it.

DONNY: Well also I'm drunk. And also you call me up and just say "Donny, here's an address. Go watch this kid." Like I'm your secretary or fucking something.

MAX: Hey, I'm sorry. I didn't think you'd mind since all you'd been doing was sitting in the goddamn parking lot for the last five hours.

DONNY: No no. Listen, let's not get into that stuff. Recrimination. I forgive you. All is forgiven. We're here now. Wanna drink?

MAX: No.

DONNY: Have one.

MAX: I don't want one.

DONNY stands.

DONNY: Join me in a drink you arrogant cocksucker or I'll kick your teeth out!

MAX just looks at him.

MAX: Sit down.

DONNY: Sure.

DONNY sits.

MAX: You're nuts aren't you. You've gone nuts on me. I can see it in your eyes.

DONNY: Can you. In my eyes. How clever you are Detective Malone. Very scientific. Well Your Honour I knew he was guilty because I could see it in his eyes.... What are you talking about, man.

MAX: You. I think you should take a leave of absence. Get help.

DONNY: Help for what.

MAX: Everything.

DONNY: Everything?

MAX: Yeah everything. Your mind. Your marriage. Your job.... Your goddamn life!

DONNY: What are you saying here. You think there's something wrong with me? You think I'm lacking something? Oh no. You think I'm not really officer material, don't you sir...*(stands)* Is that what this court martial is all about, sir. Is it sir! Is it!

MAX: Sit down.

DONNY: Sure.

He sits.

DONNY: I need a smoke.

MAX: I thought you quit.

DONNY: What are you talking about.

MAX: Oh that's right. It's Jayne that quit. Sorry.

DONNY: No. Hey. I understand the spell a woman like that can put you under.

MAX: What are you talking about.

DONNY: It's hard to think straight when you're remembering her lovin' ways.... All you see is her. You look at me, you see Jayne. I ask you for a smoke you think.... "Jayne doesn't smoke." If I walk over and kiss you right now I bet you start to feel me up and think, "God she's got nice tits."

MAX: Shut up.... What the hell is wrong with you.

DONNY: Who knows. Really.... So?

MAX: What!?

DONNY: Cigarettes! Got any? I gave my last one to the kid. Check him again will you.

MAX peers through the drapes.

MAX: He's got his eyes closed.

DONNY: Sleeping?

MAX: How am I supposed to tell that from here.

MAX throws DONNY a pack of cigarettes.

DONNY: If he's sleeping he can't be that scared.... I mean these kids are hard to read.... They can look totally fucked up one moment then you see that dumb cold killer look in their eyes.... Wish I could sleep. I can't you know.... Four hours tops.

MAX: Yeah?... Since when.

DONNY: Since since.... You know. Since I ruined my life.... You remember?

MAX: Remember what? It's not like you did it all at once. It happened over a coupla years, Donny. In fact, it's still going on even as we speak.

DONNY: Yeah.... Anyway I can't sleep.... Listen do you want me to take that kid somewhere else. I'm sorry I brought him here. It was a joke. Something to fuck you up.... I'll take him somewhere else.

MAX: You're not going anywhere. You're staying here 'til you're sober.

DONNY: That could take weeks.

MAX: Whatever.... I'll take the kid somewhere. Talk to him.... It's my favour anyway. It's just a thing I'm doing for Jayne. It shouldn't have gotta outta hand like this.

DONNY: Yeah. Sorry.... So. A favour.... So what ya get in return? She promise you something?

DONNY is opening a sampler. Drinking.

MAX: Her client's sister is Robbie Del Mar's girlfriend. She knows where he is.

DONNY: Really.

MAX: I told you that. I told you that this afternoon before I set this motel thing up with Jayne. Were you drunk this afternoon?

DONNY: You didn't notice did you.... I'm good. I'm very good. Hardly anybody notices. I'm smashed all the time, Maxie.... All the time.

MAX: Get help.

DONNY: No.

MAX: Get help.

DONNY: I don't want to. I want this. I like this. I like...wanting this. *(laughs)* Want to live in a cheesy apartment hotel. Have rough sex with professional ladies, drink vodka samplers, go prowling for criminals at night and kick the shit out of them. That's my life. It's not a good life by normal standards. But I've become fond of it.

MAX: You've got a kid.

DONNY: Shush. Don't mention the child. Not fair.

MAX: Fair? What's fair, Donny. Is it fair having you as a father.

DONNY: Shush. Off limits. Can't talk...

MAX: Is it fair for Pam.

DONNY: Pam?

MAX: Pam? Your wife?

DONNY: Careful now, commander. Wife talk doesn't come cheap. There's a price. And here it is. Who the fuck are you to bring wives into it. Who the fuck is fucking around in this very fucking fucking motel room. You fucking hypocrite. Stand up. I'm gonna kick your teeth out.... Stand up.

MAX stands.

MAX: Go ahead.

DONNY: Asshole. You bring the wife thing up.... Asshole.

MAX: I'm here once. This happened once. But for the last six months I've been.... I've tried to be...loyal.

DONNY: Loyal. Shit.

MAX: Yeah loyal...And it isn't shit. And I've tried.... So today—anyway.... It's not the same as you. I, you know, love my wife.... Okay. Look I'm sorry I brought the wife thing up. It's none of my business.

DONNY: I, you know, love my wife too. Are you saying I don't—

MAX: Didn't you hear me. I just said I'm sorry. Let's drop it.

DONNY: I blame the job.

MAX: I know you do.

DONNY: I blame the time I spent undercover.

MAX: I know.

DONNY: With the losers and everyone. And that...loser-don't-give-a-shit-way-of-life. It's seductive in its own way.

MAX: Yeah. Right.

DONNY: Anyway. I blame it.

MAX: Yeah...

DONNY: Who do you blame.

MAX: For what.

DONNY: For what you are.

MAX: What am I.

DONNY: What are you? You're a guy who's gonna go drive some kid to a quiet secluded place and convince him to plead guilty to a crime he maybe didn't commit. Convince him in a way only a man who is experienced in the art of convincing can.

MAX: Yeah.... So what are you saying. I'm as bad as you? I spent all my family's savings? Mortgaged the house? Lost the house? Deserted my wife for the company of a street walker?

DONNY: Gee, I did all that? The streetwalker had a name by the way. Clare. And I loved her.

MAX: Yeah right.

DONNY: I still love her. And she loves me.

MAX: Oh.... Good.

DONNY: We're a nice couple really once you get to know us.... So you shouldn't be saying mean things about us.... I say that just in case you're asked. You know..."How's Donny doin' with that hooker?" Then you can say "Her name is Clare and actually they're deeply in love. It's a modern urban romance."

MAX: Are you putting anything in your veins.

DONNY: Pardon?

MAX: Besides the booze, are you on anything. I think you should tell me if you are. We could find ourselves in situations. Guns could be used. I'm thinking only of my own personal safety here.

DONNY: How nice of you.

MAX: Well there's no good thinking of you. You're a goner. And apparently that's the way you want it.

DONNY: Apparently.

MAX: Get some help.

DONNY: No.

MAX: Get some help or get a new partner.... I'm gonna take that kid for a ride.

MAX is strapping on his gun.

DONNY: Yeah. You're gonna take that kid for a ride. But even so...you still feel...morally superior to me, don't you.

MAX: Get some help.

DONNY holding a sampler.

DONNY: Want one for the road? You know...something to take the edge off the violent act you're about to commit.

MAX: He won't feel a thing.

DONNY: Yeah right.

MAX: Hey Donny. It's not what you do. It's what he thinks you're gonna do. You used to know that stuff.

DONNY: Some things are good to forget.

MAX: How much gas in the car.

DONNY: How far you need to go.

MAX: To the country.... To that place. You know that place. He's gotta think I'm taking his somewhere I can bury his body.

DONNY: Right.... But I'm the one who's outta control.

MAX: That's right.... You are.

MAX leaves.
DONNY stands unsteadily...falls.

DONNY: Ah man. My back.... You've seriously fucked up my back, Maxie.... I'll have to apply for disability...(laughs) Disability.... I love that word...

Blackout.

Scene Four

The TV blares the sound of "Big Band Mariachi."
DONNY is dancing in his underwear. A knock at the door. DONNY dances over. Opens it.
PAM is standing there. Same hair colour. More natural style. Clothes still tight. But not as suggestive.
Without missing a beat DONNY grabs PAM and begins to dance with her. PAM is trying to yell over the music "Donny. Donny. Stop." She finally breaks away. And turns off the TV.

DONNY: What's wrong. You don't like Latin dancing?

PAM throws her arms in the air. Shrugs. Turns away.

DONNY: What's that mean. When you throw your arms in the air like that. I've always wondered...I mean if you didn't do that and you used words instead, would the words be something like "What the hell is wrong with you, you big drunken asshole, and what the fuck are you doing and why don't you just fucking disappear outta my life for good?"

PAM: You said on the phone you were in trouble.

DONNY: I am in trouble.... I've discovered I'm not nearly the dancer I thought I was.

PAM: I'm out of here.

DONNY gets in her way.

DONNY: No. Don't go...

PAM: Get outta my way, Donny.

DONNY: Please. I'd like.... I'd like you to stay awhile. Please.

PAM: Then stop this...this crap.

DONNY: Okay.

PAM: Get dressed.

DONNY: Get dressed. Sure.... Oh. Look that might be...not a good idea....
All my clothes are soaking in the bathtub.

PAM looks at him oddly. Goes into bathroom. Comes out.

PAM: Why'd you do that.

DONNY: Clammy.... I was feeling really clammy. I blamed the clothes. Well
that hotel I'm living in isn't the cleanest place in the world.... I thought
I might be infested...

PAM: What are you talking about. Lice?

DONNY: I don't know. Maybe.

PAM: You think you've got lice? Jesus.

DONNY: That disgusts you doesn't it. I can tell. You're such a clean person.

PAM: Jesus, Donny. Why are you living in a place where you can catch lice.
What's wrong with you. Haven't you got any self respect left.

DONNY: *(laughs)* Self respect.

PAM: You think that's funny.

DONNY: No...No, I'm flattered that you think I once had self respect. I
didn't really, you know. I mean I'm not sure I did.

PAM: Sure you did.

DONNY: Maybe I was just pretending.... When we met. When we got
married. When we lived in that nice house.... Maybe that was me
pretending.... Maybe this is me not pretending...

PAM: Yeah. Okay. Maybe it is.... Why'd you call me.

DONNY: I'm out of cigarettes.

PAM: Really.

DONNY: Yeah.... You got any? You still smoke?

PAM: Yeah. I smoke a lot. I almost never stop.

She is going through her purse. Finds a pack. Takes one. Throws the pack to DONNY.

DONNY: That must drive them nuts at work. All those prissy little academics.

PAM: I go outside. There's a place where a few of us—

DONNY: And you still wear your clothes tight. The only woman in tight clothes with a cigarette in her mouth on that whole fucking campus. I can just hear them. "There's that secretary who dresses like a slut and smokes like a Chinese gambler." You must drive them all ape-shit insane. The faculty. The students. All of them.

PAM: Yeah.... I'm a serious impediment to higher education. So.... You've got my cigarettes. If there's nothing else, I'll be going.

DONNY: I didn't call you because of the cigarettes.

PAM: Yeah I know that, Donny.

DONNY: I thought you knew.... I was just making sure.

PAM: So? What. Why did you want me here. Spit it out.

DONNY: It's hard to...just spit it out.

PAM: Spit it out anyway.... I left Emma with Jayne. But she's gotta go somewhere. I don't have a lot of time.

DONNY: Do you have time to tell me how she is.

PAM: Jayne?

DONNY: Emma.... I know how Jayne is. How's our daughter.

PAM: She's great. You should get yourself de-loused and come by for a visit sometime. Anything else?

DONNY: Ah.... So I can tell from your tone of voice you wouldn't be interested in any kind of reconciliation.

PAM: Is that what this is about. Are you outta your mind.

DONNY: Does that mean no.

PAM: You're sitting in a motel room in your underwear smelling like a distillery and you're asking me if I want to get back together with you.... Oh yeah Donny I really do.... But first I wanna go somewhere and get my brain sucked out of my skull.

DONNY: Okay so you don't want to live with me in wedded bliss.... Would you do something else for me. Would you help me kill myself.

PAM: What.

DONNY: I need help.

PAM: To kill yourself.

DONNY: I know the honourable thing is to do it alone. But I'm afraid I might botch it.

PAM: So you call your estranged wife. The mother of your child to give you a hand....

DONNY: I called my friend.... My only friend...

PAM: Donny...

DONNY: I've thought this over. It makes sense. There's some insurance. Survivor's benefits. And then there's the fact that I hate my life...a lot.... I know this will be hard for you. You don't like blood. But in the long run—

PAM: No you have to stop there. I don't know if you're serious. I don't even want to know if you're serious. I just want you to stop...I'm this close, Donny....I'm this close to doing it to myself every second day. So I don't need—

DONNY: What are you talking about. You can't kill yourself. What about Emma.

PAM: When I think about it, I think Emma would be okay.... Jayne would take her...

DONNY: Jesus Christ. You're talking about this seriously. What the fuck are you doing talking about killing yourself in a serious manner. You're all right. Look at you.... You're all right.

PAM: How do you know how I am.

DONNY: I know you're all right. You were always all right.

PAM: Oh really. Well maybe I wasn't. Maybe I was pretending too. Maybe there was just a shell around me. And maybe it's gone now. And maybe I'm not all right at all.

DONNY: It's just that end of a marriage thing. It's a thing everyone.... You're in shock or something. If you got counselling then—

PAM: Oh fuck off.... I'm sick at heart, Donny. Get it? Deep inside.... The man I loved has gone missing. He's fallen into a rotten depraved hole. And sometimes I just want to die.

They are just staring at each other.

DONNY: Jesus.

> *He goes into the bathroom. Water running.*
> *He comes out…. His face and hair are wet.*
> *PAM gets the pack of cigarettes from where DONNY left them. Lights one.*
> *Sits on the bed….*
> *DONNY gets a cigarette. Sits in a chair.*
> *They are both just sitting there. Smoking. Looking off…. Occasionally at*
> *one another. But mostly…they look away.*
> *The phone rings.*

DONNY answers it.

DONNY: Yeah…yeah…. No I'm not going anywhere…. Why not tell me now…. Okay…. How long…. You okay? *(but the phone has gone dead; hangs up)*

PAM: Who was that.

DONNY: You should leave.

PAM: Was it one of your girlfriends? She coming over?

DONNY: It was selfish the way I got you here. I didn't know how you— I wasn't really…I mean I don't think I wanted to kill myself. I just…. Look maybe we could meet later and talk.

PAM: Let's talk now.

DONNY: You have to leave.

PAM: You want me to leave because some whore is coming over here to service you but then you want to meet me later for what…. Coffee? Jesus. You have like zero respect for me, right? I mean, I'm nothing to you…

DONNY: That was Max on the phone…. Something went wrong with…a thing we were doing…. We're in trouble. Bad…trouble…. I don't want you involved.

PAM: I'm staying.

DONNY: Whatya mean you're staying. It's police stuff, Pam.

PAM: No I'm staying…. That was always the thing. You were always in some kind of trouble and I never knew what it was…. Money, depression, I never knew…. Because you always hid it…. You always sent me away…. So even though it's probably too late now anyway…. I'm staying. Just so I know.... So whatever happens I don't have to guess what made you do...whatever.... So...I know...So I can tell Emma maybe...

DONNY: You should go.

PAM: I'm staying.... When's he getting here.

DONNY: A little while.

PAM: And when he does, you gonna work this problem out with him in your underwear?

DONNY shrugs.

DONNY: I guess so.

PAM: I've got some stuff of yours in a box in the trunk of the car. I've been meaning to drop it at Goodwill.... Jeans and stuff.

DONNY: Yeah...okay...good.

PAM: I'll go get the box.

PAM starts off.

DONNY: Pam...

PAM: *(stopping)* What?

DONNY: I didn't know. I thought you were...just disappointed.... Hurt yeah, but not—

PAM: You never thought about me long enough or hard enough to know anything, Donny.

DONNY: That's not true. I just...didn't know.

PAM: Whatever.

She opens the door. Goes out.
DONNY watches her.
Blackout.

Scene Five

MAX is standing in the doorway. Not looking good. He has his hand pressed to his bloodied shirt just above his belt, to one side.
PAM is standing, staring at the blood, mildly hyperventilating...maybe about to be sick.

MAX: Don't…don't…no don't…

PAM: But…look—

MAX: No…don't…don't…just—

PAM: But…look…look it's—

MAX: No it's not as bad…as it looks.

PAM: It looks…bad…Oh…oh…

MAX: No don't…. Just…I called Jayne and she's…. Where's Donny.

PAM: Coffee.

MAX: What.

PAM: He went for coffee.. He needed to…

MAX: Sober up? Good.

> *MAX takes a step inside. Stumbles. Falls to his knees. Yells in pain.*

PAM: Ahh! …Shit.

> *PAM runs into the bathroom. Sound of retching.*
> *MAX works himself into a chair.*
> *JAYNE comes running in. Sees MAX.*

JAYNE: Oh fuck…Oh shit.

MAX: Here.

JAYNE: What.

MAX: The keys…. First aid kit. In the trunk.

> *Sound of retching.*

JAYNE: Is that Donny.

MAX: Pam.

JAYNE: Pam?…. Oh yeah…. Shit.

MAX: Get the kit.

JAYNE: Yeah.

> *She runs out.*
> *PAM sticks her head out of the bathroom. Her face and hair are wet.*

PAM: Was that Donny.

MAX: Jayne.

PAM: Jayne? ...Who's taking care of Emma.

MAX: What...I dunno...I—

He yells in pain.

PAM: Ahh...

She pulls her head in. Closes bathroom door...Retching sounds.
JAYNE comes back in.

JAYNE: Got it...

MAX: Good.... Now—

JAYNE: Yeah. Got it. Good. Yeah...yeah.... So...

She is opening the kit. Throwing stuff around.

JAYNE: What am I looking for here.... How bad is it.

MAX: Get...the...there's a bottle of pain killers. Demerol...

JAYNE: Yeah.... Demerol.... Here.

She offers him the bottle.

MAX: Can you open it.

JAYNE: Yeah...Sorry...*(fumbling with the bottle)* Yeah. Here.... You need water?

MAX: No...*(swallows four or five pills)*

JAYNE: Okay okay...So...Should we take you to a hospital.

MAX: No...no that's not gonna be possible.... Look in the kit...for...for...

JAYNE: What...For what.

MAX: There's a suturing kit...

JAYNE: A what.

MAX: Needle and thread.... It's not that bad...I think we just need to close it...

JAYNE: Close it? Like...sew it up? Me?

MAX: I'll help.

JAYNE: You'll help? Yeah but you'll help who? Me? I'm.... You think I'm gonna—

MAX: Jayne. I can't go to the hospital.... Help me get my jacket off.

JAYNE: Yeah...Pam! Pam, get out here. We need your help.

JAYNE is pounding on the bathroom door.
PAM comes out.

PAM: Yeah, yeah…okay okay. I'm okay now. I just—

JAYNE: Help me get his jacket and shirt off.

PAM: How bad is it?

JAYNE: He doesn't think it's that bad.

PAM: It looks bad.

JAYNE: Yeah…. But he says it'll be okay if we sew it up.

PAM: If we what?

JAYNE: We gotta put stitches in.

PAM: We? Us? Come on. Get serious. We can't do that…. We've gotta get him to a hospital.

JAYNE: He can't go to a hospital.

PAM: Why not.

MAX: Pam. You should leave. You shouldn't get involved.

PAM: Involved…. Involved in what…*(to JAYNE)* Where's Emma.

JAYNE: At home…. I had Mrs. Zindel come in.

PAM: Oh good. She's nice. Yeah but I should get home…. *(to MAX)* Involved in what, Max.

MAX: Just go, Pam.

PAM: Is Donny involved…. I mean I know he's involved. But is he really involved.

JAYNE: Yes, Pam he is…. He's right in the centre of it. I mean if I'm in it he's sure as hell gonna be in it with me. And that's a promise.

PAM: You. Why are you—

JAYNE: I just am.

PAM: Then I have to stay. Because you're my friend. And he's my…my…

MAX: Pam. Go. Now.

PAM: No…No I'm staying…. Right here…. I'll be—

They have his shirt off.

PAM: Ah, Jesus look at that... *(pointing at the wound)* Look how big that is. What happened to you!?

MAX: He had a knife.

DONNY comes in. Wearing a ridiculous tracksuit. And carrying a take-out tray of large coffee cups.

DONNY: Oh great.

He hands the coffee tray to PAM.

DONNY: What happened...

MAX: He had a knife!

DONNY is kneeling in front of MAX. Looking at the wound.

DONNY: You lost a lot of blood?

MAX: Well what's a lot.... Who knows.... Did you hear me. He had a knife.

DONNY: I heard ya.

MAX: You put him in our car without searching him. You musta been pretty fucking drunk when you picked him up.

DONNY: Yeah.

MAX: Sure. Or else you wouldn't have picked him up even. You would have just watched him like I asked....

DONNY: Yeah...

MAX: He had a large kitchen knife under his shirt. No way you'd have missed that if you searched him.

DONNY: This isn't deep. I think the bleeding's slowing down.... I'm gonna close it up.

JAYNE: Oh great. The drunk is gonna do the sewing.

DONNY: *(to JAYNE)* You wanna do it?

JAYNE: Yeah. I do.

DONNY: Have you done it before. No? ...So let me do it.

MAX: We were in that field about twenty miles from—I was trying to pull him outta the car.

DONNY: Pam, go home.

PAM: I'm staying.

MAX: He wouldn't get out.... I told him I just wanted to talk but he was so spooked by then—

DONNY: Pam, I don't want you to hear this.... Max stop talking 'til Pam leaves.

MAX: He was just sitting in the back seat, whining.

DONNY: Max stop talking a minute.... Pam. Get out.

PAM: No I want to hear.

MAX: Begging and whining...

DONNY: Max. Shut the fuck up! Pam you have to leave.

PAM: No!

JAYNE: Get out of her face, asshole. Why shouldn't she hear. She's gonna hear eventually.... About this. About something else. Some other fuck up of yours that effects her life...

DONNY: Hey. It was you that started this shit.

JAYNE: Yeah. I started it. But you fucked it up. It didn't have to be like this.

DONNY: Sure it did, you stupid bitch.... What do you think happens when we lean on people. You think it's like a science or something. It all goes according to some great fucking plan?

JAYNE: It does if you stay sober, asshole.

DONNY: Get away from me. I've gotta sew him up.

JAYNE: No. Go to hell. I'm gonna do it....

She is grabbing the stuff from him.

DONNY: Fine. You wanna do it? Fine. *(to MAX)* You want her to do it?

MAX: Sure. Who cares. The pills are kicking in. Why don't you all just take turns.... So Pam here's the thing you're not really gonna like knowing. You say you need to stay and you need to know but you're definitely not going to like knowing this.... I killed that kid.... Yeah. He cut me with that kitchen knife. I got my gun out.... I put two bullets in his head....

DONNY: Ah...man...

MAX: Buried him as best I could...in that field...but I was bleeding...so...

PAM: *(to JAYNE)* He killed someone? ...So...What? ...It was in the line of duty.... Or what.... No? *(to DONNY)* He just killed someone for no reason.... How are you involved, Donny.

DONNY: Ah we...we were...

MAX: So Donny.... Tell me no one saw you take that kid.... None of his friends. No neighbours.... No one just passing by. Tell me we can get out of this.

DONNY: I was...I don't know.... I was plastered. We could've been alone. There could've been a thousand people watching.... I don't know.

MAX: Well fuck you very much....

JAYNE inserts the needle.

MAX: *(groans loudly)* Aren't you...supposed to...freeze it first.

JAYNE: Sorry.

MAX passes out.

DONNY: He's unconscious.... Do it now.... Sew him up, Jayne!

JAYNE: Yeah...yeah...okay...

DONNY: You want me to do it?

JAYNE: No.

DONNY: So hurry up!

JAYNE: I'm trying!

DONNY: *(to PAM)* Heard enough, Pam? Seen enough?.... Does it feel like we're "sharing" now. You feel good knowing about how I spend my time at work? Are we more the couple you imagined we could be. Is all this bringing us "closer."

JAYNE: Shut your mouth you fucking bully. Or when I'm finished him I'll take this thing and sew your goddamn lips together.

PAM: Donny. What's happened to you. You've become some kind of... monster.

DONNY: Hey I just kidnapped the kid. He's the one who killed him. Be careful how you throw that monster word around. If you use it too soon you won't have it when you need it.... No no no look, I'm sorry.... I'm feeling all weird that you're here. I can't have you around this stuff, Pam. It's not natural for me. You're supposed to be at home. Even if you're at home hating my guts...that's when it's natural.... Or maybe even having your own life...totally forgetting about me.... But not this...not here in this mess.... It's all wrong.... So please...please listen.... Go home to Emma and let us handle it.... We can do it with some luck. But I can't think straight if you're here.... Okay?

JAYNE: He's probably right, Pam.

PAM: So if I go...You'll all "handle" it. How? How will you handle it.

JAYNE: They know how to...do things, Pam. Max and Donny.

PAM: So handling it means...what? Hiding it? Maybe even blaming someone else.

DONNY: There's no way we can move the blame here Pam. We'll just—

PAM: Hide it? Cover it up? What?

DONNY: We'll protect ourselves. That's all.

PAM: Yes but...a kid was killed. Is that right.

DONNY: Yes but—

PAM: Killed because of actions you took.

DONNY: Pam. He wasn't a kid really.... He wasn't a sweet little paper boy kid next door smiling up at you...all full of good will.... If that's the picture you've got of him in your head it's wrong.

PAM: How old was he.

DONNY: He was about twenty.

PAM: Twenty?

DONNY: Yeah. He was about twenty robbing, pimping, drug pushing, mugging, crippling, murdering fucking years old, Pam. And now he's dead in a fucking field and not one bad thing will happen in this world because of that to anyone except us if we don't do something to protect ourselves.

PAM: Did he have a mother.

DONNY: A mother? Ah shit...holy fuck. *(to JAYNE)* You. You're one of us. You pretend not to be. But you are. So you explain it to her.... I've gotta go use the car phone to book us off. We're overdue.... Explain it to her. *(to himself as he leaves)* A mother...a mother....

DONNY leaves.
JAYNE has finished sewing. She is putting a bandage on MAX's wound.

JAYNE: I think I did it all right.... Look at it.

PAM: Maybe some disinfectant.

JAYNE: Yeah. I did that earlier, didn't I…. No, maybe not.

There is a can on the floor from the kit. JAYNE sprays some on the wound.

PAM: So. Go ahead…. Explain.

JAYNE: There's nothing much to explain…. You get to a point where you start to believe that some lives just aren't worth very much…. You'll probably never get to that point…. Why should you. Most people don't. Most people think life…life itself, is pretty important. I used to think that…I was…nicer when I thought that…. You know this all started because I was trying to do a young woman a big favour. I thought she had potential…. I don't know that she does, for sure…. But I do know she has a lot more potential than that "kid" in that field ever had…. Because well…because he was basically scum.

PAM: And…that's all you feel about him.

JAYNE: Yes. I think it is.

PAM: So feeling someone is scum doesn't…kinda make you feel like you're scum too.

JAYNE: No, Pam it doesn't. It makes me sad and kind of disappointed in myself. But not like I'm scum. I've met scum, Pam. Lots of it. Scum doesn't have conversations like this with people like you. Scum grabs people like you by the throat drags you into and alley then rapes and kills you.

PAM: Jayne…. We…have tea at night before we go to sleep…. You sometimes help Emma with her homework…. You…you know…have a normal life.

JAYNE: Except when I don't.

PAM: No one said anything about reporting this. I mean it was never even discussed.

DONNY comes back in. Carrying a gun.

DONNY: *(to PAM)* Did she explain.

PAM: We have a child, Donny. She lives in this world…. You're making the world she lives in worse.

DONNY: Right. So either she didn't explain or you didn't get it. That's too bad. Because until you get it you can't help. You can only get in the way. *(to JAYNE)* He left his gun on the seat of the car…. He was so out of it…he probably left something in that field. And I'm pretty sure he couldn't have buried that kid properly…. I gotta go back there.

JAYNE: You know where it is?

DONNY: Yeah. We've used that field a few times.

PAM: You've done things like this before? You do things like this all the time…. You've got a child!

DONNY: Pam. You could come with me. Help me check for things in that field. Make sure the site is clear.

PAM: You're kidding.

DONNY: Help me bury the kid a little deeper maybe.

PAM: You're not kidding, are you.

DONNY: Then we have to go back to where I picked him up…. Find out if anyone saw me…. You could do that…. Ask around. No one knows you.

PAM: *(to JAYNE)* Are you listening to this.

JAYNE: You can do it, Pam. If you see a store nearby. Go in, ask the store owner if he saw anything. Make up a good excuse for why you're asking.

DONNY: I'll come up with something.

PAM: I can't do this.

DONNY: I think you can.

PAM: I don't want to do this.

DONNY: This is what you can do to help. Our situation requires certain actions. If we don't take them we're screwed…. Big time…. Things will happen to us…. Not you. Not directly. But Max and I are fucked…. So…so this is bad…. It's bound to affect things. It's bound to have some effect on…our child…. So you can help. Or you can go home and what…. Pray. Do you pray…. You don't pray, Pam, do you. So go home and…wait. Wait to find out if everything turns out or not. Wait to see how much of it hurts Emma.

PAM: *(quietly)* Monster.

DONNY: I'm leaving now, Pam. Coming or not.

He opens the door.

PAM: *(walking past him)* This is wrong.

DONNY stares at JAYNE.

DONNY: You started this.

JAYNE: You fucked it up.

DONNY: I'm blaming you.

He leaves. Closes the door.

JAYNE goes into the bathroom. Water running.
Comes out with a damp towel. Begins to wipe MAX's forehead. Then
wipes the blood from around the bandage.
MAX opens his eyes.

MAX: *(weakly)* Hi...

JAYNE: Hi...

MAX: How am I doing.

JAYNE: If you live you're doing fine.

MAX: Where's Donny.

JAYNE: He went to make sure the field is clean.

MAX: Yeah?...So now he gets cautious.... Asshole.

JAYNE: Total asshole.

MAX: Where's Pam.

JAYNE: She went with him.

MAX: Why.

JAYNE: I'm not sure. Stand by your asshole. Or something like that.... No
actually I don't think she knew why she was going.... She's pretty
screwed up by this.

MAX: What about you.

JAYNE: I never said I wanted him dead, Max.

MAX: I know.... He would've killed me though. He was just so wound up
with terror, and he kept yelling—

JAYNE: I don't really want to hear about it.

MAX: It was like a nightmare though. It was loud. And messy. A lot of
yelling.... Good thing we were way out there away from everything.

JAYNE: And Donny knows where it is?

MAX: Donny's the one who showed me where it is.... It's possible Donny's done some digging out there before I even met him.... Was he sober. You think he was sober when he left?

JAYNE: It's hard to tell, isn't it.... I mean he is insane.

MAX: Look in my jacket will ya...I need a cigarette.

JAYNE picks up his jacket.

JAYNE: So...how is this going to— How will you explain—

MAX: We won't. Donny will book us off.... That usually means we're working on something. They call my wife.... No on expects to hear from us for awhile.... I'll just stay here.

JAYNE: Unless you die.

MAX: Yeah. But if I don't die I'll get better.... So if Donny covers our trail...

JAYNE: The only thing you'll have to explain will be the scar...to your wife.

She puts a cigarette in his mouth.

MAX: "Honey, someone stabbed me. Don't worry. It's nothing."

JAYNE: Unless you die.

She lights the cigarette.

MAX: Yeah. But if I don't die it's nothing.

JAYNE: Yeah, right.... Just another day on the job...

MAX: Basically...

JAYNE: I didn't want him dead.

MAX: You don't have to keep saying that.

JAYNE: Yes. I do...

MAX: I mean it doesn't help...

JAYNE: Helps me...*(shrugs)* Pathetic...

MAX takes a drag on his cigarette. Grimaces.
JAYNE leans back against a wall. Her arms crossed in front of her.
Pause.
JAYNE goes over near the bed. Gets down on all fours. Looks around on the carpet.

MAX: What are you doing.

JAYNE: I lost an earring…. I think maybe it came off when…you know…

She continues to search on her hands and knees.

MAX: Was it expensive.

JAYNE stands.

JAYNE: Not really.

She pulls the bedspread off the bed. She pulls a blanket off. Another blanket. The top sheet. The bottom sheet. She shrugs. Sits on the bed. They look at each other.

JAYNE: It's gone.

MAX: *(nods)* That's…too bad…

JAYNE: Max?

MAX: Yeah?

JAYNE: Say it…

MAX: Say what.

JAYNE: You know what…. The thing you said before…. Before…

MAX: Oh yeah…I love you, Jayne.

JAYNE: Come on, gimme a break…. The other thing…

MAX: *(shrugs)* Jayne? No. She had nothing to do with it.

JAYNE: That's very good.

MAX: Thank you.

JAYNE: Because…. I've got nothing. No savings. Nothing. I told you that, right?

MAX: I don't think so.

JAYNE: Yeah. I think I told you. You probably weren't listening…. Anyway, you know…. I mean I've been a legal aid lawyer almost since I left law school…so I've got nothing.

MAX: And now you don't even have that other earring.

JAYNE smiles. Shrugs.

JAYNE: You don't look so good.

MAX: Really? I feel great.

JAYNE: Yeah, right.

MAX: No really. Maybe it's the drugs. But if I don't die, I think I'll be all right.

JAYNE: Good.

MAX: Yeah.... I killed someone before. You knew that.

JAYNE: Well I remember hearing something.

MAX: Five years ago. A domestic.... Donny and I just stumbled on it. Came around a corner and there was this guy, about sixty-five, beating the crap out of his wife with a baseball bat. Right in the middle of the street.... I'm thinking what is this fucking ugly garbage. Who needs this. But we couldn't just ignore it. So we hop outta the car, Donny goes to the old woman who's a bloody pulp by now, and I get the husband's attention to...distract him...yell at him or something.... Yeah I think I yelled "Hey you fat prick." Anyway he turns. Starts coming at me with the bat.... He's this big mean ugly old drunk, and he's got his wife's blood all over his face and his undershirt and he's coming at me mumbling some insane nonsense. And I'm backing up.... He's getting closer.... And then I hear Donny yelling. "Drop him. Drop him, Maxie! Shoot him or he's gonna crush your brains with that thing." So I do.... I shoot him. Once. Right through the heart.... And he drops like the sack of shit he is. And then...it was all over except for the paper work.... That night I got drunker than I'd ever been before...or since really.... And I'm thinking "When I get up tomorrow morning my life will be changed.... I'm gonna have trouble living with this."....But when I get up...that's not how I feel. I look around at my kids and what I feel is.... I was doing my job.... And anybody who ever comes at me and threatens my life, carrying a bat, a knife, a gun, a saw, a fucking stick...is gonna die.... That's just what has to happen... (shrugs)

JAYNE: What about the woman.

MAX: The woman?

JAYNE: The guy's wife. I mean be beat her with a bat, right? Was she okay.

MAX: I don't know.

JAYNE: You never checked?

MAX: Well...either she lived or she died.

MAX shrugs.
JAYNE lowers her head.

JAYNE: *(to the floor)* Right.

> *MAX grimaces. Adjusts himself in the chair a little…Looks at JAYNE.*

MAX: I love you, Jayne.

JAYNE: *(to the floor)* Yeah. I love you too.

> *MAX is looking at JAYNE. JAYNE is looking at the floor.*
> *Blackout.*

The End

CRIMINAL GENIUS

PERSONS
ROLLY
STEVIE
PHILLIE
SHIRLEY
AMANDA

PLACE
A slightly run-down motel on the outskirts of a large city.

Criminal Genius was first produced by Rattlestick Productions at Theatre Off Park in New York City on May 19, 1997 with the following cast:

ROLLY...Dan Moran*
STEVIE...Jim Grollman*
PHILLIE...........................Mark Hammer* / Alan Benson
SHIRLEY...Carolyn Swift*
AMANDA ....Cheryl Gaysunas*

Director ....Daniel De Raey
Set Design...Van Santvoord
Lighting Design ....Chad McArver
Costume Design..Rachel Gruer
Sound Design...Laura Grace Brown
Production Manager ....Vicoletta Arlia
Casting..Liz Woodman Casting
Stage Manager ....Elizabeth Reeves

* Member of Actors Equity Association

Scene One

ROLLY MOORE and his son STEVIE are anxiously waiting for something or someone. ROLLY paces and tugs on the medallion around his neck and tucks and untucks his tacky short-sleeved shirt. STEVIE sits fidgeting on the bed and staring at the time on the clock-radio.

ROLLY: Ah, man. Can you feel it. I can feel it.

STEVIE: I can feel it too.

ROLLY: Yeah, what do you feel.

STEVIE: I don't know. But it's not good.

ROLLY: That's what I feel too. Only I'm probably feeling it worse. Because if it happens it's gonna happen worse to me.

STEVIE: You think so?

ROLLY: Yeah. Because they'll blame me. They think you're just a moron or something.

STEVIE: Why do they think that.

ROLLY: Because that's what I told them.

STEVIE: Really? You tell them that to protect me or something? In case things went wrong?

ROLLY: No. I told them that so I could blame you in case things went wrong.

STEVIE: Thanks, Dad.

ROLLY: Ah don't get your shorts knotted up. It seemed like a good strategy. Nobody takes revenge on a moron. It's bad luck. Problem is I got a feeling they're gonna need to blame and take revenge on someone so...that just leaves me.

STEVIE: So you kinda outsmarted yourself...

ROLLY: Sure you can look at it that way. I prefer to think of myself as a victim. Everything I do almost I get punished for it.... When was the last time I did something and got away with it. There's always some kind of punishment. I always gotta take a knock. Why is that.

STEVIE: I don't know.

ROLLY: Are you saying you don't care.

STEVIE: No I'm saying I don't know.

ROLLY: But you're saying you don't know like you don't care.... Stop looking at the clock.

STEVIE: I can't. It helps keep me calm.

ROLLY: Are you.

STEVIE: What.

ROLLY: Calm. Are you calm.

STEVIE: No. Not really.

ROLLY: So stop staring at the fucking clock. You're making me nervous. It's not doing you any good and it's making me extremely nervous.

STEVIE: I...I can't.... It's like I'm...hypnotized by it. It's like it's got hold of my mind.

ROLLY: God...I hate it when you talk that shit.... It reminds me of your mother. All that mind shit.... "It's in my mind. My mind's all this. My mind's all that." Stop staring at the clock. Stop talking about your mind and stop staring at the clock.

STEVIE: I can't.

ROLLY: Yes you can!! Yes you can!!

ROLLY yanks the clock-radio viciously. Throws it on the floor. Jumps on it, smashing it to pieces.
A knock on the door.

STEVIE and ROLLY freeze. Look at each other.

ROLLY: *(whispering)* This could be it.

STEVIE: *(whispering)* Yeah.... Or...it could be something else.

Another knock.

ROLLY: Yeah. *(yelling)* Who is it?!

PHILLIE: *(outside the door)* The manager.

ROLLY: Oh yeah? *(to STEVIE)* Whatya think. What should I do.

STEVIE: Ask him something.... A question or something.

ROLLY: Whatya mean.

STEVIE: Like a test.... Ask him...what colour the lamp shades are...

ROLLY: Why.

STEVIE: They wouldn't know that. Only the manager would know that. So if he gets the colour right you'll know it's really the manager.

ROLLY: I already know it's really the manager. I recognize his voice.

STEVIE: So why were you asking me what you should do.

ROLLY: I can't fucking remember now. It was like an hour ago. All that ask him a question shit.

Another knock.

PHILLIE: *(outside the door)* Can I talk to you a minute.

ROLLY: No!

STEVIE: *(whispering)* Why not...

ROLLY: *(whispering)* I don't want to.

PHILLIE: I just need to know if you're checking out or staying another night!

STEVIE: *(whispering)* He just needs...you know, information. Tell him.

ROLLY: We're...staying! Yeah we're saying!

PHILLIE: Okay. But it's cash up front. Forty bucks.

ROLLY: *(whispering)* You got forty bucks?

STEVIE: No.

ROLLY: ...Okay! ...We're checking out!

PHILLIE: Okay! But you gotta check out now. You're already two hours late.... I gotta get the room cleaned.

STEVIE: *(whispering)* We can't leave.... If we leave.... They'll track us down.... They'll...you know...think we ran out on them and then they'll—

ROLLY: Yeah, yeah.... Okay! We're staying. Will you take a cheque?

PHILLIE: No!

ROLLY: My cheques are good!

PHILLIE: No cheques!

ROLLY: *(to STEVIE)* Gimme your watch.

STEVIE: No.

ROLLY: Gimme your watch, Stevie.

STEVIE: No Dad. No way. You gave me this watch Dad! It's the only thing you ever gave me. I can't let you give it away.

ROLLY: It means something to you? I didn't know that.

STEVIE: It's…my watch…

ROLLY: I took it off a corpse. Remember old Al Packer. I found him dead in an alley, took his shoes for myself and since you had a birthday coming up—

STEVIE: I don't care! I don't care where you got it…. In my mind it's still a gift from you to me.

ROLLY: In your mind is shit. That's what "in your mind" is. Gimme the watch or I'll come over there and kick you to death…. Our lives are in danger here…. We can't get evicted!!

STEVIE: Maybe…Maybe he'd like some merchandise…. Ask him. Let him in and ask him…

ROLLY: I don't know.

STEVIE: It's the only choice.

ROLLY: Okay. Yeah…okay.

ROLLY opens the door.
PHILLIE PHILLIPS is leaning against the frame.

PHILLIE: So…what's it gonna be…

ROLLY: We're a bit light cash-wise. We'd like to— Please…. Come in…

PHILLIE: I'd rather not.

ROLLY: Come in.

PHILLIE: No.

ROLLY: We'd like to show you something…. Come in.

PHILLIE: No. Show me here.

ROLLY: It's a catalogue…. It's a catalogue representing a line of products. Products of a particular and intimate nature. We don't like to flash it around in public.

PHILLIE: Is this public.

STEVIE: People walk by. They catch a glimpse. There goes that.

PHILLIE: There goes what.

STEVIE: That. The thing. The thing nobody knows because it's not public.

PHILLIE: What the fuck are you talking about. Do I look like I got all day here.

ROLLY: Are you drunk.

PHILLIE: Excuse me.

ROLLY: No offence. But I smell liquor. I'm just saying maybe your judgement is impaired. Maybe you should come back later and we'll do a deal when you can see things more clearly.

PHILLIE: See what? You haven't showed me anything! Maybe if you showed it to me I could see it just fine.

STEVIE: Come on in.

PHILLIE: No.

ROLLY: Come back later.

PHILLIE: No…. Give me forty bucks. Give me forty bucks or get out.

ROLLY: *(to STEVIE)* Give him your watch.

STEVIE: No…. Show him the catalogue.

ROLLY: *(to PHILLIE)* Do you wanna see the catalogue.

PHILLIE: No. I want forty bucks.

ROLLY: Can you come back a little later. Just a little.

PHILLIE: No.

ROLLY: *(to STEVIE)* Give him your watch!

STEVIE: No. No fucking way. No!

ROLLY: He doesn't take cheques. He doesn't want to see the catalogue. He won't come back a little later. You gotta give him the watch. *(to PHILLIE)* Will you take the watch as…collateral…

PHILLIE: *(shrugs)* Depends on the watch.

ROLLY: *(to STEVIE)* Show him the watch.

STEVIE: No.

ROLLY: Did you hear what I just said to him. Did you hear me use the word collateral. Don't you know what the word collateral means. It means he holds the watch 'til we get him the forty bucks. We get him the forty bucks he gives back the watch. Now show him the watch.

STEVIE: No.

ROLLY: What's wrong with you. Take off the watch and give it to this man so he can determine it's value.

STEVIE: Where are you gonna get the forty bucks.

ROLLY: Are you asking me that question in front of this man. Don't you think it's the kind of question you should ask me in private.

STEVIE: Where are you gonna get the forty bucks.

ROLLY: I'll get it.

STEVIE: Where.

ROLLY: I know where. Don't worry.

STEVIE: Where

ROLLY: I said don't worry.

STEVIE: Where. Who from. Tell me. Tell me who's gonna give it to you. Tell me where the person is.

ROLLY: Give me the watch.

STEVIE: No.

ROLLY: We have to stay in this room. You know that. Or maybe you don't know that. Do you know that.

STEVIE: Yeah I know that.

ROLLIE: Gimme the watch.

STEVIE: No.

ROLLY: If we leave the room it won't be good for us. It'll be bad.... We need the watch in this man's hands so he can determine if its resale value is equal to or exceeds forty dollars and then we can stay in the room.

STEVIE: Give him your shoes.

ROLLY: What.

STEVIE: They're not yours anyway. They're Al Packer's. They have no sentimental value to you. Give them to him.

PHILLIE: I don't want his shoes.

ROLLY: *(to STEVIE)* He wants the watch.

PHILLIE: I want forty bucks.

ROLLY: You'll get forty bucks eventually. But for now you get the watch.

STEVIE: No he doesn't.

ROLLY: If you don't give him the watch I'll kick you to death.

STEVIE: Give him your shoes.

ROLLY: What the fuck is wrong with you boy. He doesn't want my shoes. He wants the watch.

PHILLIE: I want forty bucks!

ROLLY: I'll get your forty bucks!

STEVIE: Where.

ROLLY: Don't ask me where.

STEVIE: Where.

ROLLY: I'll tell you later.

STEVIE: Tell me now.

ROLLY: *(to PHILLIE)* Can you come back. Go away? Then come back.

PHILLIE: No...No I can't.... What size are those shoes.

ROLLY: Ten. Ah...yeah ten.

PHILLIE: I just noticed them. They're unique.... Flashy...but...I like them. Okay...Okay I'll take the shoes. Give me the shoes. You can stay one more night.

ROLLY: You want the shoes? You think the shoes are better collateral than the watch?

PHILLIE: I don't want the shoes as collateral. I want them to keep.

ROLLY: That's not...sound judgement.... You see, that's what I was getting at when I suggested you return when you weren't...drunk.

PHILLIE: I'm almost always drunk. And I want the shoes.

STEVIE: Give him the shoes.

ROLLY: Stay out of this.

STEVIE: If you don't give him the shoes we have to leave the room.

ROLLY: I'm not finished negotiating.

PHILLIE: It's the shoes or nothing.

ROLLY: You don't want these shoes. I took them off a corpse.... You can't want the shoes of a man who died violently and under mysterious circumstances.

PHILLIE: Why not. You did.

ROLLY: Let's negotiate.

PHILLIE: No. Give me the shoes.

Long pause.

STEVIE: Give him the shoes.

ROLLY: Yeah.... You see this is just another example of me as a victim. *(taking off his shoes)* There are three people in this room. And I'm the only one suffering any loss. Here...take them.

Hands PHILLIE the shoes.

PHILLIE: Thanks.

PHILLIE leaves.

ROLLY: Look at me. I don't have any shoes. No...shoes.... Why couldn't you just give him the goddamn watch.

STEVIE: I didn't want to.

ROLLY: You're selfish. You're spoiled.... I've been too...generous to you.

STEVIE: No you haven't.

ROLLY: I've given you too much.

STEVIE: You've never given me anything.... Except this watch.

ROLLY: I don't want to talk about the watch. I'm too mad to talk about the watch or even think about the watch. If I keep thinking about the watch and your selfishness regarding the watch I know I'm gonna wanna kick you to death.

STEVIE: Something just came into my mind.

ROLLY: I don't wanna hear about your mind and things coming into it...or anything about your mind. Your mind is the thing that makes you selfish. If you didn't have a mind you'd be easier to get along with.

A knock on the door.

ROLLY: My shoes! They don't fit! He's brought them back.

STEVIE: Wait. Don't open the—

But ROLLY has already opened the door. And has been met by SHIRLEY "THE PEARL" KATAKIS, a lean young woman in denim who straight-arms ROLLY on the forehead and pushes him back into the room.

STEVIE: Shirley. Hi. We were just—

SHIRLEY: Shut up.

SHIRLEY has backed ROLLY against a wall.

SHIRLEY: Stay there, Rolly. Don't move. Don't move even one inch. Got that?

ROLLY: Yeah.

SHIRLEY: Stevie. Give me your watch.

STEVIE: What. Why.

SHIRLEY: Give it to me. *(she is moving toward him)* Come on, come on, come on, come on.

STEVIE, backing up, pulls off his watch frantically and holds it out to her.

SHIRLEY: Thanks.

SHIRLEY places the watch on the table. Picks up one of lamps and smashes the base of it down on the watch.

STEVIE: My watch.

SHIRLEY: Fuck your watch. Fuck you. *(to ROLLY)* And fuck your stupid fucking shoes. I've been waiting outside. Waiting right outside next to my car pretending to look for my keys listening to you go on and on with that guy about your fucking watch and your fucking shoes like you were the two biggest fucking morons in the universe. I mean I knew you were stupid. And stupid's a thing I don't usually have a problem with in a man. But come on. There are limits. You've gone beyond the limits of tolerable stupidity. You're toying with a mercy killing here. I mean I was out there thinking "They're too stupid to live. Just go on in there and put them outta their misery."

ROLLY: Ah come on—

SHIRLEY: What? You think I don't mean it?

She pulls a gun out of the back of her waist band.

SHIRLEY: *(advancing on ROLLY)* You think I'm kidding!?

ROLLY: No. No!

SHIRLEY: Come here.

ROLLY: Where.

SHIRLEY: Here. To me. Come here.

ROLLY: No.

SHIRLEY: What...

ROLLY: No.

SHIRLEY: What!?

ROLLY: Yeah...okay...okay...

> *He takes a step. She grabs him by the ear and leads him to the door.*
> *Points.*

SHIRLEY: Look. What do you see.

ROLLY: Ah.

SHIRLEY: "Ah." Nothing? Do you see nothing.

ROLLY: Ah.

SHIRLEY: "Ah"! You don't see a fire for example! You don't see large clouds
of billowing smoke rising in the clear blue sky over where a particular
restaurant is...

ROLLY: Ah no I don't.... But I can explain.

SHIRLEY: You can explain. *(to STEVIE)* Can he, Stevie. Can he explain to me
in a way that will make sense. In a way that will satisfy any concerned
individual who was waiting for a certain outcome and has not yet
witnessed this outcome?

STEVIE: Probably not.

SHIRLEY: Rolly. The plan had three parts. Part one—break into the restaurant. Part two—set fire to the restaurant. Part three—come here and
wait for me to contact you. What I wanna know is why the fuck did you
skip parts one and two and go directly to part three. Part three was the
least important part. Part three means shit without parts one and two!!!
So? ...So!?

ROLLY: I...ah...added a part.

SHIRLEY: You what.

ROLLY: No that's not right.... I ah changed a part.... I had an idea.

SHIRLEY: Oh my God.... An idea!? ...An idea... *(to STEVIE)* He had an idea?

STEVIE: I tried to stop him. He...kicked me.

ROLLY: He was whining.

STEVIE: I was begging you to keep to the plan. Parts one and two. First part one. Then part two.... In that order.

ROLLY: I had a better part.

SHIRLEY: And you told me it was Stevie we had to worry about. You told me if things went bad it would be because Stevie wasn't capable of doing his job.

ROLLY: I firmly believe I am right about that. There's no way the boy could have torched that building. He's no good with his hands.... He's clumsy. What I did, I did to save him from humiliating failure and perhaps even a painful death by fire. Why else would I change the plan.

SHIRLEY: Why else would you change the plan. Well!? ...Well?!

ROLLY: People could have gotten hurt in a fire. I'm against injury.... I've lived a criminal life for thirty-five years and no one ever got hurt in my endeavours.

SHIRLEY: You sold pornography. You stole hubcaps.

ROLLY: I did my things. Other things. Bigger things. And no one ever got hurt. I'm against human injury. I can't help it.... It's just the way I am.

STEVIE: It's true.... He kicks me every once in a while but basically he's against injury.

SHIRLEY: Yeah.... Well I didn't know that.... You never mentioned it. And it's not a well-known thing about you. When people talk about you that doesn't come up. They don't talk about Rolly Moore the great humanitarian. They talk about Rolly Moore the stupid fucking asshole. Okay I'm getting a knot in my stomach. I need immediate relief or I'm gonna barf. I mean I engaged you to carry out this task and now we're all fucked unless this other plan of yours by some miracle is actually worth something.... So? So!?

ROLLY: So?

SHIRLEY: What is it!

ROLLY: After thinking about.... I mean after having done it...then thinking about it...there are certain downsides to my plan.

SHIRLEY: *(to STEVIE)* Tell me.

STEVIE: Maybe we should just show you.

SHIRLEY: *(shrugs)* Tell me. Show me. Whatever. Just do it now! Before I eradicate you both from the face of the earth!!

STEVIE: Okay, okay... *(to ROLLY)* Okay?

ROLLY: Yeah...okay.

STEVIE goes to bathroom door. Opens it. Goes in.
SHIRLEY and ROLLY are looking at each other.
STEVIE comes out with AMANDA CASTLE, a young woman in a chef's uniform. Bound and gagged.
SHIRLEY looks at AMANDA. At STEVIE. At ROLLY.

ROLLY: She's the cook. We abducted the cook. I thought it would be better in the long run.

SHIRLEY sits. Lowers her head.

SHIRLEY: Put her back.

STEVIE: Back where. Back at the restaurant?

Without looking up, SHIRLEY points to the bathroom.
STEVIE takes AMANDA back into the bathroom. We hear him talking in the bathroom.

SHIRLEY: Stevie!!

STEVIE comes out. Closes door.

STEVIE: She's pretty scared. I was just telling her everything's gonna turn out all right.

SHIRLEY: Really. What makes you think that.

STEVIE: I don't think that. I was just taking pity on her.

SHIRLEY: Save your pity for yourself

STEVIE: Usually I do. But this time I was—

SHIRLEY: *(pacing)* Ah, this is bad.... Bad.... It hurts. It's so bad, it's hurting me. In my stomach. Knots are forming. Big ones. Do you know who that is...that woman you kidnapped.

ROLLY: The cook.

SHIRLEY: Amanda Castle. That's her name. Amanda...Castle.

ROLLY: I didn't know her name. I only knew she was the cook.

SHIRLEY: Now that you know her name does it mean anything to you.

ROLLY: No.

STEVIE: Castle. Castle. Is she related to Mike Castle.

SHIRLEY: She's his daughter.

ROLLY: Oh.... But, why's his daughter working for a rival restaurant.

SHIRLEY: The whole point, the entire reason for this fucking enterprise was that his daughter was working for a rival restaurant you pathetic weenie. The only fucking purpose in torching the rival restaurant was so that his daughter would be out of a job and come back to her father's loving embrace.

ROLLY: You see I didn't know that. You didn't tell me that. If you'd told me that the kidnapping would never have taken place.

SHIRLEY: The kidnapping shouldn't have taken place no matter what I told you unless I told you to kidnap someone. Which I didn't!

ROLLY: You see, what I'm getting at here is, if I'd known the purpose of this job I never would have agreed to do it. I just don't think that's a good way for a father to express his love for a child. It's...control.... It's...destruction. I'm against that kind of behaviour.

SHIRLEY: (to STEVIE) What am I supposed to make of him when he talks like this.

STEVIE: He's started to read these magazines.... Family magazines. They've got lots of articles.... They...you know...influence his...his.... What you call it, Dad?

ROLLY: My brain?

STEVIE: Yeah. But what I mean is it influences your you know...way of... seeing things. You're changing the way you...see...things.

ROLLY: Yeah. I'm goin' through some changes.

SHIRLEY: Jesus.... God almighty.

ROLLY: That's why I took the cook. I thought Mike just wanted this restaurant gone cause it was taking customers away from his place. So I thought if the cook was gone maybe it wouldn't be so popular. And his customers would come back and nobody could possibly get hurt like they could in a fire.

SHIRLEY: What were you planning to do with the cook.

ROLLY: Nothing bad.

SHIRLEY: No?...

ROLLY: A little scare.... You know.... "Hit the road sister. I'm giving you a break here! Scram!"....That kind of thing.... I hear that usually works.

SHIRLEY: You hear that do you. From who.

ROLLY: You. You always say that. A little scare does the trick.

SHIRLEY: I'm talking about when it's me doing the scaring. Me! Not you. People aren't scared of you. People laugh at you. Everyone. Even cooks.... *(to Stevie)* Did you know about this. Did you know he planned to do this.

STEVIE: I only know what he does when he does it. And then usually only later do I find out why. But even when I find out why I don't usually understand why. I mean why he did it.... Or didn't do it.... Or did it differently.

SHIRLEY: Shut up.... Okay, okay. I gotta think.... *(she is pacing)* What's happened here, really. What's the real damage. Is there any real damage or is it just an annoying fuck up.... Really let me think this through here.... Okay we gotta get rid of the cook.

STEVIE: Whatya mean.

SHIRLEY: She's gotta go. She saw me.

STEVIE: But she's Mike Castle's daughter.

SHIRLEY: That's only a problem if he knows we took her, isn't it.... But of course he's gonna know we took her. Who else would take her. Fuck.... We're fucked.... Unless we make it look like someone else took her. Okay.... Let's do that.... How. Any ideas?

A noise in the bathroom.

SHIRLEY: Stevie. Get in there. See what she's up to.

STEVIE goes into the bathroom.
A knock on the door.

SHIRLEY: Great... *(to ROLLY)* Find out who that is.

ROLLY: *(yells at door)* Who is it!?

SHIRLEY: Jesus.

ROLLY: What. What's wrong.

SHIRLEY: Nothing.

ROLLY: *(yelling)* Who is it!?

SHIRLEY: Stop that.... Stop...yelling.... Just open the door. I need to...I need to calm down a little.

SHIRLEY turns on the TV. ROLLY opens the door.
PHILLIE is leaning against the door frame. Holding a bottle of booze.
And ROLLY's shoes.

PHILLIE: They don't fit.

ROLLY: Okay. Thanks.

PHILLIE: Thanks for what.

ROLLY: My shoes.

PHILLIE: They're not your shoes. They're my shoes. For forty bucks, they can be your shoes.

ROLLY: Shirley, have you got forty dollars.

SHIRLEY: *(watching TV)* What.

ROLLY: You see I need forty bucks for—

SHIRLEY: See what's going on in that bathroom will ya.

ROLLY goes into the bathroom.
SHIRLEY notices PHILLIE.

SHIRLEY: What are you staring at.

PHILLIE: I'm not staring. I'm waiting for my forty bucks. You give me forty bucks. I give you his shoes and I'm on my way.

SHIRLEY: Fuck you. I'm not giving you forty bucks for those shoes. Get out of my sight.

PHILLIE: Forty bucks. Or this room has to be vacated.

SHIRLEY: Okay. Yeah. But fuck off. I'll bring it over to the office later.

ROLLY sticks his head out of the bathroom.

ROLLY: We've got a problem in here.

PHILLIE: Give it to me now.

SHIRLEY: Fuck off. We're busy here.

PHILLIE: Get out of the room.

SHIRLEY: Look. Close the door. Go away. I'll pay you later.

SHIRLEY turns off the TV.

PHILLIE: I'm not moving.

ROLLY: You better pay him.

SHIRLEY: I'll pay him when I'm good and fucking ready to pay him.

SHIRLEY slams the door in PHILLIE's face.

ROLLY: What's wrong. You don't have forty bucks on you?

SHIRLEY: Whatya mean we got a problem in there.

PHILLIE is pounding on the door.

PHILLIE: Forty bucks! Forty bucks or get out!

ROLLY: If you don't have the cash he'll probably take a cheque from you...if you've got I.D. He wouldn't take one from me but—

SHIRLEY: Shut up. What's wrong.

ROLLY: What.

SHIRLEY: You said there was a problem in the bathroom.

ROLLY: Oh...They're gone.

SHIRLEY: Gone? Gone. Stevie too? Both of them?

ROLLY: Out the window.

PHILLIE: Forty bucks!

ROLLY: He's still here. He won't go away unless you pay him. So come on, pay him.

SHIRLEY: Shut up. Gone!?

ROLLY: Gone.

SHIRLEY: Both of them.

PHILLIE: Okay. Get out. Out. Get out now!!

Pounding on the door.
SHIRLEY pounds on the door.

SHIRLEY: *(to PHILLIE)* Shut up! *(looks at ROLLY)* I have to think about this. What does this mean. Gone. What does that mean.... She's gone. Okay. You were too stupid to check the window and she escaped. No surprises there. But why is he gone.

ROLLY: Maybe he went after her.

SHIRLEY: Maybe. Yeah maybe...Or...

A pounding on the door.

SHIRLEY: Shut up! Go away!

PHILLIE: Get out!

SHIRLEY: Fuck off!

PHILLIE: Pay. Or get out!

ROLLY: What's the problem. Don't you have forty dollars. You gotta have forty dollars. You're Shirl the Pearl. You're the boss. Come on. You've got forty dollars. Give it to him and he'll go away. Just give it to him. Why won't you just give him forty dollars.

SHIRLEY: *(sitting)* Shut up!

ROLLY: Why. Tell my why.

SHIRLEY: I don't have forty dollars. Okay!? Satisfied? I don't have forty dollars.

ROLLY: Why not. Why don't you have a crummy forty dollars.

SHIRLEY: It's a love story.... I mean a long story.

ROLLY: Tell me. I need to know.

SHIRLEY: No. Fuck off.

ROLLY: But I need to know.

A pounding on the door.

PHILLIE: Out! You gotta get out!

SHIRLEY: Tell him to go away. I need to think. He's making too much noise. I can't concentrate.

ROLLY: Tell me the story. It's really important to me. You're the tops. You're the most I can become. And if the most I can become doesn't even have forty dollars what's the point.

SHIRLEY: What's the point of what.

ROLLY: I don't know. That's what I mean.

SHIRLEY: What are you talking about. Shut up. Tell him to shut up. Everyone shut up. I gotta think.

A pounding on the door.

SHIRLEY: Go away! Please!

PHILLIE: No way, sister!

A pounding on the door.

SHIRLEY: *(sitting)* I can't think...I can't think.... They're gone and I just can't...think what that means. What does it mean, Rolly. What does it mean that they're gone. How bad is that. What position does that place us in. You know, what does it mean...

ROLLY: *(shrugs)* What's the point... Look... I don't even have any shoes.

A pounding on the door.

PHILLIE: Get out! Get out! Get out!!

SHIRLEY leans against the door.

SHIRLEY: *(calmly)* Please. Go away. Stop pounding on the door. I can't think.... Rolly please tell him to stop pounding.

ROLLY just shrugs. Stares off. A pounding on the door.

PHILLIE: *(laughing)* Fuck me? No fuck you! Me go away? No you go away! Fuck you and get out of here! *(laughs)* Out! Out!

SHIRLEY rubs her temples.

Blackout.

Scene Two

Later. PHILLIE is sitting on the bed. Drinking. Watching TV.
SHIRLEY comes out of the bathroom. Wrapped in towels. Her hair is wet.

SHIRLEY: Okay. Let's see. Sometimes a shower helps. Sometimes it's almost like a fresh start. There's life before the shower. And then sometimes it's a whole new thing afterwards.

She turns off the TV.

PHILLIE: I was watching that.

SHIRLEY: We need to talk.

PHILLIE: That was the weather channel. I was waiting for the long-range forecast.

SHIRLEY: We need to talk.

PHILLIE: I've got big plans for the weekend.

He belches.

SHIRLEY: We need.... Look at me. How drunk are you.

PHILLIE: How drunk are you.

SHIRLEY: I'm not.

PHILLIE: Well I'm so drunk I thought you were drunk too.

SHIRLEY: Are you always drunk.

PHILLIE: I...don't know.... How about that. I don't know. *(chuckles)*

SHIRLEY: What I mean is can you function. Just because you're drunk doesn't mean you can't function does it.

PHILLIE: When you say "function" what exactly do you mean.

SHIRLEY: Do things.

PHILLIE: When you say "do things" what—

SHIRLEY: We have to make an arrangement. I need you to make a couple of phone calls. If you help me out I'll be able to pay for the room. Plus.

PHILLIE: Plus? Plus what. Plus another room?

SHIRLEY: No not another room. Plus more money. I'll give you forty dollars plus.

PHILLIE: Plus what.

SHIRLEY: Money! More money! I'll give you more money!!

PHILLIE: For what.

SHIRLEY: For helping me. Just help me and I'll pay you. I'll pay you one hundred dollars.

PHILLIE: Plus?

SHIRLEY: Plus what.

PHILLIE: Ah…plus forty plus.

SHIRLEY: Plus what!?

PHILLIE: I don't know. It was your idea. All this plus stuff…. I don't know!

SHIRLEY: Okay. Forty dollars for the room. One hundred dollars for your assistance.

PHILLIE: So we're just forgetting the plus then?

SHIRLEY: That is the plus. One hundred is the plus. Okay?

PHILLIE: Sure. Whatever.

SHIRLEY: Okay. You're calling a guy named Mike. And this is what you're gonna say.

PHILLIE passes out on the bed.

SHIRLEY: Jesus.

She goes into the bathroom.
PHILLIE groans. Rolls over. Groans. Rolls over again. And falls off the bed down into a small space between the bed and the wall. Where he can't be seen.
The door is pushed open. ROLLY is standing there. Covered in soot. His clothes a bit charred. Still without shoes.

ROLLY: Help! Help I'm…smoldering. I'm smoldering.

SHIRLEY comes out of the bathroom. Just finishing getting dressed.

SHIRLEY: Oh what the—

ROLLY: Help me, Shirl. I'm…on fire or something.

SHIRLEY: Oh for… *(approaching)*

ROLLY: I'm…hot, burning, burning hot.

SHIRLEY: No it's, it's—

ROLLY: Burning, burning—

SHIRLEY: No no. It's just the shirt. Take off the shirt.

ROLLY: Help! I can't move. I'm smoldering.

SHIRLEY: Take off the shirt! The shirt!

ROLLY: The shirt? Oh my God. My shirt's on fire!

SHIRLEY: Take it off!

ROLLY: Take it off, Shirl! Take off my shirt!

SHIRLEY: You take it off.

ROLLY: Help. Help!

SHIRLEY: Shut up! *(she slaps him)* Take off your shirt! Just take off your shirt. Okay?! Okay?!

ROLLY: Okay.

He takes off his shirt. Holds it by the collar. It is smoking. SHIRLEY takes it from him. Goes into the bathroom. We hear the shower running.

ROLLY: Good idea!

SHIRLEY comes out of the bathroom.
ROLLY is standing in the doorway. Staring off.

ROLLY: Look...

She goes to the doorway.

SHIRLEY: Smoke.

ROLLY: Yeah...

SHIRLEY: You did it.

ROLLY: Yeah.

SHIRLEY: When did you do it. Just now?

ROLLY: Yeah...I just did it. I burned the joint down. Look.

SHIRLEY: *(vaguely)* I'm looking.

ROLLY: It was easy. Well not exactly easy. I almost got burned to death.... But I made my mind up to do it and I actually did it.... I'm proud of that.... Lots of smoke, eh?

SHIRLEY: Yeah...

ROLLY: I had to do it. When I found out you were as broke as we were I got depressed. I felt like giving up.... I felt like what's the point.... But really what's the point of that.... So I had to do something.... Get us some results..... So I did. I did it. And I did it without shoes...

SHIRLEY: *(looking down)* Yeah...without...ah...shoes...

ROLLY: So...So okay. It's done.

SHIRLEY: But...

ROLLY: What. What...but, Shirl.

SHIRLEY: I'm just thinking...ah...what's it mean. What's it mean that you burned it down now. Instead of before.... How does that play out.... I mean...*(concentrating)* You didn't burn it down the first time. The first time you kidnapped Amanda Castle. Then you let Amanda Castle escape. A person who saw us all and knew what we were planning to do.... And then knowing that there was this person out there who knew what our plans were and who could identify us...you did it anyway.... So what does that mean. What I'm getting at is, does it mean you're the biggest fucking retard on the planet and I'm totally fucked for having anything to do with you. Or does it mean you're the biggest fucking retard on the planet but we can still get out of this if we think clearly for a minute.

ROLLY: So...so what you're saying is...what...what are you saying... I shouldn't have burned it down?

SHIRLEY: Shush. I'm thinking.

ROLLY: So...well how was I supposed to know that. Did I hear instructions from you telling me not to burn it down. Never. Never in all that occurred did I ever hear you tell me not to burn it down.

SHIRLEY: She escaped! She can identify you. Didn't that mean anything to you.

ROLLY: Obviously not! I follow instructions.

SHIRLEY: No you don't.

ROLLY: Yes I do.

SHIRLEY: Did I instruct you to kidnap the cook.

ROLLY: I explained that.

SHIRLEY: No you didn't.

ROLLY: I thought I did.

SHIRLEY: An explanation is something that makes sense.... Now just shut up I'm thinking.

ROLLY: Usually...Almost always...I follow instructions. I was under instructions to burn that place down.

SHIRLEY: No. You weren't.

ROLLY: Yes. I was.

SHIRLEY: Shut up.

ROLLY: I'm not taking the blame for this. Whatever happens. I'm not taking the blame.

SHIRLEY: Yes. You are.

ROLLY: No. I'm not.

SHIRLEY: Shut up.

She is pacing.

ROLLY: I thought you'd be pleased.... I did it to please you as much as anything.

SHIRLEY: You have to stop talking. I'm thinking.

ROLLY: Where's Stevie.

SHIRLEY: How should I know.

ROLLY: He didn't come back?

SHIRLEY: No. Now please be quiet.

ROLLY: Because I thought for sure he'd come back. I thought he'd catch her and come back with her. Or he wouldn't catch her and he'd come back and tell us he couldn't catch her.... But I thought he'd come back... .Where is he.... Where is he, Shirley.

SHIRLEY: Okay. Okay here's where we are. We had a job. We had a contract... We didn't fulfill this contract on our first attempt... But we went back and did it later. It got done. That's the bottom line. It got done. Right? Well, right or not right.

ROLLY: I can't pay attention to you and worry about my kid at the same time. And every father's got a a duty to worry about his kid. I'm just learning how to worry. I'm new at it. I didn't care before. I didn't know about...caring. Then one day I picked up one of those magazines and I read "Having Trouble Caring?" and I thought "Yeah."

SHIRLEY: Okay the bottom line is...good. There are complications that aren't so good.... But at least the job got done. That's my position. That's the positive spin I'm putting on this.... The job got done.

ROLLY is staring off at the open doorway.

ROLLY: Stevie, Stevie where are you. Man, I hate this caring shit! ...Oh... Look...

SHIRLEY: What.

ROLLY: More smoke... Different smoke at a different place. Close to my smoke but...different.

SHIRLEY is standing next to ROLLY. They are staring off.

SHIRLEY: I have kind of a bad feeling about this.

Sound of a car roaring into the parking lot screeching to a stop. Door opens. Closes. Another door opens and closes. People coming.... *Suddenly...AMANDA CASTLE pushes past SHIRLEY and ROLLY and comes into the room.*

AMANDA: Outta my way!

STEVIE is following AMANDA.

STEVIE: Excuse me.

He comes in.

AMANDA: Close the door. Come on. Close the door.

SHIRLEY closes the door.

AMANDA: Okay. It's good that you're still here. I thought you'd have pissed off by now but it's a bonus that you're here.... Man that was awesome. That was one thrilling life experience.... Entirely new. A whole new thing for me.... Hey I burned a canoe when I was twelve but that was nothing. It was on a lake up north. No one was around to see it. It just burned and sank. Birds screeched. Big deal. But this... Look. Did you see. Did you. Did you see.

SHIRLEY: See...what exactly.

ROLLY: We saw smoke.

AMANDA: Yeah. My smoke. You saw my smoke.

ROLLY: Yeah... It's near my smoke.

AMANDA: Very near, yeah. It's across the street from your smoke.

SHIRLEY: Across the street. Oh my God...

ROLLY: What did you do, Stevie.

AMANDA: He didn't do it. I did it.

SHIRLEY: You torched your father's restaurant?

AMANDA: Yeah. It was amazing. I should have done it years ago. The sense of freedom and well being that swept over me was awesome.... It's almost...almost.... Look I'm feeling very aroused and since there's no one in this room I really want to have sex with I think I'll have a shower. Man. Awesome. Seriously.

She goes into the bathroom. Closes the door.
ROLLY and SHIRLEY look at STEVIE.

SHIRLEY: She set fire to her father's restaurant. Really?

STEVIE: Yeah…. Well you can see the smoke, right.

SHIRLEY: And you were with her.

STEVIE: Ah…yeah.

SHIRLEY: But you didn't stop her.

STEVIE: I didn't think it was any of my business. It was…personal…. She hates her father. Her mother killed herself when she was eight. She thinks her father drove her to it. Ever since then she's been looking for ways to get back at him. She's tried to poison him three or four times. When she was eleven she ran off with an actor and they got married in Mexico or on some island that sounds like Mexico. But her father had the actor killed by a retired vice cop and Amanda had to come home. She's always taking off with someone. Her father is always getting the guy killed and Amanda is always coming home. It's a thing that's gone on for years. The restaurant thing is different. It's hers. She went to school in Italy. Her plan was to become a great chef and open a restaurant across the street from her father and put him out of business…. So killing all her boyfriends and husbands was one thing but this attack on her restaurant was different. Kinda personal. So when she saw my dad here set fire to her restaurant and she knew he was doing it for her dad well there was no stopping her.

SHIRLEY: How do you know all this, Stevie.

STEVIE: I was there.

SHIRLEY: I mean the mother. The husband. The school in Italy…

STEVIE: She told me.

SHIRLEY: Why.

STEVIE: Well I don't know…. We were sitting in her car. Talking.

SHIRLEY: Talking? Talking about what. Were you talking about why you let her escape and what a great a guy you were for doing that even though it was going to throw your dad and your boss into serious shit and how basically you didn't give a damn.

STEVIE: Hey, listen. I had to let her go. There was no other choice. My dad and I can't do violence! We couldn't have hurt her so I had to let her go.

ROLLY: He's right. When you think about it. From our point of view letting her go was the only choice.

SHIRLEY: Your point of view is shit.

STEVIE: But we can't do violence. We can't.

ROLLY: It's always been a problem. Being into crime I mean, and having this problem doing violent things. We know that. It's a thing we live with every day.

STEVIE: The violence thing.

SHIRLEY: Okay okay you can't do violence. But how do you feel about violence being done to you. Are you cool with that.... I mean if I were to smash your brains in with that chair would that be okay with you.

STEVIE: Not really.

SHIRLEY: Or if Mike Castle finds out you're responsible for letting his daughter burn down his restaurant and has some ex vice cop come and put a bullet in your ear, would that be okay. Would it.

STEVIE: I'm not responsible for that fire. She is.

SHIRLEY: You let her go!

STEVIE: I had no choice.

SHIRLEY: You could have not let her go!

STEVIE: Oh sure. But for how long. How long could I have not let her go until you would have wanted us to not have her live. I mean come on.

SHIRLEY: Come on, what.

STEVIE: Come on.

SHIRLEY: You're fucked. I'm telling Mike Castle on you and you're fucked.

STEVIE: Well I think you're fucked.

SHIRLEY: Yeah?

STEVIE: Yeah. You hired us. So you're fucked.

ROLLY: He's right.

SHIRLEY: Shut up.

ROLLY: Yeah, but he's right.

SHIRLEY: You don't think I know he's right? You don't think I know I'm fucked? All I'm saying is that if I'm fucked you're really fucked. If I'm taking a fucking then you're taking the fucking of all time. Get it? *(She grabs STEVIE's hair)* Do you get it!?

STEVIE: Sure.

AMANDA comes out of the bathroom. Wrapped in towels.

AMANDA: I need a smoke... Hey what's going on. A little family feud?

SHIRLEY: Family? I'm not related to these goofs.

AMANDA: Sure you are. In a larger sense you're definitely family. Anyone got a smoke? Come on. I could really use a smoke.

PHILLIE sits up.

PHILLIE: I've just got menthol. *(He is searching in his shirt pockets)* But you're welcome to one.

SHIRLEY: Jesus...

AMANDA: Who's that. *(smiles)* Another relative?

SHIRLEY: *(to PHILLIE)* I thought you'd.... What are you doing here.

PHILLIE: *(standing)* Beats me.... Last thing I remember I was making plans for the weekend. *(hands AMANDA a cigarette)* Here. It's menthol. Did I tell you that.

AMANDA: Yeah.... Got a light?

PHILLIE: Ah...no...

AMANDA: Anybody got a light?

They all shake their heads. Shrug.

AMANDA: *(to PHILLIE)* What's the good of a cigarette without a light.

PHILLIE: I...don't know. Something to hold?

AMANDA: Fuck it. Sit down. Everyone sit down. We've got some planning to do.

SHIRLEY: Wait a minute.

AMANDA: Why.

SHIRLEY: What's goin' on.

AMANDA: I'm about to tell you.

SHIRLEY: I mean what's goin' on now.

AMANDA: Right now what's goin' on is you're preventing me from telling everyone what's goin' on. Now do you want to know or not.

SHIRLEY: Ah...ah...

AMANDA: I'll take that as a yes. Everyone sit down.

SHIRLEY: *(pointing to PHILLIE)* He can't sit down.

AMANDA: Why not.

SHIRLEY: He's not one of us.

AMANDA: Sure he is.

SHIRLEY: I'm telling you he's not.

AMANDA: Really. *(to PHILLIE)* You.... What's your name.

PHILLIE: Phillie.

AMANDA: Phillie. Are you a fucked-up pathetic individual with a bleak past and almost no potential.

PHILLIE: Ah... yeah.

AMANDA: *(to SHIRLEY)* See? Fits right in. Sit down, Phillie.

SHIRLEY: He's gotta go.

AMANDA: No. He's gotta stay.

SHIRLEY: Why.

AMANDA: Because I want him to stay. Because I like him. I like his style. I like that he smokes menthol. I like where he sleeps. But mostly I like saying he can stay when you say he can't.

SHIRLEY: Are you fucking with me now.

AMANDA: Definitely. I'm definitely fucking with you.

SHIRLEY: Why.

AMANDA: You know why.

SHIRLEY: What is this. *(to STEVIE)* Do you know what this is.

STEVIE: No. Not really. I mean—

ROLLY: I know what it is. She's challenging your authority.

SHIRLEY: Obviously she's challenging my authority. But why. Do you know why.

AMANDA: He doesn't know why. You know why.

SHIRLEY: Yeah? Well if I know why, why am I asking him.

AMANDA: You know why.

SHIRLEY: Fuck you and this "you know why" shit. I think there is no fucking why. I think you've just got it all wrong. You've made a big mistake. I'm the boss here. You're not the boss here. I mean just a few fucking hours ago you were a hostage. And now you're standing here saying who can sit down and who can't.

AMANDA: I never said anybody couldn't sit down. I invited everyone to sit down.

SHIRLEY: You know what I fucking mean.

AMANDA: And I was never a hostage.

SHIRLEY: Oh so now you were never a hostage. Whatya mean by that. What are you saying. Are you fucking with me for a purpose or what.

AMANDA: You know I am. You know the purpose.

SHIRLEY: I told you to stop all that "you know" shit. I hate that.

AMANDA: Sit down.

SHIRLEY: No.

AMANDA: Come on. They're all sitting down.

They are.

SHIRLEY: Stand up!

They all look at each AMANDA.

AMANDA: Stay where you are.

SHIRLEY: Stand up!

No response.
SHIRLEY walks over to ROLLY. Bends down.

SHIRLEY: *(whispering)* Rolly. What's happening here. When I tell you to stand up. Why won't you stand up.

ROLLY: *(whispering)* She doesn't want us to.

SHIRLEY: But...I'm in charge.

ROLLY: I...don't know if that's true.

SHIRLEY straightens. Turns. Walks to AMANDA.

SHIRLEY: Why are you fucking with me.

AMANDA: You know why.

SHIRLEY: Why are you challenging my authority.

AMANDA: Come on. You know why.

SHIRLEY: Is it because you want to be in charge.

AMANDA: You know it is.

SHIRLEY: Is it because you've got some plan. And you feel I'm not capable of implementing this plan.

AMANDA: That's exactly how I feel.

SHIRLEY: Because I can't handle things.... Because I don't understand what's going on. Because I hired the wrong guys to do the job and because they thought you were a hostage but really you were just observing. Because you had this plan to burn down your father's restaurant all along and this was just a good opportunity. And now if you've got some other plan to do something else I won't understand so you have to take charge.

AMANDA: It's something like that, yeah. So...will you sit down now, Shirley?

SHIRLEY: Probably. Probably I will sit down. I'm tired. I'm confused. I'm worried about your father and what he's going to do to me for fucking up so bad. And also well I've had a rough month. I met a guy at the track and I fell for him in a huge way. He was pretty. Extremely pretty. And in one month he'd taken me for everything I had and disappeared.... I mean everything.... Everything.... So.... Any help you can give would be appreciated.

AMANDA: Sit down.

SHIRLEY: Sure.

SHIRLEY sits down next to PHILLIE on the bed.

AMANDA: So here's what we have to do.... In a nutshell we have to strike fast. I mean there's a force being directed at us at this very minute so we have to do something pre-emptive.

PHILLIE: No.

AMANDA: What.

PHILLIE: No match.

He has all his pockets turned out.
AMANDA throws away her cigarette.

AMANDA: Okay. Here's the plan. *(she looks at them all)* But first I'd like to make an observation. I look at you people and I think nobody really understands you. They misdiagnose your problem. They observe you in your natural habitat. Doing the things you do and they think "Drugs. Heavy drugs." But it's not drugs is it. It's something else.... What is it.... Stupidity? Help me out here. What is it. Some common thing that binds you all together.... Well?

PHILLIE raises his hand.

PHILLIE: Excuse me.... Not stupidity. Bad luck. I think bad luck binds all the unfortunate of the earth...and makes us...unfortunate.

ROLLY: Yeah. Bad luck.

STEVIE: *(looks at ROLLY)* Definitely... And...sadness.... The sadness of...

AMANDA: The stupid?

PHILLIE: The poor.

STEVIE: Yeah. The poor.

ROLLY: Definitely.

SHIRLEY: Kindness.

AMANDA: What.

SHIRLEY: Kindness. Every time I get into trouble it's because I've been too kind. Usually to a man I forgave when I should have punished.... I haven't punished people enough.... I've been too...kind.

AMANDA: Anyway here's the plan.... We have to kill him. Kill him as dead as a doornail. And fast. If we kill him we'll be in good shape. We might even be in a position for a takeover. I can assume the throne. I can rule his criminal empire. You can be my...assistants. But we have to kill him. If we kill him he won't be coming after us. He won't be hiring anyone to come after us, any cops, or ex-cops, or any of his friends in the Asian gangs or any other ethnic gang. He'll be dead. But for him to be dead we have to kill him. If we kill him, he won't be able to get married again and father any other children and dominate and ruin their lives. But we have to kill the son of a bitch. If we kill the son of a bitch...and maybe if I take control of the criminal empire and hire you as assistants you'll have money and prestige and people won't be able to observe you in your natural habitat and think "Drugs" or "Stupidity" or "Bad luck." Or any combination of those things because you won't look the same or act the same because money and prestige can change the way people look and act..., But we have to kill him. We really do.... We have to.... So whatya say.

PHILLIE: I'm in. Kill the son of a bitch. Whoever he is.

SHIRLEY: Yeah. Punish the bastard. Whack him before he whacks us.

AMANDA: And whack us he will. Make no mistake. That's how he thinks. He's making plans to whack us right now.

PHILLIE: You know this guy pretty well then.

AMANDA: He's my father.

PHILLIE: Yeah?... Well I gotta say and you have to understand that everything I hear think and say is filtered by a very thick alcoholic fog but I gotta say nonetheless that if there's only one person that you kill in your life I think a dominating murderous criminal father with gangland connections is a good choice.

ROLLY: I'm sorry. But you have to count us out. We don't do violence. Under any circumstance.

AMANDA: Really?

ROLLY: It's a thing.

AMANDA: That right, Stevie?

STEVIE: Yeah it's a non-violence thing.... We're not proud of it or anything.

ROLLY: No we're not proud of it. We never said that. It's just a thing we have.... And we've always had it.

AMANDA: Well I'm afraid you're gonna have to lose it.

STEVIE: We can't lose it. It's our thing. If we lose it we don't have a thing.

ROLLY: And without a thing, what are you. I'll tell you.

AMANDA: Don't bother.

ROLLY: No. I wanna tell you.

AMANDA: You don't have to tell me. I know. I really do know. You're afraid this one...quality, if you can call it that, this "thing" is something that keeps you special in some way. It's the "thing" that prevents you from becoming inconsequential, insignificant nothings. But you're wrong. It doesn't do that at all. It just limits your options. Because you are inconsequential nothings. You really are. With or without the thing. So lose this non-violence hang-up before it gets us all killed.

STEVIE: We can't.

ROLLY: That's right. We can't.

AMANDA: Sure you can. Think about it.

ROLLY: I have. Really. But I can't. Especially now. Because now I'm goin' through these changes.... Serious changes. I've been reading articles about...life.... Sometimes there's a quiz. I always fail it.... It's depressing. It's a quiz about life. And I'm not good enough at life to pass. I wanna change. I do.

STEVIE: He does. He really does.

ROLLY: So we can't do violence. We just—

AMANDA: (to SHIRLEY) Tell them to shut up.

SHIRLEY: (to ROLLY) Shut up.

AMANDA: (to SHIRLEY) How come you hire guys who have an issue around violence. I mean how do you work with that.

SHIRLEY: It's never come up before. I've always just hired them as carriers, messengers, snitches, that kind of stuff. This was the first thing that required action, balls.

AMANDA: And they fucked it.

SHIRLEY: Royally.

ROLLY: Hey I burned the thing. It's burning.

SHIRLEY: Yeah but you fucked it. Because you were seen.

ROLLY: No one saw me.

AMANDA: I saw you.

ROLLY: No one else saw me.

STEVIE: I saw you.

ROLLY: So what that you saw me. Why are you piping in with "I saw you." You don't count.

AMANDA: Well I count. And I saw you. Got annoyed. And burned my father's restaurant down. And that was a mistake. I'm admitting that now. That's the thing that's gonna make him wanna kill us. And so because you let me see you, all of this is really your fault.

ROLLY: Oh sure blame me.

AMANDA: I am.

ROLLY: Oh sure go ahead and blame me. Like it's my fault.

AMANDA: It is your fault. Didn't you hear me just say it was your fault.

ROLLY: Oh sure go ahead. I don't care. It doesn't matter. Look okay I'm willing to help. I'll do anything short of hurting anyone. And so will my kid. We're good messengers. Give us a message to take somewhere.

STEVIE: We're good snitches too.

ROLLY: Yeah send us somewhere with a message. Let us snitch on someone while we're there. Stuff like that we can do.

STEVIE: We're excellent with those things. We've even got a thing we do. A way of doing a good snitch. We do it together. It's like an act or something. I pretend to say something I shouldn't about someone and then Dad cuffs me real hard on the head.

ROLLY cuffs STEVIE.

ROLLY: Like that.

STEVIE: And then I cry. Like this. *(he cries)* Sorry Dad. Sorry.

ROLLY: And then I beg the guy.... Like this... *(in a whisper)* Please don't tell so and so that Stevie said such and such because so and so will be real ticked off.... And then I cuff him again.

ROLLY cuffs STEVIE.

STEVIE: *(crying)* Sorry Dad... *(smiles)* And that usually works.

ROLLY: It always works.

STEVIE: That's what I said.

ROLLY: You said usually.

STEVIE: Usually, always. What's the difference.

AMANDA: *(to SHIRLEY)* Tell them to shut up.

SHIRLEY: *(to ROLLY and STEVIE)* Shut up.

AMANDA: Okay. Look maybe if we just think of this as an act of defence. We're just defending ourselves.... You're not against defending yourself are you.

ROLLY: Well...what do you mean.

AMANDA kicks him quickly in the groin.
ROLLY doubles.

STEVIE: Ah man. That was...ah man that was.... Dad, you okay?

ROLLY: Ahhhh...

AMANDA: What I mean is if you knew I was about to do that again would you try to stop me.

ROLLY: Ahhh...yes.

AMANDA: How about you.

STEVIE: Definitely...

AMANDA: Okay. Just think about what my father's gonna do as a big kick in the crotch.

STEVIE: I'd run.

AMANDA: We're not gonna run.

STEVIE: But...I'd run.

AMANDA: Running is not an option.

PHILLIE: What's wrong with running.

AMANDA: You got a non-violence thing too?

PHILLIE: Definitely.... Violence is bad.... Let's run.

AMANDA: No one is running.

PHILLIE: I am.

AMANDA: No you're not.

PHILLIE: Yeah, definitely. You're scary. If your father's even a bit like you I'm running.... I mean I haven't even done anything and I'm running.

AMANDA: You're not going anywhere. I need you.

PHILLIE: Me? How can you need me. You don't know anything about me.

AMANDA: I know that I need you. Five is better than four. Especially when two of the four are these two goofs.

PHILLIE: Yeah but...the way you kicked him in the groin was scary. It lacked...heart.... I'm running.

ROLLY: So am I.

STEVIE: Me too.

AMANDA: No one's running. *(to SHIRLEY)* Tell them.

SHIRLEY: Maybe running isn't such a bad idea. I mean your father kinda scares me. I mean I'm really just a small time player and he—

AMANDA: We're not running! If anyone runs they get tracked down like a dog kicked in the groin and then have their hearts cut out.... No one is running. This is a battle. You are an army. You are my army in the colossal battle I am about to have with my father and his army. It's a battle for control over a colossal empire of evil corruption and I'm gonna win this fucking battle and put my father in the fucking ground. And you're gonna help me do it!! You're not much. You're a bunch of pathetic nothings. But you're all I've got. And you're gonna fight! I have a plan. We're going to implement this plan. Anyone who fails to implement his or her part in this plan gets kicked in the crotch and loses a heart. I mean it. Everyone look at me and see if I mean it.... Well do I mean it.... Is everyone looking.... Do I mean it.... Do I!?

SHIRLEY: Yes. I think you do.

ROLLY: You really hate your father don't you.

AMANDA: Yes. Yes. I do.

ROLLY: I hope you never hate me like that Stevie. I couldn't stand it if you hated me like that.

STEVIE: Come on Dad. If I was gonna hate you I'd already hate you.

ROLLY: Whatya mean by that.

AMANDA: Okay shut up. Here's the plan.... No wait.... *(she paces for a moment, talking to herself)* Okay got it.... Here's the plan.... No...Ah. I'm...Something's happening to me here. I'm losing self confidence. Yeah. I'm feeling a bit unsure of myself. *(to SHIRLEY)* That's what happened to you isn't it. Do you think it has something to do with being in charge of this particular group of zany individuals.

SHIRLEY: Probably...I mean look at them.

AMANDA: Yeah...it's not like you feel you've got a strong support system in place...

SHIRLEY: No.... Definitely not.

AMANDA: Yeah well.... Here's the plan anyway.

She begins to pace.
Blackout.

Scene Three

Later. Night. Sounds of car screeching up and down the street.
STEVIE by the window. Peeking through the blinds. ROLLY is pacing
nervously.

STEVIE: Nothing. I don't see them. I just...don't see them.

ROLLY: Get away from the window.

STEVIE: I gotta keep lookin'.

ROLLY: Get away from the fucking window. It makes me nervous.

STEVIE: I gotta keep lookin'. It makes me nervous when I'm not lookin'.

ROLLY: Get away from the window.

STEVIE: I can't.

ROLLY: I'm nervous when you're at the window.

STEVIE: I gotta keep lookin'.

ROLLY: But I'm so nervous I can't think.

STEVIE: What are you thinking about.

ROLLY: I'm thinking about a lot of things.

STEVIE: Like what.

ROLLY: Like why won't you get away from the window when I ask you.

STEVIE: I can't.

ROLLY: And also I'm thinking, what happened. What the fuck happened.

STEVIE: Who knows what happened. No one knows.

ROLLY: Someone's gotta know. Nothing happens in this world without
someone knowing. You mean we don't know.

STEVIE: That's right, we don't know.

ROLLY: So what's new. When do we ever know. I can't remember the last
time I knew what happened when something happened.... Get away
from the window.

STEVIE: I can't.

ROLLY: I can't think when you're at the window. Don't you understand. I can't fucking think.

STEVIE: Too bad. I can't think if I'm not at the window.

ROLLY: So now your thinking is just as important as my thinking. So now you're some big shot thinker or something. Get away from the window.

STEVIE: No.

ROLLY: Get away from the goddamn window, or I'll come over there and kick you to death.

STEVIE: Someone's coming.

ROLLY: Who.

STEVIE: I can't see.

ROLLY: Who is it.

STEVIE: I can't see. It's too dark.

ROLLY: What's the point of looking if you can't see. You're standing at that goddamn window all this time and you can't even fucking see. What's the point of that!?

STEVIE: Someone's coming. Whoever it is…is coming…real close.

ROLLY: Who is it!

STEVIE: I can't see.

ROLLY: Even real close you can't see?

STEVIE: No.

ROLLY: So get away from the window!

STEVIE: No!

ROLLY: I'm nervous with you there and someone coming. Get away from there. What's the point of being at the window, Stevie. What's the fucking point!!

STEVIE: Ah Jesus. Someone's coming. Real close, real fast…

And PHILLIE bursts into the room. His forehead is bleeding.

PHILLIE: Where are they

ROLLY: They're not here.

PHILLIE: Did they get out.

ROLLY: We don't know.

PHILLIE: There were gun shots.

STEVIE: We heard them.

PHILLIE: Lots of them. It was like a battle. Lots of gunshots, serious commotion. Chaos and fear.... Chaos and fear.... I ran.

ROLLY: So did we.

STEVIE: Well not right away.

ROLLY: Yeah not right away. We stood there a moment wondering what to do...

STEVIE: Then we ran.

PHILLIE: I ran right away. I heard all that commotion. I ran. I ran right into a wall. I knocked myself out. When I woke up one of the guards had an Uzi trained on my head. He made me get up. Started to march me back to the house. I tripped in the dark. The guard tripped over me. I got up fast kicked him in the head...and took off.

STEVIE: Ah shit. Why didn't something like that happen to us, man. Then we could say we...did our part.

ROLLY: Hey we did our part... Our part was to stand guard. We stood guard.

PHILLIE: But you ran.

ROLLY: Yeah. But we did our part first.

STEVIE: Dad, our part was to stand guard and take out any of his men who came along.

ROLLY: Okay so we did part of our part. That's not bad.... We did something. So they can't totally blame us. They can only blame us a little.

PHILLIE: I don't think they're into blaming a little. I think they're into blaming a lot.

STEVIE: We ran. They told us not to run. We ran. We're screwed. Say anything you want about it but we're still screwed.

ROLLY: I don't think we're screwed.

STEVIE: You can say we're not screwed but we are.

ROLLY: We're not screwed.

STEVIE: You can say that.

ROLLY: Yeah I can say that because I've been thinking about it.

STEVIE: You can think all you want but we're screwed... *(to PHILLIE)* Aren't we.

PHILLIE: Definitely.

STEVIE: *(to ROLLY)* See?

ROLLY: What's he know about it.

PHILLIE: Well I must know something or I wouldn't have a fucking opinion, would I. I heard them say if you run you're screwed. You ran. You're screwed.

ROLLY: Yeah? Well so are you.

PHILLIE: I never said I wasn't.

ROLLY: Well you are.

PHILLIE: I have to take a piss.

PHILLIE goes in the bathroom. Closes door.

ROLLY: I don't like his attitude. It's kinda superior. Who is he to feel superior to us.

STEVIE: Everyone feels superior to us, Dad.

ROLLY: Yeah. Why is that.

STEVIE: Someone's coming.

ROLLY: Who.... Oh that's right I forgot. You can't see. You stand there. But you can't fucking see.

STEVIE: This time I can see.

ROLLY: Yeah?

STEVIE: Yeah.

ROLLY: Yeah so who the hell is it!?

The door flies open SHIRLEY and AMANDA are standing in the doorway. They are a mess. Filthy, torn clothing. A few cuts.
STEVIE and ROLLY look at each other.
AMANDA and SHIRLEY step into the room.
STEVIE and ROLLY look at each other.

AMANDA: No. Don't look at each other. Look at us.... Look at us! Look at our clothes. Our faces. Our hair. Now look at each other.... See the difference? We look...fucked up.... You look okay. But we look fucked up.... Why is that.... We went to the same place at the same time to accomplish the same task. But we came back looking like this. And you didn't.... Why.... Why!?

STEVIE: Because we...ran.

SHIRLEY: You ran like dogs.

STEVIE: Yeah we ran like dogs.

ROLLY: Not right away.... We did our part at first and then—

SHIRLEY: Shut up! You ran like pissing little puppy dog cowardly shiteaters. And now you're gonna have to pay.

ROLLY: Yeah but—

SHIRLEY pulls out a gun.

SHIRLEY: Shut up.

STEVIE: Dad she's got a gun.

ROLLY: She always had a gun.

STEVIE: She's got a bigger gun.

ROLLY: Yeah... Hey, Shirley why you got such a big gun all of a sudden.

AMANDA: She took it off a guard she killed.

STEVIE: Dad, she killed a guard.

SHIRLEY: I put a knife in his head.

ROLLY: In his head. You stabbed someone in the head?

STEVIE: Dad.

ROLLY: What.

STEVIE: Dad.

ROLLY: Dad, what? What!

STEVIE: In his head, Dad. She stabbed him in the head. I mean, I can't even imagine stabbing someone in the head.

AMANDA: She was magnificent. She was brave. And angry. She fought like a demon. We both did. We fought. And we killed. My father had twelve guards. We killed seven. That's what we did. What did you do. You didn't fight. You didn't kill. You ran. You ran and now you're screwed. Where's Phillie.

STEVIE: In the bathroom.

SHIRLEY: Tell him to come out here and die like a man.

STEVIE: I can't.

SHIRLEY: Tell him!

STEVIE: I can't. I can't say that. Come out and die like a man. It's too scary a thing for me to say. Really.

SHIRLEY: *(to STEVIE)* Shit! ...You're shit. *(to ROLLY)* And you're shit too...

She pounds on the door.

SHIRLEY: Phillie, you in there!?

PHILLIE: Yeah!

SHIRLEY: Come on out here.

PHILLIE: No.

SHIRLEY: Come on out and die like a man.

PHILLIE: No way.

SHIRLEY: Are you shit, Phillie. Are you a shit-eating cowardly shit like these two. Come on out here and I'll kill you fast. Make me come in there and you die slow.... Which way do you want it. Fast or slow.

PHILLIE: I don't want it either way. I don't want it fast and I don't want it slow. Just kill them. Leave me alone.

AMANDA: You ran, Phillie. You ran just like them.

PHILLIE: Okay I ran. But first I fought. I took out a guard. I kicked him in the head.

AMANDA: *(to ROLLY)* That true?

ROLLY: That's his story.

STEVIE: I believe him.

ROLLY: Why you saying that.

STEVIE: Because I do.

ROLLY: Yeah but now maybe they won't kill him.

STEVIE: So?

ROLLY: Yeah but they're still gonna kill us.

STEVIE: So? Why's it better if they kill us that they kill him too.

ROLLY: It just is.

STEVIE: Why.

ROLLY: It just is. I don't know why. It's like…okay I know. It's because I'd feel better…. And I'd feel better because I'm tired of being the only one who gets it, who gets caught, and gets screwed and gets killed…

STEVIE: You're not the only one, Dad. They're gonna kill me too.

ROLLY: Big fucking deal.

STEVIE: Come on, Dad. Be big about this. Go out with some class. Come on. Pass the quiz of life, Dad. Come on.

ROLLY: Yeah. Yeah… Okay. *(to AMANDA)* You can let Phillie live.

SHIRLEY: You don't make that decision. Who the hell do you think you are to make that decision.

ROLLY: It was only a suggestion.

AMANDA: Phil! It's Amanda.

PHILLIE: Hi.

AMANDA: Did you really take out a guard.

PHILLIE: I kicked him in the head. I kicked him…twice.

AMANDA: Okay okay. Stay there for a moment…. We're thinking about it…. *(to SHIRLEY)* Whatya say.

SHIRLEY: No, let's kill him. Let's kill him just like we kill these two. Kill them all and then let's go out and kill some more. I like it. I'm sorry I didn't start doing it sooner. There's dozens of guys who have fucked me over who could've been dead now. Killing is a good thing. It's cleansing. I like it. Let's do as much of it as we possibly can.

AMANDA: You know, I kinda feel the same way. It's like…sex.

SHIRLEY: It's better than sex.

AMANDA: Yeah but it's like sex. It's exciting like sex. It makes you hot.

STEVIE: Oh shit. Man, I'm getting fucked up by this.

AMANDA: What's your problem.

STEVIE: I'm gonna die. I'm gonna die but I'm listening to you talk to each other about sex and I'm getting excited. So I'm gonna die but I'm excited and I'm fucked up by that.... Help me, Dad. I'm confused! Really confused!

ROLLY: *(to AMANDA)* Kill him! Kill him now! Put him outta his misery.

SHIRLEY: I'll kill him when I wanna kill him.

ROLLY: Kill him now.

SHIRLEY: Stop telling me who to kill and when to kill them. Who the hell do you think you are. Maybe I'll kill you now.

ROLLY: He's the one who's confused. What's it to you who you kill first. Show some kindness. What's happened to you Shirley. You used to be a pretty decent person.

Suddenly the room is riddled by gun fire. The windows shatter. Pictures fall of the walls. SHIRLEY is hit in the shoulder. And drops her gun.

AMANDA: Hit the floor. Everyone down.... Get the lights someone get the lights.

ROLLY: I'll do it.

ROLLY crawls over. Reaches the wall switch. Hits it.
Darkness. Cars screeching away. Silence.

AMANDA: They're gone.

ROLLY: Maybe.

AMANDA: No, they're gone.

ROLLY: Maybe.

SHIRLEY: Hey! She says they're gone. They're gone!

AMANDA: Get the lights.

ROLLY: Let's wait.

AMANDA: Get the lights. They're gone.

ROLLY: Maybe.

SHIRLEY: Rolly, get the fucking lights!

ROLLY gets the lights. Light.
SHIRLEY is holding her bloodied arm. AMANDA is on the floor. Against the wall. STEVIE is gone.

ROLLY: Where's Stevie... Stevie!?

ROLLY pounds on the bathroom door.

ROLLY: Phillie, is Stevie in there with you.

PHILLIE: No.... Sorry.

> *STEVIE appears from the space between the bed and the wall. On his knees. Holding SHIRLEY's large gun.*

STEVIE: Here I am, Dad.

ROLLY: Stevie. You got the gun, boy.

STEVIE: Yeah.

> *AMANDA gets up.*

AMANDA: Stevie. Give me the gun.

STEVIE: No way.

AMANDA: Stevie, I need the gun.

STEVIE: Sure you need the gun. You need the gun to kill us then talk about sex. Or talk about sex while you're killing us. Or have sex while you're killing us. Or some kind of confusing shit like that.

AMANDA: I need the gun for protection. Those people are coming back.

ROLLY: They're not coming back.

AMANDA: Yes they are.

ROLLY: I don't think—

SHIRLEY: If she says they're coming back they're fucking coming back. Why are you always contradicting her. Who the fuck do you think you are. She's the smart one. You're the idiot! Now just shut the fuck up and tell that other idiot to give her the fucking gun. They're coming back. She needs the gun to protect us. Give her the gun, Stevie.

STEVIE: No.

SHIRLEY: Give her the fucking gun.

STEVIE: No. If I give you her gun she'll kill us.

SHIRLEY: She's not gonna kill you. I won't let her kill you. Because I'm gonna fucking kill you.

AMANDA: How about if I promise neither of us will kill you.

ROLLY: Don't believe her, Stevie.

STEVIE: I don't believe her.

ROLLY: You looked like you might be believing her.

STEVIE: Well I wasn't.

ROLLY: Well don't.

AMANDA: Stevie we were never really going to kill you. We were just playing with you, scaring you because you let us down, you know.... As for the sex stuff, well it's just talk. Women talk like that. It's nothing personal. Don't let it scare you. Anyway it's perfectly safe for you to give me the gun.... Do you believe me.

STEVIE: No.

ROLLY: Don't.

STEVIE: I'm not.

ROLLY: So don't.

AMANDA: Ah fuck it.

> *And AMANDA lunges over the bed at STEVIE. The gun falls. ROLLY heads for it. SHIRLEY stands. ROLLY grabs her. They fall together. AMANDA, STEVIE, SHIRLEY and ROLLY are all crawling toward the gun. They get there at the same time. Roll in a heap.*

AMANDA: I need the gun—

STEVIE: No way.

> *And the following nine lines overlap:*

ROLLY: Don't let her get it.

STEVIE: I'm not.

AMANDA: I need it. They're coming back.

ROLLY: No they're not.

SHIRLEY: Get off me.

ROLLY: You first.

AMANDA: I need the gun. Just for protection.

STEVIE: I don't believe you.

ROLLY: Don't believe her.

> *Sounds of several cars approaching quickly.*
> *AMANDA pulls herself free.*

AMANDA: Listen— Listen!!...

They all listen.

PHILLIE pounds on the bathroom door.

PHILLIE: What's going on out there.

AMANDA: Listen!... They're back.

SHIRLEY sits up.

SHIRLEY: *(to ROLLY)* You hear that? They're back. Ah shit, I'm hurt bad...

STEVIE crawls to the window.

AMANDA: Whatya see.

STEVIE: Nothing.

AMANDA: Nothing?

ROLLY: Send someone else.

SHIRLEY: I'll go...

Shirley begins crawling to window.

SHIRLEY: Ah...I'm hurt.... I've got stomach cramps.... I'm agitated and depressed.... I felt a hell of a lot better when I was killing people.

Shirley is at the window.

AMANDA: So?

SHIRLEY: It's them.... Two cars.... Six guys with guns.

AMANDA: Is my dad with them.

SHIRLEY: Yeah.

STEVIE: I thought you killed her dad.

SHIRLEY: He was in his bedroom. We never got that far. We were stopped by his guards.

STEVIE: You blame us for that.

SHIRLEY: Yes we do.

ROLLY: I think it's too late for blame. What good is blame anyway. I mean when you get right down to it no one's really to blame.

SHIRLEY: Wrong! You're to blame! I'm blaming you. Blame is good. I love blame. You fucked up the original deal and you caused all this shit, Rolly. So I'm blaming you!!

ROLLY: We used to be friends, Shirley. I think it's sad the way you've turned on me. I'm not responsible for all your misfortune.

SHIRLEY: Yeah you're just one of the many men who has fucked me over Rolly. Just one. But since you're the only one here, I'm feeling all my feelings about them for you. So shut up and take the fucking blame.

AMANDA: We need a plan. Six guys with guns are walking towards us. We need a plan. Where's the gun.

STEVIE is holding it.

STEVIE: Here.... No bullets.

AMANDA: Okay we need a plan that doesn't involve a gun.

STEVIE: *(looking out the window)* Are you sure there are six. I only see two.... Oh no there's another one.

SHIRLEY: *(looking out the window)* What's wrong with you. Are you blind. There are six of them. Fifty feet away.

STEVIE: It's the neon. And it's the darkness around the neon. And the neon spilling into the darkness... It's hard to see.

AMANDA: What are they doing.

STEVIE: I can't really—

SHIRLEY: They're talking! They're checking their weapons. They're pointing at various things. I think they're formulating a plan.

AMANDA: Okay. They've got weapons. They've got a plan.... What have we got.... What have we got.... Okay let me think...

ROLLY: Maybe we should—

SHIRLEY: Shut up and let her think.

A long pause.

PHILLIE: What's happening out there. Why is it quiet all of a sudden.

AMANDA: Please. I'm thinking.

PHILLIE: Sorry.

STEVIE: *(to SHIRLEY)* What are they doing now.

SHIRLEY: They're coming this way.

STEVIE: *(to others)* They're coming this way.

AMANDA: I don't know…. There's something about the dynamic of this particular group. I used to be able to plan things with a certain flair. I had imagination. A kind of devil may care confidence…. I don't know…

SHIRLEY: They've stopped again. I…don't think they like their plan. They're talking again.

AMANDA: Okay. They're talking. Revising their plan. That gives us more time. We can still come up with a plan of our own. I mean anything's better than just sitting here and letting them slaughter us. Any ideas?

No response. She knocks on the bathroom door.

AMANDA: Phillie! Any ideas?

PHILLIE: About what?

They are all just looking at her. AMANDA notices ROLLY's feet.

AMANDA: You're not wearing shoes.

ROLLY: No.

AMANDA: Where are they.

ROLLY: I don't know. Phillie took them. And he wouldn't give them back because we didn't have forty dollars for the room.

AMANDA: No one had forty dollars?

ROLLY: Not even Shirley.

AMANDA looks at SHIRLEY. SHIRLEY shrugs.

AMANDA: How long have you been without shoes.

ROLLY: A long time.

AMANDA: Did you go to my father's house without shoes. I mean were you standing guard in your socks like that.

ROLLY: Yeah.

AMANDA: Do you think you might have behaved differently in shoes.

ROLLY: Oh, definitely.

AMANDA: You might not have run, you might have done your part thereby allowing us to successfully complete our task and kill my father?

ROLLY: Well I was feeling kind of…

AMANDA: Vulnerable?

ROLLY: Yeah.

AMANDA: Yeah. So I guess if we really need to blame something…. I mean if it helps us feel better we can—

SHIRLEY: That's bullshit. Blaming the shoes is bullshit…. Don't let him blame the fucking shoes.

STEVIE: You don't know. You weren't there.

SHIRLEY: I was there.

ROLLY: Yeah but you were there in shoes.

SHIRLEY: Ah shut up. *(to AMANDA)* They're getting pretty close.

AMANDA: So…. Any ideas? Any at all?…. So we're just gonna wait here and let those guys come in here and blow our brains all over the walls. Is that it. I hate that. We can do better than that. We can. Come on think…. Think!

They all just stare blankly. PHILLIE bangs on the bathroom door.

PHILLIE: Hey! The shoes are under the bed. I left them there. All you had to do was look.

The door is kicked in. Then silence. They move cautiously toward the open door. Get near it…
Four gunshots. SHIRLEY, ROLLY, STEVIE and AMANDA all fall. Dead.

PHILLIE: Hey! What's happening out there. Were those gunshots…. Well? …Well? Ah the hell with you all…. I'm sorry I ever met you…. You're just like everyone else…. You take advantage…. You see that I'm a not-well man, that I'm addicted to alcoholic beverages, prone to bad luck, you see that I'm not a very strong person and you take advantage. Get me involved in something I'm too impaired to fully understand. Whatever happens to me, I'm blaming you. You thought you were gonna blame me, well I'm blaming you. The forty buck thing, the shoes thing, the running thing, I'm not taking responsibility for any of it. Who said we were bound together…. That's crap. We're not bound. It's every man for himself. Dog eat dog. Fuck you. Did you hear me. Fuck you. Talk about bad luck. Bad luck loves me like I'm it's mother…. Ever since I was a kid…. No. You know what? It's not bad luck. It's people. Since I was five, six years old nothing good has ever happened to me. I blame my parents and my teachers. I blame everyone I ever met. Everyone.... You know if there was any justice in the world they'd kill you all and leave me alone. But they won't. They'll kill me too. I didn't do anything to them, okay I kicked one of them in the head, but is that any reason to kill someone. No. Unless of course that person is me. Sure kill me for any old reason. Who am I. No one. Nothing. Fuck all. Phillie Fuck-All.... You can kill him anytime you want. Kill him, fuck him, kill him fuck him, kill him. Who cares. He's just a pathetic asshole.... Well isn't that a sad commentary on our society... I mean really. I blame society for producing that kind of callous indifference to fucked-up individuals.... I really do.... I really really do.

Long pause.

PHILLIE: Looking back I never had a chance. My parents were idiots, my teachers were idiots, all my friends were idiots, everyone, every single person I ever met in my whole life was a mean-spirited, demented idiot. And I never complained. Never. Not once.... Not until now. I've been a fucking saint!

A noise from the bathroom.

PHILLIE: Oh look. Great. Someone's at the window in here. He's trying to climb in. No he changed his mind. He's happy just looking at me. Mean-looking prick is just staring at me. Oh great, he's got a gun. Yeah here he is, some other demented idiot in my life for no good reason and this one is going to shoot me. Well go ahead, asshole. Shoot me. Why not. Who cares.

A gunshot.

PHILLIE: Great.

Sound of a body falling. Pause.
STEVIE's body twitches slightly.
Blackout.

The End

FEATURING LORETTA

PERSONS
LORETTA
SOPHIE*
DAVE
MICHAEL

*SOPHIE speaks with a Russian accent.

PLACE
A slightly run-down motel on the outskirts of a large city.

Scene One

Motel room. LORRIE is on the phone. She is dressed like a cowgirl.
Something is cooking in a frying pan on a hot plate.

LORRIE: *(into phone)* Nah. No way am I here longer than another month.... Well there are things happening.... Sure there are.... I might go to Tokyo for a few months. I met some guy who says I can do modelling over there. Modelling and dancing.... He says they love women who look like me, whatever that means.... No it's not white slavery. It's modelling.... Okay it's posing. It's posing maybe without clothes. And dancing a bit. But it's not white slavery. And even if it was I might go anyway.... Well because it's a change.... No it's not stupid. And even if it is stupid I might go anyway.

A knock at the door.

Look I gotta go.... I gotta go. Say hi to Mom for me.... I do call her.... Okay I call you. It's the same thing... .Because you're her daughter too. So...you say hi to her.... Yes it does make sense...

(A knock at the door)

Lots of things. No not just the Tokyo thing. Other things. A...partnership. I was offered a kind of partnership in something. Look it's complicated. I'll tell you later.... I don't wanna come home. There's nothing for me there.... He's nothing. He's just something that happened to me.... No he doesn't. He doesn't love me. And you know what, even if he does love me I don't care. So what if he loves me. Being loved isn't the only thing in the world.... Adventure, experience... Yes Jane. I'm a waitress... That's right minimum wage... That's right I wear a dumb costume.

(A knock on the door)

I gotta go.... Say goodbye, Jane. Say goodbye Janie. Janie...Janie...Janie, I gotta go.... Yes I'm happy.... Because things are good. I mean I feel things could be good and I've got...a feeling about other...good things...too.

(A knock on the door)

Yes it does.... Yes it does make sense. If you were here feeling the feeling you'd know. No maybe you wouldn't know. I gotta go. Goodbye.... No goodbye. I gotta go...Jane, I gotta go. Goodbye.

She hangs up. Goes to door. SOPHIE, the young Russian immigrant
daughter of the owner, is at the door.

SOPHIE: They have sent me.

LORRIE: Hi.

SOPHIE: They smell cooking.

LORRIE: Really? All the windows are closed.

SOPHIE: They smell. They send. They say, "Say not to be cooking in room."
Okay? Goodbye.

LORRIE: Sure. Bye.

LORRIE closes the door. A knock on the door. SOPHIE is standing there.

SOPHIE: I am sorry.

LORRIE: It's okay.

SOPHIE: Cook.... Still cook.... I say mistake. I tell them...you know.... Hey!
She's not cooking. Mistake.

LORRIE: No it's okay.

SOPHIE: No cook.

LORRIE: No. It's almost done. So I can turn it off in a.... You see, they gave
me a steak at work so I thought I'd just.... Usually I just use the hot
plate for boiling water for coffee.... See? Coffee.

SOPHIE: Cannot look. Cannot see hot plate. I see hot plate...I know hot
plate is here.

LORRIE: Oh yeah...right.

SOPHIE: Gotta go.

LORRIE: Okay.

SOPHIE: Need towels?

LORRIE: No... I'm fine.

SOPHIE: Okay. Sorry. Goodbye.

SOPHIE leaves. LORRIE closes the door. Opens it.

LORRIE: Hey. Wait a minute. Please.

SOPHIE comes back.

SOPHIE: Hello.

LORRIE: Yeah, hi. Ah. Come in for a minute...

SOPHIE steps in.

SOPHIE: Hello.

LORRIE: Yeah. Hi…Ah… I was wondering. What do you know about Tokyo.

SOPHIE: I am Russian.

LORRIE: Ah, yeah but—

SOPHIE: Tokyo is Japan.

LORRIE: Yeah I know.

SOPHIE: Why would I know about Tokyo.

LORRIE: I thought…maybe you'd been there.

SOPHIE: I am Russian.

LORRIE: But that's…over there…. And Japan is…over there. People travel over there, don't they.

SOPHIE: Not me. I was in Russia. Now I'm here. That's it.

LORRIE: I might go there. Tokyo. I met a guy. He wants me to go there.

SOPHIE: Japanese guy?

LORRIE: No. But he works for a Japanese man over there. He's his representative here.

SOPHIE: Careful! You could be white slave.

LORRIE: No way.

SOPHIE: Japanese man. Western woman. White slave. Careful…. Steak burning.

SOPHIE points to hot plate which is smoking. LORRIE goes to hot plate. Holds up charred steak.

LORRIE: Shit…. White slave…. Really?

SOPHIE: Ask questions before you go…. What work you will be doing there.

LORRIE: Dancing.

SOPHIE: Ask many questions…. What is your age anyway.

LORRIE: My age? *(takes the charred steak from pan)* Oh I get it. It's the costume isn't it. You think I'm some goofy kid with a rodeo or something. It's the thing they make me wear down at Buffalo Blow-Hole's.

LORRIE drops the steak in a waste basket.

SOPHIE: Buffalo what. Oh Buffalo Bob. *(laughs)* Buffalo Blow-Hole. *(pats Lorrie's arm affectionately)* You are funny. I don't know what means blow hole though…

LORRIE: It's just that I'm looking for adventure. I'm not naive. I'm not a fool. I've got an education. Two years of community college…

SOPHIE: I study also.

LORRIE: Yeah?

SOPHIE: Physics. Two years.

LORRIE: Physics. Yeah?

SOPHIE: Two more years. Then two more. Then three for big finish. P…H…D.

LORRIE: Yeah? Physics. What…kind. I mean…to learn what.

SOPHIE: Beginning of the universe.

LORRIE: Yeah? So…how'd it begin.

SOPHIE: *(laughs)* Silly… I don't know. *(hits her)* I'm studying just two years. Later for that…. Okay I'm leaving…. Remember no more cooking or my father says…you out.

She makes the safe at the plate gesture with her arms.

SOPHIE: You know. Baseball game.

LORRIE: That means safe.

SOPHIE: Father says out.

LORRIE: He's wrong. It means safe…. This means out. *(jerks her thumb up and over her shoulder)*

SOPHIE: *(laughs)* He's wrong? For years he's saying "Careful or you're *(makes safe gesture)* out."… He's really saying "Be careful or you are safe?"

LORRIE: Yeah.

SOPHIE: *(laughs)* That's funny. Look I'm laughing. *(turns serious)* Don't tell him.

LORRIE: I won't.

SOPHIE: He will be getting mad…. Yelling.

The phone rings.

LORRIE: Have to go.

SOPHIE: Me too.

SOPHIE leaves. LORRIE answers the phone.

LORRIE: *(into phone)* Hi…Hi Mom…. Yeah, okay but…maybe we could talk about it later…. Yeah, yeah…. But Japan's just one option. There are others. Look I gotta get ready. I'm going out…. Out…Out. Just out…. Yeah…Yeah…. Well it's *(looking around)* a room. A motel room. It's fine…. No. It's fine…It's fine! …Great. Goodbye.

She hangs up. Starts to undress as she goes to the bathroom. A knock on the door.

LORRIE: Who is it.

DAVE: Me.

LORRIE opens the door. DAVE is standing there. DAVE is in his late twenties. Dressed in sports jacket and tie.

LORRIE: Come on in.

DAVE: You're not ready.

LORRIE: Almost.

DAVE: We'll be late.

LORRIE: I just need two minutes.

DAVE: We'll be late. I can't be late. If I'm late I'm screwed.

LORRIE: Two minutes.

She goes into the bathroom.

DAVE: He hates lateness. There are only two or three things he actually hates. Lateness is one of them.

LORRIE: I'm just washing my face, running a brush through my—

DAVE: Lateness and…two other things I can't remember now…. But definitely lateness.

LORRIE comes out of the bathroom in her slip. Brushing her hair.

LORRIE: Hand me that dress on the bed.

DAVE: Which one.

LORRIE: There's only one.

DAVE: There's two.

LORRIE: Oh right.... Well which one do you like.

DAVE: I don't care. This one. No this one. I mean they're both.... Look we haven't got time for this. I thought you wanted to help me get this job.

LORRIE: I do.

DAVE: So hurry.

LORRIE: Look if we're late, say it was my fault.

DAVE: Ah...no I can't do that.

LORRIE: Why not.

DAVE: Because I just remembered one of the other things he really hates is passing the buck.

Phone rings.

LORRIE: Will you get that.

DAVE: There's no time.

LORRIE: I'm expecting a call.

DAVE: Now? You're expecting a call now. When you knew you were going out you arranged to have a call?

LORRIE: He said he'd call. That promoter. About Japan.

DAVE: Oh that guy. Sure I'll talk to that guy.

LORRIE: Dave don't—

DAVE: It's okay.

DAVE answers the phone.

DAVE: *(into the phone)* Hello.... No she can't come to the phone right now.

LORRIE: Yes I can.

DAVE: She's busy.

LORRIE: Dave...

DAVE: Getting dressed.

LORRIE: Dave, give me the phone.

DAVE gestures "relax."

DAVE: What's my name. What's your name. No forget your name. Who cares about your name.... Okay. Tell me your name. That's not your name.

She told me your name and I can't remember what it is, but it's definitely not that…. *(to LORRIE)* Is the guy's name Michael.

LORRIE: Yeah.

DAVE: Come on. Michael?

LORRIE: Just give me the phone.

DAVE covers the receiver.

DAVE: You said he was from Japan.

LORRIE: No I didn't. I said he represented Japanese interests. Give me the phone.

DAVE: Why. So you can listen to more of his crap. His lies. His false promises. So you can ruin your life? *(into phone)* Michael. About Japan. Forget it. *(hangs up)*

LORRIE: Oh…Jesus. What did you just do. You just…took away one of my options.

DAVE: It had to be done. You're thousands of miles from your family so I had to do it.

LORRIE: You had no right. What the hell made you think—

DAVE: Wait. Let's go. We'll talk about it in the car.

LORRIE: No way.

DAVE: Well we can't talk about it now. We'll be late. Come on.

LORRIE: No way.

DAVE: Come on, Lorrie.

LORRIE: *(sits)* I'm staying.

DAVE: We gotta go. It's time to go.

LORRIE: So go.

DAVE: We gotta go.

LORRIE: No we don't.

DAVE: You promised.

LORRIE: Forget it.

DAVE: But you promised. I asked you to come to dinner with my boss. To be charming. To say nice things about me. To say nice things about my boss. And you promised you would. Remember? We said it could be the beginning of a...partnership of some kind.

LORRIE: Forget it. I'm not coming. You stepped over a line. When you stepped over that line all deals were off.... Goodbye.

DAVE: Goodbye? Whatya mean goodbye.

LORRIE: Goodbye.

DAVE: Goodbye for now?

LORRIE: Goodbye.

DAVE: Goodbye until you calm down? Goodbye for awhile?

LORRIE: Go away.

DAVE: Go away? Like...go...away? Okay, okay how about if I apologize.... I mean I think I was right to do what I did. I really do because well I just do and you will too eventually. But for now I'm willing to apologize.... So can we just go now. Can we just go and have this dinner with my boss like we were supposed to.

LORRIE: *(stands)* No, Dave. We can't.

LORRIE walks to door.

DAVE: I need this promotion. If I don't get this promotion now I'll never get it. I'll miss my opportunity.

LORRIE: That's...too bad.

DAVE: But you don't understand.

LORRIE: Yes I do.

DAVE: No you don't understand about promotions and opportunities. You're a waitress for chrissake.

She opens the door.

LORRIE: Get out.

DAVE: Come on, let's go.

LORRIE: Get out.

DAVE: Come on. Let's go eat. Suck up to my boss. Get me that promotion. Later we'll walk. We'll talk. I'll apologize. You'll forgive me. I'll explain how what I did was for the best and you'll—

LORRIE: You have to leave now.

DAVE: I need you to come with me.

LORRIE: That's not gonna happen.

DAVE: I won't get the job. I'm no good in one-on-ones.

LORRIE: I've noticed.

DAVE: If I don't get the job, I'll…blame you.

LORRIE: Really.

DAVE: Yeah. I'll blame you.

LORRIE: Leave.

DAVE: I'll blame you big time! Very big time!

LORRIE: Leave now or I'll call someone. Leave!

DAVE: I'm leaving. Look at me. I'm leaving…I'm…leaving…. *(he gets outside…turns)* Okay. I'm giving you one more chance. Are you coming or not.

She slams the door in his face. The phone rings. LORRIE answers it.

LORRIE: *(into phone)* Yes…. Oh hi, Michael… No. That was just Dave…. He's…an idiot. He's a friend from work…well a customer. And we…. Look. Forget him. He was just passing by and he— Yeah weird. I think he was drunk or something.

A knock on the door.

DAVE: Lorrie. It's Dave!

LORRIE covers the receiver.

LORRIE: Go away!

DAVE: Lorrie. Please!

LORRIE: No!

DAVE: I hate you! I thought I liked you! But I don't! I hate you! *(starts to cry)* Please, Lorrie. Please. I need this job. Please. Please forgive me. Please!!

He is pounding on the door.

DAVE: Lorrie. Please!!! Pleasssse!!… I don't hate you! I really don't!

LORRIE: *(into phone)* Can you call back in five minutes? …Thanks….

LORRIE hangs up. Moves closer to door.

DAVE: But you promised, Lorrie.... I thought we had something. Something to build on. A beginning of something.

LORRIE: You have to leave, Dave. You can't just stay there crying and pounding on the door.

DAVE: Come with me!

LORRIE: No. You ruined it. You messed with one of my options. I hate that. My options are all I've got.

DAVE: I thought I was one of your options.

LORRIE: You were. But now you're not. When you answered that phone and said those things you stopped being an option. Go away.

DAVE: I hate you!

LORRIE: I hate you too.

DAVE: I love you!

LORRIE: Go away.

DAVE: I love you. Can you hear me. I love you. Come with me. Help me get the job. Let's build on the something we have. Let's keep our options alive! Please. Please.... Oh God I hate you. I really hate you!

LORRIE: Just...go away.

DAVE: Don't worry I'm going.

LORRIE: So go.

DAVE: I'm going.

Pause.

LORRIE: Are you gone...

Silence. LORRIE sighs. Leans her head against the door.
Blackout.

Scene Two

Later. LORRIE and MICHAEL are eating takeout Chinese food from cartons. MICHAEL is mid-thirties. Expensive sweater. Blue jeans. Leather jacket on one of the chairs.

MICHAEL: Oh this...this is good. Try this.

LORRIE: I've got some.

MICHAEL: No try this.

LORRIE: I've got some on my plate.

MICHAEL: Have you tried it.

LORRIE: Yeah. It's good.

MICHAEL: Oh.... Try this one.

LORRIE: I don't like fish much.

MICHAEL: Shrimp.

LORRIE: Shrimp? I don't like it.

MICHAEL: Try it though.

LORRIE: I don't...want to.

MICHAEL: Close your eyes. Try it with your eyes closed. Come on be a trier.

LORRIE: No.

MICHAEL: Come on. I won't stop until you try it. That's the way I am. I just won't stop.

LORRIE: Okay. I'll try it.

LORRIE closes her eyes. MICHAEL puts some shrimp in her mouth.

MICHAEL: Like it?

LORRIE: Yeah.

MICHAEL: Want more?

LORRIE: No.

MICHAEL: I thought you liked it.

LORRIE: I like it a little.

MICHAEL: I really like it. I like it all. I like everything here. A lot.

LORRIE: Great.

MICHAEL: I usually like everything. Almost always. Everything I eat. Everything I see…. Everything.

LORRIE: Really? That's great.

MICHAEL: Look I gotta tell you something. It's been on my mind. You look like the kind of person I can tell this kind of thing to. Are you.

LORRIE: I don't know.

MICHAEL: I hope you are. Are you.

LORRIE: I don't know.

MICHAEL: You probably are…. Okay. Look when I first saw you in that restaurant I got an immediate erection.

LORRIE: Oh…Really?

MICHAEL: Yeah…Was it okay to tell you that.

LORRIE: Ah. Sure. I guess.

MICHAEL: Because it's the truth. Absolutely. I saw you. I got hard. Just like that. Just like I described it. I walked in. You were there. My eyes took you in. Bingo. Now look like I said. I like things. Food. People. I'm, you know, sensual. I see someone I'm attracted to, it's not unusual for me to get aroused. But never before immediate. The eyes see, the penis hardens. Never before like that. So later I got to thinking. You have a special quality. A quality I can market. That's why I suggested the Tokyo thing. I've got business partners over there. I thought I could put you in a position over there to be involved with very large money situations.

LORRIE: Look if you're talking the escort business I'm not really—

MICHAEL: I was thinking escort, I'm not thinking that now.

LORRIE: Anyway when we first talked you said it would only involve dancing. Private dancing.

MICHAEL: Well dancing, escort. Whatever. I was thinking…I'm not thinking that now. None of it. Now I'm thinking I don't want you in Tokyo. You're quality is not something I feel like exporting. It's homegrown. It's of this place. Look there's nothing special about me. I'm average really. I mean I like things more than most. But the things I like are what everyone likes. I like you. Everyone will like you. Look I'm thinking something. And it's something I need to tell you. Can I.

LORRIE: I guess…If you need to.

MICHAEL: Well if I don't what's the point. I mean even if I tell you and you don't agree, what's the point. But I won't know unless I tell you. So...

LORRIE: So I guess you better tell me.

MICHAEL: Okay. I want to feature you in a series of erotic movies.

LORRIE: You do?

MICHAEL: Okay let's be honest here. I don't know what the hell erotic movies are. Maybe I do. But I'm not sure so let's say what I mean. I mean let me say what I mean then you can say something...about that. Okay?

LORRIE: Yeah, okay.

MICHAEL: Pornographic movies. By that I mean this. Simply. You're lying on the bed naked. Naked men come in, see you, get an erection, and then have sex with you. Now maybe that's pornographic *and* erotic. I don't know. But it's what I want to do. So there it is.... I thought I'd like to make about five of these to start with. Each one about forty minutes long. Each with a different guy. So other than the guy everything is the same. Even the immediate erection is the same. They all need to do that. Get hard fast. I think I'll pay you two thousand five hundred dollars for each one. Okay so that's what I want to do.... I hope you agree. Do you.

LORRIE: I don't know.

MICHAEL: If you agree to the basic idea, we can work on the details. Condoms, medical exams, lighting intensity, percentage of profits, foreign sales, approval of the "co-stars." But why bother with all that unless you agree. I hope you do. I think you'd make an impact. It could be the start of something.

LORRIE: What...something?

MICHAEL: Something...else. Big things...I don't know exactly.

LORRIE: You don't.

MICHAEL: No. I've never done it before. I'm a booker. I find girls. Book them into bars...clubs.

LORRIE: So when you say it could lead to...big things, you don't really know what you're talking about.

MICHAEL: But does that mean it's a bad idea.... I mean just because I don't know what I'm talking about doesn't mean it can't happen.

LORRIE: What can't happen.

MICHAEL: Whatever. Look. I like you. You're a sexy individual. Let's make six naked sex movies and see what happens. Will you at least think about it. What's the harm in thinking about it. Come on, say you'll think about it.

LORRIE: Okay. I'll think about it.

MICHAEL: Excellent. *(puts on his jacket)* By the way who was that guy on the phone before.

LORRIE: No one.

MICHAEL: Boyfriend?

LORRIE: Sort of.... But it's over.

MICHAEL: He sounded like an asshole. I mean I didn't like him. And usually I like people.... So I can only assume he's an asshole. By the way if we do this I don't want boyfriends hanging around. It creates a bad atmosphere.

LORRIE: I thought you'd never done it before.

MICHAEL: It's not hard to imagine them creating a bad atmosphere.... Okay. I gotta run. Are you gonna eat the rest of this food.

LORRIE: I don't think so.

MICHAEL: Mind if I take it?

LORRIE: Go ahead.

MICHAEL is putting the cartons in a bag.

MICHAEL: I just messed up your head a bit, didn't I. Admit it. Just a bit. Come on. I was brutally honest and told you I wanted you naked and having sex on film. And that kind of set you back a bit. I mean you thought I was kind of sleazy, that maybe I had a hidden agenda or something. But I don't. I just have an idea. Maybe it's good. Maybe it's not good. Maybe it's good but it needs refinement. Just think it over. And call me.

LORRIE: I don't have your number.

MICHAEL: I'll call you.... Bye.... Can I kiss you. I feel like kissing you. Can I.

LORRIE: I...guess.

MICHAEL: Never mind. It's okay. No. It's a bad idea. If I kiss you I get excited. Just looking at you I'm getting excited so no way can I kiss you.... Hey look. It's not like I don't want to...but we've got a business thing hanging in the air. Let's get that business thing worked out first. Then maybe.

LORRIE: Maybe what.

MICHAEL: Oh right. That was extremely presumptuous. Just because I get excited looking at you doesn't mean you get excited looking at me, does it.

LORRIE: No.

MICHAEL: No. Well that answers that.... No, no it's okay. Strictly business. That's better. Is that what you meant when you said "no."

LORRIE: When.

MICHAEL: Just now. Just then. Never mind. Forget it. Call me. I'll call you. See ya.

MICHAEL leaves. LORRIE sits on the bed. Stands. Goes to a wall mirror. Looks at herself. Shrugs. Goes to TV. Turns it on. Flicks. Finds the weather station. The phone rings. LORRIE answers it.

LORRIE: *(into phone)* Yeah.... Hi.... Yeah she called.... Tell her not to worry. Japan's out.... Well it just got replaced.... As an option that's what.... You call her. It's cheaper for you to call her.... No you call her.... Okay don't call her.... No I'm not.... I'm not hard, Jane.... No I haven't become hard since I got here. I only got here a month ago. Even if I was gonna get hard I wouldn't be hard yet.... Freedom.... Freedom.... Yes, freedom.... Look it up. F-R-E-E-D-O-M... Yes from her. From you. From everyone.... Yes from Tommy's family. That's right.... Yes they were.... They were trying to run my life.... Oh no they don't. They have no right.... He's dead.... Yes, yes he was my husband but he's dead.... No I never let him make those decisions so why would I let his father and mother make them.... Whatya mean why not. You know why not.... Okay you don't. But that's your problem not mine.... Because if you don't know why it's important not to let other people make your decisions in life, that's a problem.

A knock on the door.

I gotta go. Someone's at the door.... Yeah I get visitors. I'm meeting as many people as I can...I told you why. Because I'm in a hurry.... Because I've only got so much time to make the decision that's why.... I told you! If I've got prospects then yes. If not then no.... No.... No I'm not showing yet.... No not even a little.

A knock on the door.

I gotta go.... No you call her.... You call her.... Okay, okay, I'll call her....
Later.... Goodbye.

LORRIE answers the door. SOPHIE is standing there with a vacuum.

SOPHIE: Something strange happened.

LORRIE: To you?

SOPHIE: No to you.

LORRIE: To me? When. What are you talking about. What's with the
vacuum cleaner.

SOPHIE: I have to clean. Is now bad for cleaning.

LORRIE: You have to clean now?

SOPHIE: Usually now is okay. Now you are usually out.

LORRIE: Yeah well I— Come in.

SOPHIE comes in. Plugs in the vacuum.

SOPHIE: Did I tell you something strange happened?

LORRIE: Yeah, what.

SOPHIE: I told you something strange happened but not what it is.

LORRIE: No.

SOPHIE: *(hits herself on the head)* Stupid. I'm so tired. Physics you know is
hard work. Then I have to clean rooms. I'm so tired.... Father wanted to
be a physics man. Became Red Army KGB man instead. Now he owns
motel. I tell him. Motel is fine for me too. Forget physics. I clean motel.
He screams like when he was KGB screaming at dissidents. Okay now I
tell you what happened before I forget again because I'm so tired... You
know man who was just here who just leaves.

LORRIE: Yeah what about him.

SOPHIE: Man who was here before that man who just leaves...that before
man comes up to this man and they have a large argument...

LORRIE: Just now?

SOPHIE: Yes. Then before man makes just now man get in car and they
leave.

LORRIE: Made him? Made him how?

SOPHIE holds up her hand and makes a gun.

LORRIE: A gun?

SOPHIE: Looks like. Maybe not.... But yes, I think so.

LORRIE: So Dave...kidnapped Michael?

SOPHIE: Is Dave man from before.

LORRIE: Yes.

SOPHIE: Then yes. Dave kidnapped Michael.

LORRIE: Jesus.... I gotta do something about this. What.... Call the police. Are you sure he had a gun.

SOPHIE: Maybe not.

LORRIE: Maybe he...didn't have a gun?

SOPHIE: Maybe I'm sure.

LORRIE: So you're not sure.

SOPHIE: They are friends, these two men?

LORRIE: No.

SOPHIE: So why one would leave with other one. It looks strange.

LORRIE: Did you see a gun. Actually see it.

SOPHIE: It's dark.

LORRIE: So you didn't see it?

SOPHIE: I'm tired...

LORRIE: I can't call the police unless we're sure. What do we do. We have to do something.

SOPHIE: We?

LORRIE: Me.

SOPHIE: Good. Not me. My father won't like me to do something. Not official something. Because well he is ex-KGB man in this country with enough money to buy motel. You understand what I'm saying here?

LORRIE: Sort of.... Yeah I guess. Okay.... But what should I do. I should do something.

SOPHIE: Call him.

LORRIE: Call him. Who, Dave?

SOPHIE: You know his telephone number? He lives close?

LORRIE: Yeah...yeah.

SOPHIE: Call him. See what he says. Maybe he will say something.

LORRIE: Ah...okay...yeah.

She goes to phone. Punches in a number.

LORRIE: Dave that you? ...It's Lorrie.... Dave did you just kidnap Michael from the motel parking lot.... *(she is listening)* Okay. *(she hangs up)*

SOPHIE: Did he do it.

LORRIE: Yeah he did.

SOPHIE: That's all he says..."Yeah I did?"

LORRIE: He said he was just about to call me and tell me. He said not to call the police. He said to wait for him to call back and tell me what he wants me to do.... Strange.

SOPHIE: I told you strange.... What will you do.

LORRIE: I...don't know.... Wait. Or...maybe I should...call the police.

SOPHIE: Dave said no.

LORRIE: Yeah but...so what. Dave is a kidnapper. Obviously he's going to say no police.... Wow. Dave is a kidnapper. I mean I haven't known him that long but I never would have pegged him as a kidnapper. I have to think about this...*(she sits on the bed)*

SOPHIE: You mind if I clean room?

LORRIE: Ah...no it's—

SOPHIE turns on the vacuum. Vacuums for awhile. Looks at LORRIE a few times. Turns off vacuum.

SOPHIE: Excuse me.... You...you are...you are pregnant, aren't you.

LORRIE just looks at her.

LORRIE: Pregnant?

SOPHIE: Pregnant.... Yes?

LORRIE: Yes. How could you tell.

SOPHIE: I don't know.

SOPHIE turns on the vacuum. LORRIE watches her vacuum.
Blackout.

Scene Three

SOPHIE and LORRIE sit on the end of the bed, holding hands.

LORRIE: He was stubborn. He liked doing things I didn't understand. He liked climbing rocks. He liked going fast in boats and cars. He liked going by himself to dangerous places and seeing how scared he'd get. And then seeing how long he could stay even though he was scared. That's just the way he was. You can't understand it if you're not like that. You just can't. He knew that was bear country. He knew it had been a hard winter with not much food for those bears. He knew what he was doing was foolishly dangerous. He went anyway. He was excited about going.... I thought about trying to talk him out of it. But I didn't. I was tired of trying to talk him out of things. It never worked. He always went anyway. And I was always really angry. And so was he. This time I just smiled and said "Have a blast." And he smiled and said "Yeah okay" or something.... And then he left. He went off...and got...eaten by a bear.... I mean eaten by a fucking bear.... Almost entirely eaten. Jesus... And no life insurance. Nothing. Nothing but debts.

SOPHIE: I am crying. This is okay if I'm crying?

LORRIE: Yeah...sure.

SOPHIE: *(crying harder)* Oh good.... Because it is so sad.... And horrible. Because your husband was eaten by bear without knowing you had a baby inside. Yes?

LORRIE: Yes.

SOPHIE: *(crying harder)* Horrible. Horrible and sad.... *(stops crying suddenly)* You know something? I believe I too had relative eaten by a bear.

LORRIE: No way.

SOPHIE: Yes. I believe that's true. Long time ago. Hundred years.... Relative goes on expedition into China. Eaten by bear. No not bear really. Panda.

LORRIE: A panda? No way. A panda. Come on.

SOPHIE: Please. You people think panda is toy. Panda eats just bamboo you probably think. Sure panda eats bamboo. Bamboo gone. Panda eats you.

Anyway this is a...a...thing we share. Someone eaten. We share that feeling...

LORRIE: Ah yeah...I guess.

SOPHIE: I'm sorry. What am I saying. I lose some relative over one hundred years ago. I have no feeling at all about this. And you lose husband and you have his baby inside. And I'm saying we share.... But you are sadder than anyone in the world is sad.

LORRIE: Life is...more complicated than that for me. Most people have things happen to them in a certain order in a certain way. That's never really been true for me. You see I kinda...left my husband for awhile a few weeks before he was killed.... I left him for a.... You see this baby's father isn't my husband. It's another guy. You see, my husband was sleeping with this friend of mine. And I found out. So I went out and slept with a friend of his. And he found out. And then we had a fight. And I left. And then I came back. But we kept fighting. And then he went and got eaten by a bear. And then I found out I was pregnant. And then my husband's family found out. And they think it's my husband's kid. But the guy whose kid it is knows it's his. And he wants to...I don't know...get involved. And my husband's family wants to get involved. And my mother wants to get involved.... So I left.... I just left.... Because they were all trying to...control everything. And...get involved.

SOPHIE: And so now...I know all this. I didn't want to know all this.

LORRIE: I'm sorry. I just—

SOPHIE: People kill themselves when they are knowing things like this. This is too much.

LORRIE: I'm sorry.

SOPHIE: No. I'm sorry. I'm so sorry I might have to kill myself.

LORRIE: You're kidding, right?

SOPHIE: Why do people kill themselves. Wake up one day. A heavy sadness comes down on them. Presses down on the head. Maybe they just say "too much." Then die.

LORRIE: But you see—

SOPHIE: This could be it for me. Tomorrow morning I am waking up. Hearing my father yell. Thinking of your baby. Dying.

LORRIE: No you see it's not sad. Not really—

SOPHIE: Husband is dead or not.

LORRIE: Okay that's kinda sad. I mean even then I'm still so pissed off at him for sleeping around I haven't really felt the pain of his death.

SOPHIE: Tomorrow.

LORRIE: Tomorrow?

SOPHIE: Or day after. Pain always comes. My mother died.

LORRIE: I'm sorry.

SOPHIE: Not today. Before.

LORRIE: Yeah but I'm still…never mind.

SOPHIE: My father yelled her to death. In Russia. He yelled and yelled and my mother died. Then he said "Come on we're leaving this place." He and brother. Not mine brother. His. Also KGB man. My uncle. He has money put away. So they are just saying come on. I am saying mother just died. But they yell at me very loud very much so I go. I forgot Mother for a long time. Because leaving is difficult enough. But…later the pain comes. I remember Mother. And the pain…comes.

LORRIE: I'm sorry.

SOPHIE: I'm sorry too. Hungry? You can cook in room something.

LORRIE: It's okay… It's nice of you to stay with me. You're nice.

Pause.

SOPHIE: Thank you.

Pause.

LORRIE: I…don't know how long I should just wait here.

SOPHIE: Did he say how long you should just wait here.

LORRIE: I don't remember. I mean even if he did…. Why should I. What's the point. I mean these guys. Dave. Michael. I hardly even know them. I don't want them hurting each other but…. You know these guys are like the guys at home really. I mean they've all got…opinions about what I should do…. I mean really when it comes down to it it's the same. Guys telling me in one way or another…what I should do.

SOPHIE: Yelling at you?

LORRIE: No not yelling…well sometimes. But mostly just…yacking. And giving their opinion like I'm supposed to…listen…. And then…agree or something.

SOPHIE: Yelling is worse! Talking is okay. When men talk you can smile. Close your...brain. This is harder when they yell. Brain won't close.

LORRIE: I want to see, you know, just see how things work out for awhile. Before I decide.

SOPHIE: Decide what.

LORRIE: Everything.... Where to go. What to do.... Whether, you know...whether to have this baby.

SOPHIE: Decide to have baby? Baby is there. Baby is coming.... Oh...oh you mean decide. You will kill the baby?

LORRIE: Kill?

SOPHIE: Kill.

LORRIE: Kill? It's not...It's not killing.

SOPHIE: Is something wrong with baby!

LORRIE: What? No. I don't think so.... I mean it's just—

The phone rings. LORRIE answers it.

LORRIE: *(into phone)* Hello...ah... What...ah... Wait. *(to SOPHIE)* I think it's for you.

SOPHIE: Me?

LORRIE: Your father maybe? How'd he know you were here?

SOPHIE: Ex-KGB man. He knows where I am everywhere.

SOPHIE takes the phone. Holds it away. As her father yells. She has a brief conversation in Russian about having to clean the bathroom again. Hangs up.

SOPHIE: You hear him yelling?

LORRIE: Yeah.

SOPHIE: Someday he will be yelling so loud.... His brain...it... *(gestures)*

LORRIE: Explodes?

SOPHIE: Yeah. Boom! Or maybe my brain.... I have to leave now.

LORRIE: I understand.

SOPHIE: I want to stay.

LORRIE: I understand.

SOPHIE: But I have to leave.... *(she goes to door)* I'm leaving but...I want to tell you not to kill the baby.

LORRIE: It's not a baby...yet.

SOPHIE: It is.

LORRIE: No it's not...

SOPHIE: What is it. If not baby? What?

LORRIE: You know there's time before it's...actually a baby. And anyway it's my choice. Isn't it my choice.

SOPHIE: No.

LORRIE: If it's not my choice whose is it.

SOPHIE: Not a choice for anyone. Baby is coming.

LORRIE: Maybe.

SOPHIE: I'm telling you. I'm not man yelling at you. I'm telling you.

LORRIE: What's the difference.

SOPHIE: Big difference.

LORRIE: Yeah but what is it, the difference.

SOPHIE: I'm not yelling!.... Sorry. Have to go.

> *SOPHIE opens door. DAVE is standing there.*
> *SOPHIE looks at DAVE. Back to LORRIE. Back to DAVE.*

DAVE: Well are you going or not. I can't wait here all night.

SOPHIE: *(to LORRIE)* I can go?

DAVE: Yes. You can go.

SOPHIE: She says I can go. Not you. *(to LORRIE)* It's okay? I can go?

LORRIE: I'll be fine.

> *SOPHIE leaves. DAVE comes in.*

DAVE: Who is she? The maid or something?

LORRIE: Her father owns the place.

DAVE: So...you tell her what's going on? She looked...like she knew something. Or something.

LORRIE: She saw you Dave. She saw you kidnap Michael.

DAVE: Really.... Is that right.... She did, eh. Okay...so...okay. What do you think I should do about that.

LORRIE: Oh I don't know Dave. Maybe you should kill her. Slit her throat and bury her in a tar pit. I mean, you're leaving quite a trail of evidence.... Jesus.

The phone rings.

DAVE: My throat's really dry. I'm having trouble swallowing...I need a glass of water.

LORRIE answers it. DAVE goes into the bathroom.

LORRIE: *(into phone)* Hi.... Yeah.... Shit.... How'd you get this number, Steve.... My mother. My mother gave you my number.... Why would she do that.... Oh great. That's really great.... No she didn't have to know, Steve.... No.... Because who the father of the baby is, is none of her business. At the moment it's only my business.... So great. You told her and she gave you my number so you could call and harass me. So go ahead.... Yeah yeah...yeah...yeah...yeah.... No no I'm not coming home.... No you're not coming here either.... No you're not going to have a say in it... .None.... That's right. None...None! ...No you're not!

She hangs up. DAVE comes out of the bathroom with a glass of water.

DAVE: Who was that.

LORRIE: What do you want.

DAVE: I...just want to know who that was.

LORRIE: No I mean what the fuck do you want, Dave. Why are you here.

DAVE: You know why I'm here. I told you I was coming.

LORRIE: That's why you're here? Because you told me you'd be here?

DAVE: Well sort of. I mean.... Well there's this question about my hostage...I mean—

The phone rings. LORRIE answers it. Listens.

LORRIE: *(into phone)* Look. Steve. Let's do it this way. You hang up. I'll call you later when you're less upset. I'll call and try my best to explain my point of view. And then maybe you'll understand.... My point of view, that's what. Maybe you'll...understand what I need to— Listen, are you at home...I'll call you back. Yes Steven I will.... Soon.... Soon.... Later than that. But soon. Goodbye.... Yeah. Yeah. Goodbye...

She hangs up.

DAVE: Who was that Lorrie. I mean who is Steve. Do I know him. Is he a guy from the restaurant. Is he the manager's son. Or that other guy…the food inspector…. I heard something about a baby before. What baby were you talking about.

LORRIE: Dave…Dave you have to let Michael go. It's a serious crime. Kidnapping. You could be ruining your life here.

DAVE: Who's Steve.

LORRIE: Where's Michael now.

DAVE: In the trunk. Is…Steven someone from home? Is he your boyfriend back home, Lorrie.

LORRIE: In the trunk of your car? Outside?

DAVE: Yeah… Do you love Steven. Is Steven the man you're in love with, the man you're devoted to. Is…Steve the man you're thinking of when you get that far away look in your eye.

LORRIE: Dave. Go out to your car. Unlock the trunk. Bring Michael in here. We'll all work it out together.

DAVE: Does…Steven think you're as special I think you are. Just ask yourself that Lorrie. Is Steven a man who can elevate you in his estimation as high as I can.

LORRIE: *(shrugs)* Go get Michael. He might be getting really uncomfortable in that trunk. Maybe he's even running out of air…. Go get him.

DAVE: Okay.

LORRIE: Thanks, Dave

The phone rings. DAVE looks at the phone.

LORRIE: Go ahead.

DAVE leaves reluctantly. LORRIE answers the phone.

LORRIE: *(into phone)* Hi…Yes he did. Did she tell you she was going to do that…. Did you try to stop her…. She's not anyone's grandmother…. There is no baby…. He's not anyone's father, she's not anyone's grandmother, and you're not anyone's aunt. Look, Jane…Jane. Jane. You're my sister. You're not my conscience. And neither is Sophie. And I'm gonna have to tell her that…. Sophie is Sophie. Her father owns— She's my friend…. I just met her…. She's…the friend I just met. Forget it…. No Tokyo is out, I told you. Listen, I'm really tired, Jane. I'll call

you tomorrow.... No not later. Tomorrow. Okay? Tomorrow...
tomorrow...tomorrow.

She hangs up. The door opens.
MICHAEL comes in. DAVE is right behind him.

DAVE: Okay...I did it.

MICHAEL: Lorrie. Thank God you're—

DAVE: Don't talk. Don't say anything.

LORRIE: Dave, just relax now.

MICHAEL: Be careful. He's got a gun.

LORRIE: No he doesn't.

MICHAEL: I can feel it.

LORRIE: It's his finger.... That's just your finger, isn't it Dave.

DAVE: Ah...yeah.

MICHAEL: Asshole...

MICHAEL turns and knees DAVE in the groin. DAVE crumbles to the floor.

MICHAEL: All this time I thought the asshole had a gun. *(to DAVE)* Asshole. Not only did you kidnap me, you did it with a finger.... I feel kind of...humiliated by that.

MICHAEL sits on the bed.

LORRIE: Are you all right, Dave.

DAVE: Ahh...I...

MICHAEL: Excuse me, Lorrie. But do you really care if he's all right or are you just being polite. I mean I'm the one who's been in the trunk of a car for almost—

LORRIE: Are you all right, Michael.

MICHAEL: I'm okay, yeah. Thanks for asking.

LORRIE: Dave, why did you do this. It was a really stupid thing to do.

DAVE: Desperate. *(he is getting up slowly)* The act of a desperate man. I couldn't stand the idea of losing you to this sleaze.

MICHAEL: My knees are wobbly from being in that trunk. My knees are wobbly or I'd stand up and make you pay for that remark.

DAVE: Look at him, Lorrie. He's a total sleaze. Look at his leather jacket. It's the jacket of a sleaze. What'd it cost. A hundred and fifty tops. I couldn't lose you to him.

LORRIE: First of all, Dave, you can't lose me to anyone because you don't have me.

DAVE: Yeah but I—

LORRIE: No look.... Whatever we might have had which probably wasn't much, you wrecked it when you crossed that line.

DAVE: What line was that Lorrie.

LORRIE: It's the same old line, Dave. The one that gets crossed when someone makes decisions for me they have no right to make. Like removing Michael from my life.

DAVE: From your life? Is Michael in your life, Lorrie. In what way is he in your life.

MICHAEL: I'm her agent.

LORRIE: No you're not.

MICHAEL: I'm gonna be her agent.

LORRIE: No you're not.

DAVE: Agent. Why don't you call it what it is.

LORRIE: What is it.

MICHAEL: Yeah, what is it.

DAVE: You know what it is.

MICHAEL: What is it.

DAVE: Pimp. Pimp is what it is. Pimp. Yuk. Just saying it sickens me.

LORRIE : So don't say it.

DAVE: Sure. I bet it sickens you too.

LORRIE : It doesn't bother me at all.

MICHAEL: It bothers me. I prefer agent. Actually I prefer business manager. But I'd settle for agent.

DAVE : Pimp!

MICHAEL: Hey. Be careful. My knees are firming up.

LORRIE : Pimp, agent, business manager. What's it matter really.

MICHAEL: It matters to me.

LORRIE: The point is you're none of those things. You're a contact. An option. A partner in a business transaction maybe…. All the decisions will be mine.

MICHAEL: Sure. I know that. What decisions.

LORRIE: All of them. Where. When. For how long and with whom.

DAVE: What are you talking about.

LORRIE: Sex films.

DAVE: Oh my God. I knew it. I knew it! Sleazy pimping sleaze.

MICHAEL: Shut up, asshole. We're talking about erotic videos.
Pornographic, yes. But also very special in the way they will feature—

LORRIE: Sex films.

DAVE: You can't.

MICHAEL: Special in the way they will feature Loretta and—

DAVE: You can't, Lorrie.

LORRIE: Sure I can. Why can't I.

The phone rings.

LORRIE: I can do whatever I want. What I want to do right now is make as much money as I possibly can. Money is the only thing that expands your options. No matter what anybody says, it's money. Only money. It's not love and respect and intelligence and hard work. The world doesn't give a shit about any of those things if they're not also connected to the ability to make money.

DAVE: Aren't you going to answer the phone.

LORRIE: No.

DAVE: Why not.

LORRIE: None of your business.

MICHAEL: Want me to get it?

LORRIE: No.

MICHAEL: I don't mind.

LORRIE: Let it ring…. I'm going out for awhile.

DAVE: Where are you going.

LORRIE: Out.

DAVE: Out where.

LORRIE: Out.

DAVE: Can I come.

LORRIE: No.

MICHAEL: What about me.

LORRIE: No Michael, why don't you just stay here. When I get back we'll talk about your…idea.

DAVE: What about me.

LORRIE: What about you.

DAVE: Well what should I do.

LORRIE: Well for one thing you should apologize to Michael for kidnapping him.

DAVE: I meant should I stay here…

LORRIE: I don't care.

DAVE: You don't care…. What, if I stay or if I go?

LORRIE: That's right. *(leaving)* Just don't answer the phone…. Michael, don't let him answer the phone.

MICHAEL: I won't. Don't worry…. And…have a blast.

> *LORRIE leaves. Closes door.*
> *DAVE looks at the ringing phone.*

MICHAEL: Don't even think about it, asshole.

DAVE: Pimp! Slimeball. Pimp!

> *MICHAEL stands. Steadies himself.*
> *DAVE steadies himself.*
> *Blackout.*
> *The phone continues to ring.*

Scene Four

DAVE and MICHAEL...are eating a pizza. MICHAEL is drinking a beer.

MICHAEL: The thing is, she arouses me to such an extreme degree.

DAVE: Tell me about it.

MICHAEL: She turns me on to such an extremely high point—

DAVE: You can't think.

MICHAEL: No I can think.

DAVE: You can't talk.

MICHAEL: No I can talk and I can think. It's just that it's rare. Extremely rare.

DAVE: Tell me about it.

MICHAEL: I mean I like people. I like women. I like food.

DAVE: What's that got to do with it. Food?

MICHAEL: I'm saying I'm sensual.

DAVE: You mean sexual. You're sexual.

MICHAEL: Everyone's sexual.

DAVE: Loretta is really sexual.

MICHAEL: Yeah she's rare. She's got a quality. I recognized it and—

DAVE: And now you just want to exploit it.

MICHAEL: Exactly.

DAVE: You see I can understand that. I can. I mean as soon as you put it in business terms for some reason I stopped having a problem with it.

MICHAEL: Well it is business.

DAVE: I thought it was love.

MICHAEL: It's never love.

DAVE: Well in your business it's never love.

MICHAEL: No it's never love ever. It's always business!

DAVE: I love her!

MICHAEL: You need her. You need her for your life. To enhance your life. To expand your operations. To make a more complete impression on people. It's business.

DAVE: It is business.... Wow.... Okay, you're right.

MICHAEL: I mean, okay it's love too.

DAVE: You love her?

MICHAEL: Well you know what, I think I do. Yes.

DAVE: You see, I have a problem with that. That's personal. It's...threatening...

MICHAEL: She doesn't love me.

DAVE: She doesn't?

MICHAEL: No.... She wouldn't even kiss me.

DAVE: She wouldn't? She kissed me.

MICHAEL: Yeah well...you had that kind of thing...for some reason. We began our relationship in a different way... Strictly business.

DAVE: Yeah.

MICHAEL: She doesn't love you either by the way. I can tell.

DAVE: How?

MICHAEL: In a hundred little ways.... Just take my word for it. She doesn't love you. Let go of that part of your relationship. I mean put it in the back. Bring the business into the front and put the love into the back.... We can do this together. I've got plans for her. You can be involved.... You're in marketing, right?

DAVE: No. Sales.

MICHAEL: I thought you were in marketing.

DAVE: Sales.

MICHAEL: What's the difference.

DAVE: I'm...not sure..... But I don't do marketing. I know that.

MICHAEL: But you could. Probably you could.

DAVE: Probably yeah.... You mean Lorrie? Market Lorrie?

MICHAEL: Sell Lorrie. Sell Lorrie's quality.... Sell the thing in Lorrie that gives men an immediate erection.

DAVE: I'm not comfortable when you say that, when you talk about your erection.

MICHAEL: Did you get one. Did you get an immediate erection when you saw her. Come on this is important. Within five seconds of looking at her, taking her in were you hard? Yes or no.

DAVE: Yes...ah...yes pretty hard.

MICHAEL: Pretty hard.... How hard is that. How hard do you usually get.

DAVE: I get as hard as anyone.

MICHAEL: Well some men only get...pretty hard. You know what I mean?

DAVE: No.

MICHAEL: Did you get as hard as you can get.

DAVE: Which is as hard as anyone can get. I mean I didn't mean that pretty hard wasn't really hard. It was hard.

MICHAEL: Okay. So okay.... She's got a quality. This is a quality we can feature in a series of endeavours that run the gamut of exploitation possibilities. It can run from sex videos up through low-grade movies into magazines and television right into major motion picture stardom.

DAVE: You know this?

MICHAEL: I feel this.

DAVE: But you don't really know anything about any of it.

MICHAEL: Not a thing.... I'm a booker for topless bars. I'm nothing. But look...so what.... What are you. You sell shoes.

DAVE: Screws.

MICHAEL: What.

DAVE: Not shoes. Screws.

MICHAEL: I thought you told me shoes.

DAVE: No. Screws. Big industrial screws. This big. They use them for—

MICHAEL: Hey, hey who cares. The point is even if we are a couple of losers, maybe we can do this thing, if we pull together.

The phone rings.

DAVE: There it is again. I hate this. Why does that phone keep ringing. Who the hell is calling her.

MICHAEL: Don't answer it.

DAVE: Who is it. I have to know.

MICHAEL: Don't do anything to alienate her. You're already in her bad books. If you want in on this deal I'd stay put. Just forget the phone.

DAVE: I'm trying.

MICHAEL: Have another piece of pizza.

DAVE: Okay.

LORRIE comes in carrying a couple of department store shopping bags.

LORRIE: Hi.

MICHAEL: Hi.

DAVE: Hi.

LORRIE: Has the phone been ringing all this time.

MICHAEL: No. Whoever it is calls about every ten minutes.

DAVE: Who do you think it is, Lorrie.

LORRIE: Could be anyone. Well you two look like you've settled your differences. Pizza and beer. Man. There's a sight for sore eyes.

DAVE: He's drinking beer. I've got a Diet Pepsi…. See?

MICHAEL: Imported beer. And it's gourmet pizza. It's got smoked chicken on it.

DAVE: So Lorrie…. You've been shopping. Did you have fun. What did you get.

LORRIE: I'll show you.

She goes into the bathroom.

MICHAEL: When you asked her about shopping just now, your voice sounded all mushy. You looked like you were going to cry.

DAVE: I don't know what you're talking about.

MICHAEL: I think you were having a domestic fantasy about her. Something involving the two of you shopping together in some mall. I told you to put that stuff in the back of your brain.

DAVE: Leave me alone.

MICHAEL: Can I have this last piece of pizza.

DAVE: Let's split it.

MICHAEL: I don't wanna split it. It's mine. You've already had four pieces.

DAVE: So why'd you ask if you could have it. By asking, you make it sound like you really think it's mine.

MICHAEL: No. I'm just polite.

DAVE: Yeah, right.

MICHAEL: Yes it is right.

DAVE: Polite.... You manage topless dancers.

MICHAEL: Is there some reason why you think those two things don't go together.

LORRIE sticks her head out of the bathroom.

LORRIE: Pizza and beer. What's up with you guys anyway. You friends now?

DAVE: Hardly. He's a pimp.

MICHAEL: And he's some asshole who sells shoes.

DAVE: Screws.

MICHAEL: The thing is we've decided to work together. On...our project.

LORRIE: What project.

MICHAEL: You. You're the project. The amazing physical thing you have, that quality—

DAVE: You see, he thinks it's just physical. I think it's deeper.

MICHAEL: I think it's deeper too.

DAVE: I think it's deeper than you do. *(to LORRIE)* I think you're special in a lot of ways and if you want to make a living from your...specialness then I want to help.

LORRIE: Maybe we should talk. You sound like you're making plans.

MICHAEL: We are. We're making very big—

LORRIE: No. We should talk. I'll be right out.

She goes back into bathroom. The phone rings.

LORRIE: *(from bathroom)* Get that will you.

DAVE: Did she say get that.

MICHAEL: I think so.

DAVE: Ah...okay I'll—

MICHAEL: No wait. You should make sure.

DAVE: Yeah.

He knocks on the door.

DAVE: Lorrie. Did you say get that. Or don't get that. We thought you said get that. But we're not sure. Because before you were pretty definite about us not getting it. So we're—

LORRIE sticks her head out.)

LORRIE: Get it.

She disappears back into the bathroom. MICHAEL is heading for the phone.

DAVE: Where you going.

MICHAEL: I'm getting the phone.

DAVE: She told me to get it.

MICHAEL: You should grow up. You're too...needy.

DAVE: I need to get the phone.

MICHAEL: You should grow up fast. We can't work with her if you're going to be like that. Can't you tell she has no patience for that kind of behaviour. She's losing respect for you by the minute.

DAVE: But I...need to know who's calling her. I need to know if it's this guy Steven. And if Steven is the guy she thinks about when she gets that really faraway look she gets.

MICHAEL: Get ahold of yourself. Fast.

LORRIE sticks her head out.

LORRIE: Are you gonna get the phone or not.

MICHAEL: Got it.

LORRIE disappears into the bathroom. MICHAEL answers the phone.

MICHAEL: *(into phone)* Yeah.... Ah...Michael.... A friend.... Who is this.... Okay sorry I was just— Lorrie it's for you!

DAVE: *(whispering)* Who is it.

MICHAEL: He wouldn't say.

DAVE: Do you think it's Steven. I bet it is. I bet it's Steven. Jesus. Steven.

MICHAEL: Calm down. What the hell is wrong with you.

LORRIE comes out of the bathroom. She is wearing a bathrobe.

LORRIE: Who is it.

MICHAEL: I don't know.

LORRIE takes the phone.

LORRIE: *(into phone)* Hello…. Yeah… Hi, Mr. Vokitch…. How's Mrs. Vokitch…. Oh hi Mrs. Vokitch…. *(to MICHAEL and DAVE)* It's Mr. and Mrs. Vokitch. My dead husband's parents. They're calling me from their rec room. They have two phones in their rec room. I could never understand why. Two phones. Ten feet apart. I guess it's so they can both get on the phone and then…. What…. Signal each other?… *(into phone)* Are you both in the rec room Mrs. Vokitch. *(to MICHAEL)* Yeah. They're both in the rec room…. Sitting on the couch. Signalling. *(into phone)* I'm sorry Mrs. Vokitch. I was just…. A friend. He's a friend…. No not a good friend…. Just…just…. Well I'm working in a restaurant…. Waitress, yes…. No…. No I don't think I'm coming back any time soon. *(to MICHAEL and DAVE)* A long cold silence… *(into phone)* Hello? Are you still there? …Go ahead I'm listening…. Ah…. Yes. Yes I'm pregnant…. No I'm not sure what I'm going to do…. Yes yes I…might…get an abortion. *(long long pause)* Well those are all interesting opinions. But really I have to do what I think is right…. No I don't share your religious beliefs…. Because I don't…. Because I think they're wrong…. Yes I think your religious beliefs are wrong…. Because for one thing you believe you can tell other people what to do…. Yes what to do with their lives, their bodies, everything…. Yes that is the problem. Look look let me spare you any more pain. Okay?…. Listen ah…this baby is not Tommy's…. That's right…. No…No it's Steven's. Steven Dysart. Yes…. Yes it is! No I'm not lying…. Listen I know this is a hard thing…. A hard thing for you to…. Mr. Vokitch? Did he hang up, Mrs. Vokitch…. Well maybe you should hang up too…. Mrs. Vokitch Tommy was not a saint. Tommy was…. No he wasn't even a really good guy…. Tommy was a prick, Mrs. Vokitch…. Yes he was. He was a prick. A stupid prick who fucked around on me from almost the first day I met him. And then went out to play with the wildlife and got eaten. He was a really stupid guy Mrs. Vokitch. Stupid and mean. *(to MICHAEL and DAVE)* She hung up too…. They're sitting on the couch now. Side by side. Staring at a picture on the wall of Tommy…and his canoe. *(she sighs)*

LORRIE puts the receiver down.

DAVE: So…who's Steve.

LORRIE: What. You heard me. The father of the—

MICHAEL: You're pregnant. Really?

LORRIE: Really.

MICHAEL: That could be a problem.

LORRIE: Tell me about it.

MICHAEL: I mean I've got plans.

LORRIE: Really.

MICHAEL: Well almost.

DAVE: So Steven is still in the picture or is he—

LORRIE: Okay listen. Both of you. Here's the deal. I've got some decisions to make. But first I have to make a lot of money. Because I want to make sure money isn't a factor in my decisions. So what I need from you two is any help you can give me with making this money. Fast. Because I figure I've only got a couple of months. I don't know if it's videos or dancing in Tokyo or some high-end call girl work. I don't care. I'll go the best and fastest route we can find. But I want to be in charge. You can help. You'll get paid even. But I want to make all the final decisions. Okay?

MICHAEL: Okay. Sure. I just—

LORRIE: Dave? Dave, do you want to help me. I mean Michael and I can probably do this alone. You can just go.

DAVE: I don't want to go. I want to stay.

LORRIE: Okay, but if you stay you have to—

DAVE: Can I ask you about Steven.

LORRIE: No. No you can't ask me about anything like that. You can be my friend.

DAVE: By friend you mean?

LORRIE: Friend.

DAVE: Nothing else.

LORRIE: No. Well...we'll see how you do as a friend.

MICHAEL: What about me. Can I be your friend too.

LORRIE: Sure.

MICHAEL: And will we see about me too.

LORRIE: I...*(shrugs)* think of you as a...

DAVE: Pimp?

LORRIE: No I mean—

MICHAEL: Never mind. It's...okay. Strictly business is okay.

LORRIE: So...okay.... Business. The money problem. We have to get on that right away. And really.... *(She drops her robe. She is wearing a very revealing undergarment)*...this is all we've got to work with. I mean if they want it, we'll be fine. I mean if they really want it, if it's something that will generate...income...then we'll be...okay I guess.

MICHAEL and DAVE look at each other.

LORRIE: Well? This is my product.... So?

MICHAEL: I think your product is...a good product. A special product.

DAVE: If I had a million dollars I'd give it to you right now. If I knew someone with a million dollars I'd go and steal it from them and give it to you. I'd kill someone to give you a million dollars. I'd kill my mother.

MICHAEL: Get ahold of yourself. You're no good to us if you're going to take this personally.

DAVE looks at MICHAEL's crotch.

DAVE: You should talk.

The phone rings. Blackout.

Scene Five

SOPHIE and LORRIE. SOPHIE is moving around in an agitated manner. LORRIE is sitting on the bed in her bathrobe.

SOPHIE: My father yells and yells and yells.... He is yelling so much Uncle leaves. And Uncle is a man who yells himself so yelling is usually no problem for him. But this time my father yelling is too much even for Uncle. My father is yelling this close to my face. Usually Father is yelling farther away. But this time this close. I'm scared. I tell him I'm scared. He yells louder. He yells and yells. And then he dies. He dies yelling. He dies on his feet. Standing up. Yelling.... He falls. But he is already dead.... Anyway ambulance comes. You heard it?

LORRIE: Yes.

SOPHIE: That was me. Police came. You heard?

LORRIE: Yes.

SOPHIE: Also me.... Fire department. Call 911 and everyone comes. It's like...party. My father is dead on the floor. But I'm looking at all these people and I'm thinking I should cook something.

LORRIE: Are you all right.

SOPHIE: I think I killed my father.

LORRIE: He had a heart attack.

SOPHIE: He yelled himself to death.... Because I am a bad student.

LORRIE: I thought you were a good student.

SOPHIE: I am a good student. He thought I was bad student.

LORRIE: So he was wrong.

SOPHIE: He was wrong. And now he is dead.... I told him. I'm good student. There is no reason to be yelling.

LORRIE: He didn't believe you?

SOPHIE: Didn't hear me. Yelling too loud.

LORRIE: Can I...get you something.

SOPHIE: Do I need something.

LORRIE: Do you want me to call anyone.

SOPHIE: No one to call. Just Father, me, and Uncle are here. Uncle is gone.

LORRIE: Gone for good?

SOPHIE: Oh yes. When Uncle leaves when Father is yelling he takes suitcase full of money. He's gone.

LORRIE: So you're alone.

SOPHIE: Are you my friend.

LORRIE: Yes.

SOPHIE: So I'm not alone.

LORRIE: I meant...Never mind. Do you need help with the arrangements...The funeral?

SOPHIE: Father atheist. No religion. Was big shot Communist. Funerals no big deal. Loved parades though. Maybe I get a few peoples. March up and down street for awhile.... That was joke. I'm sorry.

LORRIE: Ah...where did they...take his body.

SOPHIE: Somewhere.

LORRIE: Do you want me to find out. Don't you think you should know.

SOPHIE: You know all I'm thinking now? No more physics! Father is dead! No more physics! *(she begins to cry)* Father yelled me into physics.... I hate that thing physics. So my father is dead. And physics is dead too. And I'm happy about that. *(she is crying, having trouble breathing)* And I am also...happy...very... happy... because no one is...yelling anymore at me. Excuse me.

SOPHIE goes into the bathroom. Runs water. We hear her vomiting. A knock on the door. The phone rings. LORRIE goes to phone.

LORRIE: *(yelling to door)* It's open! (picks up phone) Hello.

MICHAEL and DAVE come in with some photographic equipment. A lighting umbrella. Stuff.

LORRIE: *(into phone)*... Yeah Mom. I did... Because I had to. They made me...Yes it was cruel. Sometimes you have to be cruel to people...When the people are insensitive and stupid that's when... I gotta go. Call me later. No I'll call you. Goodbye.

She hangs up.

MICHAEL: Okay we're loaded up here. I consulted a few friends. Guys who've done this stuff before.

DAVE: Other pimps.

MICHAEL: Producers. Entrepreneurs.

DAVE: Fucking pimps.

MICHAEL: Are you gonna help or what. This attitude of yours is starting to wear me down, Dave.

LORRIE: He's right, Dave. No attitude. No judgement. No opinion. Just help. Okay?

DAVE: Definitely.... I was just taking exception to calling his buddies anything except what they are. Which is pimps. I mean I'm just saying let's not be hypocritical here.

LORRIE: Yeah let's not.

DAVE: Whatya mean by that.

LORRIE: Forget it.... *(to MICHAEL)* Where's the video camera.

MICHAEL: In the car. *(to DAVE)* Get it.

DAVE: You get it.

MICHAEL: It's your car. You've got the keys.

DAVE: I'll give them to you.

MICHAEL: Get the goddamn video camera. Gimme a break here. I'm setting up the lighting.

LORRIE: Why won't you get the camera, Dave.

DAVE: I didn't say I wouldn't get it. I just didn't like being ordered to get it. I'll get it.

DAVE leaves.

MICHAEL: That guy is a problem.

LORRIE: Every guy is a problem in some way.

MICHAEL: He loves you.

LORRIE: I've been loved before. I can handle him. Maybe he can help. Let's see.

MICHAEL: Well, anyway I'm ready to go in a number of directions here. I've got several avenues to explore.

LORRIE: I was thinking about a calendar. The twelve months of me. How fast could we do that.

MICHAEL: That could be done fast I guess. What. Twelve shots of you in...what.

LORRIE: Nothing.

MICHAEL: Yeah. In nothing. Doing what.

LORRIE: Doing...nothing. Naked.

MICHAEL: Naked. And doing nothing... Okay. We could do that. That's one idea.

LORRIE: Guys hang those in garages. Taxi offices. Barber shops. Locker rooms. Everywhere guys go. We could get them printed up fast. Take them around.

MICHAEL: Yeah. But...

LORRIE: But what.

MICHAEL: I was thinking of something bigger. More adventurous. More...

LORRIE: What. What is it. You don't think the calendar's a good idea, do you. You think we need to do something else. Don't you.

DAVE comes in with the camera.

DAVE: Okay. Here it is. What now.

LORRIE looks at DAVE. At MICHAEL. At DAVE again.

LORRIE: Take off your clothes.

DAVE: What.

LORRIE: Hand him the camera. Take off your clothes. He's going to film us having sex.

DAVE: I'm not...I'm not...

LORRIE: I'll understand if you say no.

DAVE: I'm not...saying no.

MICHAEL: She means it's okay if you're not up to it.

DAVE: Fuck off.

LORRIE: So is this it, Michael. You think this is the way to go? I thought a calendar. Something like that. Then maybe a few high-class clubs somewhere. Headlining. A stripper thing. But no. You think this. This is really what you think we should do, isn't it.

MICHAEL: Well I'm not totally sure. But a calendar isn't the kind of dollars we were both thinking. I was thinking thousands. A calendar is hundreds. Also this is just an intro. A sample. A kind of audition. I'll use this tape as an introduction to the industry.... I know some guys. We'll show it to these guys, and then I know things will happen.

LORRIE: Can you do this, Dave.

DAVE: Can I do it. Definitely I can do it. There's no doubt I can do it. I just don't know if it's the way to go. It...lacks class.

MICHAEL: It doesn't lack anything. It hasn't been done yet. If we do it with class it has class...We just have to do it. So... Can you do it.

SOPHIE comes out of the bathroom. Drying her face with a towel.

DAVE: Stop asking me if I can do it. I can do it.

SOPHIE: Sorry. I am using your towel. Because I had to clean up myself. I was a very sick girl.... What are you doing with these men.

LORRIE: A sex video.

MICHAEL: You wanna watch?

SOPHIE: Thank you for asking. But I have to go. *(she starts off, stops)* You are making some joke about sex video?

LORRIE: Ah...yes.

SOPHIE: I don't understand it.

SOPHIE leaves.

MICHAEL: She's very attractive... *(to LORRIE)* Do you find her attractive.... I liked her very much. What do you think about her.

LORRIE: She's pretty.

MICHAEL: Are you attracted to her.

DAVE: You're outta line.

MICHAEL: No I'm not. It's business. Maybe we could get her involved.

LORRIE: No. I don't think so. Her father just died a couple of hours ago.

MICHAEL: Well maybe in a week or two.

DAVE: You're disgusting.

MICHAEL: Oh shut up and take off your clothes.

DAVE: I'll take off my clothes when Lorrie tells me to take them off.

LORRIE: Do you want to take them off in the bathroom, Dave.

DAVE: That'd be better.

LORRIE: *(to MICHAEL)* Then maybe while he's in there we could do some nice things with the lighting so that when he comes out it's more...more you know...nice. There's a nicer mood.

MICHAEL: Gotcha. A mood. A nicer mood. I'm on it.

MICHAEL begins to set up a lighting thing.

LORRIE : Go ahead, Dave.

DAVE: Thanks Lorrie. Thanks for suggesting the bathroom I mean.

The phone rings.

DAVE: You want me to get that Lorrie?

LORRIE: No thanks. You just go in there and...

DAVE: Okay.

DAVE goes into bathroom. LORRIE answers the phone.

LORRIE: *(into phone)* Yeah.... Hi, Jane.... Really...Really. Well good that they're praying for me. It never hurts to have people praying for you.... Good let them tell everyone. Let's get the whole town praying for me.... No...No Jane I won't apologize to anyone. I won't.... It's my life.... Yes yes yes. Well that's.... Right now? Right now I'm getting ready to make a sex film.... No. I'm not kidding.... For the money.... The money.... The money! ...Yes I can... It's an audition. If people like it I could get lots of work.... Yes I do. I have plenty of time. *(to MICHAEL)* How many of these could I do in two, two and a half months.

MICHAEL: Dozens.

LORRIE: *(into phone)* Dozens. I could do dozens of them. And then I'd have money. And then whatever choice I made I'd be making it with money.... Yes it is. It's everything.... Well I think it's everything.... Because...Because I can't trust anyone except myself.... No not Mom, not you, not the Vokitchs.... Steven? No no definitely not Steven.... Just me. I can trust me to make the choice that's best for me. And nobody else.... Okay. Listen I gotta go.... No. This is not all happening because my husband got eaten by a bear.... I gotta go. I have to...trim my pubic hair.

She hangs up.

MICHAEL: I don't think you have to do that.... That thing you said...about your—

LORRIE: That was my sister. She's...she's...well I just like saying things like that to her. Because she thinks she's got it all figured out. Married. Four kids. Sings in a choir. Serves as a school trustee.... Blah blah blah.... And all that just makes her feel so fucking...right.

MICHAEL: Was your husband really eaten by a bear.

LORRIE: Yeah. But you know what. It wasn't the most important event in my life.... I mean everyone back home thought it was. But they were wrong. They were so wrong I just couldn't stand being around them anymore.

MICHAEL: I think you're a truly interesting person. I hope our relationship flourishes beyond the business aspect and we're able to form a lasting friendship.

LORRIE: Yeah well, we'll see.... So do you think I should be fully naked when he comes out.... Or like this.

She takes off the robe. She is wearing bra and panties.

MICHAEL: That's good.... I mean I like it. I look at you and I like it..... So...that's good.... Let me just adjust this lighting a bit. You know I'm going on instinct really. I've never really done this before.

LORRIE: That's not true is it. You do it all the time.

MICHAEL: Ah...well...I do it...sometimes. Yes.

LORRIE: How many times.

MICHAEL: Several times.

LORRIE: Have you ever sold one. I mean have any of your other...women gone on to—

MICHAEL: I've come close. A girl I filmed last year was close. They liked her. A few companies gave her a few small things.... But...you're different. You're the one.

LORRIE: I don't need to be "the one," Michael. I just need to make some money.

MICHAEL: It would be great if you were the one though. Because I'm...I'm pretty broke.

LORRIE: I thought your dancer booking business was going well.

MICHAEL: Well what's well.... Not real well, I'm too.... I'm not.... I used to be... .But now I'm.... Anyway I think you could do well. You're special. This could be a big start for you. Erotica is a starting point.... Porn I mean. Whatever. Yeah, whatever. *(gestures helplessness)* Well you gotta start somewhere... *(gestures again)*

MICHAEL is standing there. Smiling a bit sadly. Gesturing at LORRIE.

LORRIE: What's wrong.

MICHAEL: Look at you. You deserve someone better than me. You deserve a better situation. With someone who would know for sure how to highlight your qualities.... I'm really not very good at this.

LORRIE: Well do your best.

MICHAEL: Oh I always do my best. My best just isn't very—

LORRIE: Is there a tape in the camera.

MICHAEL: Yeah.

LORRIE: Well that's a start.... Should Dave come out.

MICHAEL: Ah...yeah. Tell him to come out.

LORRIE: Should I get on the bed.

MICHAEL: On the bed.... Yeah.... Or...

LORRIE: Maybe...just waiting here.... Or maybe sitting over there.... Or there.

MICHAEL: Yeah.... Or.... You know as long as we see you. And we see him see you. And see him get aroused. That's all we need...to see...to start with.... So really it's up to him to get...you know...

LORRIE: Yeah.... That's...I mean that could be a...

LORRIE knocks on the door.

LORRIE: Dave. Listen to me. I'm telling you this now so you're prepared. Michael is going to turn the camera on you at some point and tape you...getting aroused. Do you think you can do that.

DAVE: *(from bathroom)* Definitely.

LORRIE: Can you, Dave.

DAVE: No problem.

LORRIE: Because I'd understand. It's perfectly natural to have.... I mean we could do it differently if you want.

MICHAEL: We could just skip ahead to the bed part. He could be covered up.

DAVE: What's he saying. Is he saying I can't do it.

LORRIE: No he's—

DAVE: Because I can do it. So tell him to just shut up.

LORRIE: He's just saying we could skip ahead.

DAVE: I'll do it... I'll do it. *(he starts to cry)* I will. I will. I'll do it for you, Lorrie. I will.

MICHAEL: Is he crying in there.

LORRIE: Yeah.

MICHAEL: Jesus.

LORRIE leans against the wall.

LORRIE: Dave...Dave come out. I want to talk to you.

DAVE: I need a minute here. I'm trying to compose myself.

LORRIE: It's okay. Just come on out.

The bathroom door opens. DAVE is in his underwear.

LORRIE: We can get someone else, Dave.

DAVE: No way. No way is anyone else doing this with you.

LORRIE: Yeah eventually, Dave. Eventually maybe lots of guys are gonna do this with me.

DAVE: Yeah. But not now. Now it's me. Then maybe later you'll change your mind so it'll still only be me because you only did it once. That's possible. Don't tell me it's not possible. You don't know how you'll feel. Maybe you'll feel ashamed and depressed and you won't want to do it anymore.

LORRIE: Maybe.

DAVE: So...okay...But you still wanna do it this time, right?

LORRIE: Yes I do.

DAVE: Okay then I'm your man.

MICHAEL: No you're not.

DAVE: Yes I am.

MICHAEL: No you're not. The thing I had in my mind is very specific. I told you. A very specific thing which demonstrates her very special quality. A look. An erection. That's the thing. Are you saying you can do that thing. Because I think you can't. And if you can't you should step aside for someone who can.

DAVE: Who.

MICHAEL: Me.

DAVE: You pig! You just wanna fuck her.

MICHAEL: That's right. I do. I wanna fuck her more than anything in the world. And that's the thing we need on tape. That's the kind of erection we need. We don't need a mushy romantic erection. We need a big hard nasty erection.

DAVE sticks his fingers in his ears.

DAVE: I'm not listening to this, pig.

MICHAEL pulls DAVE's fingers from his ears.

MICHAEL: You just wanna cuddle her or go shopping with her or something.

LORRIE is sitting on the bed. Her head lowered.

DAVE: You're not doing this. I'm doing this.

MICHAEL: You can't.

DAVE: Watch me.

MICHAEL: No, I think you should watch me.

DAVE: In your dreams, pimp.

MICHAEL: Look I've tried to be nice to you when you call me these names. But I'm running out of patience.

DAVE: Pimp.

MICHAEL: Asshole.

They grab each other.

DAVE: Pimp!

MICHAEL: Asshole. Limp dick. Loser!

They are trying to knee each other in the crotch. SOPHIE comes in.

SOPHIE: Lost! He is lost. My father. His body is not anywhere!… Oh look… *(points to DAVE)* Sex video was not a joke.

LORRIE: Actually I guess it was.

MICHAEL: *(to DAVE)* You hear that? Now she thinks it was a joke. A pathetic joke.

DAVE: If she says it was a joke it was a joke. I knew it was a joke. *(he laughs)*

MICHAEL: Not that kind of joke, you asshole.

DAVE: A joke's a joke.

MICHAEL: Shit. Shut up.

DAVE: *(laughs loudly)* The joke is on you. She was just...joking.

MICHAEL: It's not that kind of joke!!

DAVE: Let go of me. I have to get dressed. Let...go...of me.

> *DAVE frees himself. Goes into bathroom.*

MICHAEL: Lorrie this can work with the right individuals involved.

LORRIE: Is he right Michael. Was this a scheme just so you could have sex with me.

MICHAEL: No. No. Come on. No. Well I wanted to have sex with you. But first and foremost I'm in business. I really mean that. It's a project. A project requiring certain individuals...Not certain other...*(points to bathroom)* individuals who aren't up to the task.

LORRIE: Go for a walk.

MICHAEL: Does that mean get out and stay out.

LORRIE: No it means go for a walk. I'll deal with Dave. Come back later.

MICHAEL: Okay. Should I leave the camera.

LORRIE: Leave everything.

MICHAEL: Leave everything and come back later. What? An hour or so.

LORRIE: A few hours. Maybe tomorrow.

MICHAEL: Tomorrow is...okay for me. I mean I'll clear my schedule. And ah...tomorrow should be okay.

LORRIE: If not...the day after.

MICHAEL: No tomorrow. Tomorrow okay?

LORRIE: Yeah. Or the day after.

MICHAEL: Okay. Whenever. We'll start again. Without Dave.

LORRIE: Maybe. We'll see. I'll talk to him. I'll work it out. Maybe with Dave. Maybe without Dave. Maybe a video. Maybe the calendar idea. Maybe something else.

MICHAEL: The calendar idea was okay. I wasn't against it or anything.

LORRIE: Good.

MICHAEL: Whatever. I just want to do a project with you whatever it is. Strictly business.

LORRIE: I know.

MICHAEL: Good…. Tomorrow…. Or the next day. *(to SOPHIE)* Goodbye. Nice to meet you.

He leaves.

SOPHIE: *(to LORRIE)* That man loves you.

LORRIE: I know…

SOPHIE: You love him?

LORRIE: No.

SOPHIE: He's the father of…? *(points to LORRIE's stomach)*

LORRIE: No.

SOPHIE: Good. He looks like…pimp.

DAVE comes out of the bathroom. Dressed.

DAVE: Lorrie we have to talk.

LORRIE: Yeah.

DAVE: *(to SOPHIE)* Can you excuse us.

LORRIE: Not now, Dave. Tomorrow. No…. Next week.

DAVE: I have to talk to you. It's important. I have to get a few things straight. This thing about Steve. These plans you have to make. The need you have for money.

LORRIE is leading him towards the door.

LORRIE: I really appreciate what you were willing to do for me.

DAVE: I knew you were kidding. I just played along. We really got him, eh.

LORRIE: Dave, I want you to think about—

DAVE: Lorrie, I love you.

LORRIE: Dave don't say I love you when you really mean I want you.

DAVE: I want you.

LORRIE: You want me how? Sexually. And how else?

DAVE: I love you. I want you in my life. But I have to know more about you. Who's this guy Steve. Are you really pregnant. Or is that a joke too. Do you really need money so bad that you'll make porn movies or were you really teaching that pimp a lesson. Was your husband really eaten by a bear. And are you really pregnant with his best friend's baby. If you could answer these questions properly I think we could have a pretty fantastic relationship. I really do. Will you think about answering these questions, Lorrie. Will you.

She has him outside the room.

LORRIE: Next week.

She closes the door on him. She comes and sits next to SOPHIE.

SOPHIE: You don't love him either do you. Thank God.

LORRIE: No.... Your father's body has disappeared?

SOPHIE: Disappeared? No. Gone.

LORRIE: I meant...they don't know where he is.

SOPHIE: Sad. I feel sad. But also happy.... I am.... What am I.

LORRIE: Free?

SOPHIE: Free? Oh.... Yes. No more physics.

She laughs.

LORRIE: I meant...well your father can't yell at you anymore.

SOPHIE: And no more physics.

LORRIE: Yeah.

SOPHIE: But I'm having no one else...

LORRIE: You mean you're alone... Me too.

SOPHIE: *(points)* Baby.

LORRIE: Listen. I told you. I don't know about the baby.

SOPHIE: You want it.

LORRIE: I don't know.

SOPHIE: I know. You want it.... You were making sex film for baby.

LORRIE: No.

SOPHIE: Yes.

LORRIE: No! I was making sex film for money!

SOPHIE: Money for baby!

LORRIE: For me!

SOPHIE: And baby!

LORRIE: No!

SOPHIE: Yes! Yes! Yes! For baby! Okay I know something. Forget it. Give me
the baby.

LORRIE: What.

SOPHIE: I am…alone. Give me baby.

LORRIE: No!

SOPHIE: Yes! Give me that baby!

LORRIE: No! And stop telling me what to do.

SOPHIE: You're not wanting it. Give it to me.

LORRIE: No! I won't!

SOPHIE: Because you are wanting it.

LORRIE: I need money.

SOPHIE: Yes. Okay. I have money. My father's KGB money. How much you
want for baby?

LORRIE: What?

SOPHIE: I buy baby. How much.

LORRIE: You can't buy the baby.

SOPHIE: Sure I can. I have money!

LORRIE: I don't want your money!

SOPHIE: I know. You want baby! Ha ha! You are working in Buffalo Bob's
restaurant for baby. You are making sex film for baby. You are going to
Tokyo to be white slave for baby. You want baby. I'm telling you—

LORRIE: Don't tell me.

SOPHIE: I'm telling you.

LORRIE: Everyone tells me. Don't tell me.

SOPHIE: I'm not…everyone. I'm me. So I can tell you.

The phone rings. LORRIE gets up. Goes to phone. Looks at it.

SOPHIE: You're answering the phone?

LORRIE: I...don't think so.

A knock on the door. DAVE is outside.

DAVE: Lorrie! It's me. I've just got a couple more questions.... Could I come in.

He knocks on the door again. The phone is still ringing.
He knocks on the door again.

SOPHIE: You are answering the door?

LORRIE: No.

Pause.

SOPHIE: What a day. Father is dead. Body is gone. Uncle is gone. No more physics. You are making sex film for baby. We have big fight. You cry.

Phone stops ringing.

LORRIE: I didn't cry.

SOPHIE: Soon you will cry, I think.

LORRIE: Don't bet on it.

SOPHIE: I'm your friend. I'm telling you. You will cry.

LORRIE: Why.

SOPHIE: For me. For you. For baby. For my father.

LORRIE: Your father was an asshole. I'm not crying for him.

SOPHIE: For your husband eaten by bear.

LORRIE: Another asshole.

Pause.

SOPHIE: My father has died today. I think I am scared.

LORRIE goes and sits next to her.

LORRIE: Scared. But free.

SOPHIE: But scared.

LORRIE: But...free.

SOPHIE: You too.

LORRIE: What...free?

SOPHIE: No. Scared.

LORRIE: Yeah. Maybe.

Knock on the door.

DAVE: *(from outside)* Lorrie it's me! I'm still out here. Did you forget that I was still out here. What about those questions. Are you gonna answer them.

SOPHIE: You will be okay.

LORRIE: You think so?

SOPHIE: Men are loving you so much, they will help you.

LORRIE: They help you. But they take away your options. And then they want you to love them back. Eventually...they don't want you to do anything else except love them back. I want to do other things.

Knock on the door.

LORRIE: Go away Dave! I mean it!

DAVE: *(from outside)* Okay.

SOPHIE: What things are you wanting to do.

LORRIE: Things...no one told me to do. Or expects me to do.

SOPHIE: What.

LORRIE: It doesn't really matter what.

SOPHIE: It doesn't matter what you do? Then have baby.

LORRIE: Maybe.

SOPHIE: Have baby!

LORRIE: Maybe! Maybe I'll have the baby!! Maybe!!!

SOPHIE: You are yelling like my father.

LORRIE: Sorry.

SOPHIE: Now maybe I will cry.

LORRIE: I'm...sorry.

LORRIE hugs her.

SOPHIE: You are...nice person... I think you will be good mother.

LORRIE takes away her arm. The phone rings.
They both look at it. Look away.

SOPHIE: What a day…. When Father died…I am thinking of my mother. I'm ashamed. Because I'm thinking joke is on you Father. You yelled my mother to death. Now you are…*(makes the thumb over the shoulder gesture)*…outta here! I am ashamed. But I feel pretty good thinking that anyway.

LORRIE: Sure…

SOPHIE: Don't make sex film.

LORRIE: I might.

SOPHIE: You will be ashamed after.

LORRIE: Maybe.

SOPHIE: For sure!

LORRIE: Maybe! But then maybe not. I don't know. I won't know until I know!

Pause.

SOPHIE: Your husband was really eaten by bear?

LORRIE: Yeah. But I don't have any bad feelings towards the bear. I'm sure it had its reasons. *(she chuckles)*

SOPHIE: This is a joke?

LORRIE: No…. Well…. But when I first found out I laughed a little. I did.

SOPHIE: No.

LORRIE: Yes…. To myself…. A little. *(she shrugs)* I couldn't help it. I found it a bit funny… I mean, from the bear's point of view. It's just the way I am.

SOPHIE shrugs. Pause. They are both lost in thought.

SOPHIE: *(smiles)* Me too…

The phone rings. They look at it. It rings six times. Then…
Blackout.

The End

THE END OF CIVILIZATION

PERSONS
MAX
HENRY
LILY
DONNY
SANDY

PLACE
A slightly run-down motel on the outskirts of a large city.

Scene One

Night. Detective MAX MALONE is leaning back against a wall. Arms folded. Watching HENRY CAPE finish his whiskey and water. HENRY puts the glass on the table. Stands. He is just a little drunk.

HENRY: I'm going to the bathroom. Do you have any problems with that.

MAX: *(shrugs)* None that I can think of.

HENRY: I mean…I'm starting to feel a little persecuted here. I'm starting to think you have something to say to me you haven't said. Some question or something…. So?

MAX: So…what.

HENRY: So do you.

MAX: Why don't you just go to the bathroom if you have to go.

HENRY: I will…. I'm going right now. Is that okay with you. I mean it's not like I need your permission or anything…. Is it?

MAX: No it's not.

HENRY: So okay then.

HENRY goes into the bathroom. Closes door. MAX knocks on the door. HENRY opens it.

HENRY: What.

MAX: Leave the door open, okay?

HENRY: Why.

MAX: I'd feel better with it open.

HENRY: Yeah. But why… Ah forget it. What's it matter. It doesn't mean shit to me. Open or closed.

HENRY backs into the bathroom. MAX looks around the room a bit.

HENRY: *(from bathroom)* You searching the room now?

MAX: Yeah.

HENRY: You kidding? Or what? You really searching? Or are you…just kidding me.

MAX: I'm just kidding you.

HENRY: Like hell you are.

MAX is looking at the dresser top. He picks up a small object. Puts it in his pocket. HENRY comes out of the bathroom.

HENRY: Find anything?

MAX: No.

HENRY: What were you looking for.

MAX: Nothing in particular.

HENRY: I need another drink.

MAX: I think you've had enough.

HENRY: You do, do you? Well here's what I think…. I think I need another one. Maybe two.

MAX: Why don't you just sit down for a minute, Mr. Cape.

HENRY: Suppose I don't wanna sit down.

MAX: Then you can stand. You look a little unsteady that's all.

HENRY: Really…. Why don't you just take me down to the police station. If you're going to treat me this way why not just take me down there and really give me a going over.

MAX's cell phone rings. He takes it out.

MAX: *(to HENRY)* Excuse me. *(into phone)* Yeah… Really… Okay…

He puts the phone back in his pocket.

HENRY: Was that about Lily.

MAX: No.

HENRY: Come on. Was it about Lily. Have they found her.

MAX: It wasn't about your wife.

HENRY: Are you lying. You are, aren't you. Fuck you, if you're lying about this. She's my wife. I've got a right to know anything you find out.

MAX: It was my partner. He's over at the plant with the supervisor.

HENRY: What. What plant.

MAX: Where you applied for work today…. Anyway my partner's with this guy…Gerrard.

HENRY: Gerrard? *(smiles)* Oh yeah. Manny Gerrard. Big fat guy. I mean huge. Yeah I'll never forget that guy. Looked like hell. Like he was about to die or something. And he smelled.

MAX: He remembers you too.

HENRY: Well he should. I smacked him in his big fat face. Is he pressing charges or something.

MAX: He says this afternoon, five minutes after the bomb went off, he got a call.

HENRY: There was a bombing at the plant?

MAX: You didn't know.

HENRY: Well how could I.... Was it on the news

MAX: It was just a little bomb. And there wasn't any damage. It was in the dumpster out back. Anyway the call the supervisor took.... The guy told him this was just a little taste of what was to come.

HENRY: Really.

MAX: Yeah.... And the thing is, the supervisor, Manny...says he recognized the voice of the caller as being yours.

HENRY: Really. That's odd. Because...when I was there I hardly said anything to him. I think I said hi. He mumbled something back. I asked for the personnel manager. He told me he was on vacation. I asked when he was coming back. He told me it was none of my fucking business.... I thought to myself what a strange and ugly thing to say to someone who's just looking for work. So I punched him in his big fat smelly face. And left.

MAX: He says it was you who called. He says he's sure.

HENRY: Really.

MAX: I'm just...telling you.

HENRY: You're just telling me. You're not taking me in. You're just telling me. Well that's large of you Detective.... You're all heart.

HENRY goes over to the dresser.

MAX: What are you doing.

HENRY: Getting something... In the dresser.

MAX: No. Don't.

HENRY: Whatya mean "no don't." What the hell is—

MAX: Just back away from it, Mr. Cape… Come on.

HENRY: Why.

MAX: Do it!

HENRY: Okay…okay.

HENRY puts his hands up. Backs off. MAX goes over. Opens the drawer. Brings out a bottle of whiskey.

MAX: This what you were after?

HENRY: You betcha.

MAX: How about a coffee instead.

HENRY: How about not…

HENRY grabs the bottle from MAX.

HENRY: *(pouring a drink)* I think you've got a choice to make here Detective. It's simple. Believe me or don't believe me. If you don't believe me take me in and beat the fucking truth outta me. If you do believe me get outta my face. And get out there and help find my wife who has now been missing for…*(looks at his watch)* thirty-seven and a half hours…. That's the choice, man. All this other stuff is crap. Some little fucking bomb…. Making sure I don't close the door when I take a piss. Asking questions without asking questions. Searching the room without searching the room. Either you think I had something to do with my wife's disappearance or you don't. Come on, be a man. What is it. Spit it out. You think I what, killed my wife then went out, put a bomb in the dumpster of some stupid factory somewhere…. *(sits on the bed, propped up against the pillows)* I mean is that the…"scenario."

MAX: I'm sure they'll find your wife and she'll be fine…. I mean I really hope so. I thought she was a nice person.

HENRY: What are you talking about.

MAX: I met her last week.

HENRY: Yeah right.

MAX: No. Really. My partner and I were here last week. She didn't tell you? Maybe she told you and you just forgot.

HENRY: What is this. Are you yanking my chain here?

MAX takes out his notebook. Looks through it.

MAX: Tuesday. Late afternoon.

HENRY heads for the bathroom.

MAX: Where you going.

HENRY: I want a little water in this. That okay with you?

MAX: Sure. The more the better.

HENRY goes into the bathroom.

HENRY: *(from bathroom)* So go ahead. You were here…. Are you sure it was Tuesday.

MAX: Yeah…. Around four thirty…. Donny my partner got here first. I was booked off visiting my kid. Anyway when I got here…there was no one in the room. So I just…waited…

Lights change.

Afternoon.MAX is looking around the room. Voices outside. Laughing. Door opens. LILY CAPE and Detective DONNY DEVERAUX come in.

DONNY: Hey, Maxie…. Everything cool? With the youngsters I mean.

MAX: It was just a thing at school. I have to go back later and meet the teacher but—

DONNY: Great…. Lily this is Detective Malone.

LILY: Hi.

DONNY: Lily and I were just out looking at her husband's van.

MAX: He's not around?

DONNY: No she doesn't know where he is.

LILY: Well I know he's out looking for work. That's what he does every day. He gets up. And goes out to look for work.

DONNY: They've been here for three weeks.

LILY: Three weeks today. Three very long weeks.

DONNY: Lily's going a little stir-crazy. They left their spacious home to come here.

MAX: Really.

LILY: Well we had to. We won't have our spacious home much longer if he doesn't find something soon.

MAX: *(to DONNY)* Did you tell her why we're here.

DONNY: Well I told her what I knew, Max. I told her some guy had left some very strange writing on a bathroom wall at Horton Manufacturing. And I told her we were asked to talk to all the people who'd passed through that building today.

LILY: But you don't mean all the people. You mean the people who were there looking for jobs and got told there was nothing for them. And there never would be.

MAX: Is that what they told your husband.

LILY: Probably. That's what they all tell him. What kind of things were written on this wall. Some kind of threat?

MAX: Yeah. They're taking it that way.

DONNY: They gotta take it that way, Lil. I mean suppose someone does blow the place up and all they had to do to prevent it was hire fifty people.

LILY: That's what it said? Hire fifty people or your factory will get blown up?

DONNY: But with more poetry. This guy had a way with words. What were the exact words Max. Something about concrete rain…

MAX: Can't remember.

DONNY: Sure you can. Wasn't there some joke…or something from the Bible?

MAX: I…can't remember, Donny. *(to LILY)* Did your husband seem all right to you this morning, Mrs. Cape.

DONNY: Guess what, Max. We know each other. I forgot to tell you. Lily and I went to high school together. What a neat fucking coincidence, eh.

MAX: Yeah. *(to LILY)* So…your husband…. Did he seem all right or not.

LILY: He's been looking for work for two years. He never seems all right. Not really.

DONNY: It's a sad story. But it's happening everywhere. Some guys take it better than others. Henry sounds like he's taking it okay. I mean he still gets up and goes out looking.

MAX starts looking around the room.

LILY: Yeah. He does.

DONNY: Too bad you had to leave your home though. That must be rough. Well it's part of the story. When there isn't much work you gotta go where it is.

LILY: It isn't anywhere.

DONNY: That's just how it seems, Lil. But it's out there. You gotta keep the faith. Be strong…. Is that the kind of man Henry is. I never met Henry, did I.

LILY: He's not from here. I met him after I left.

DONNY: Right. So what's he like, Lil. Is he the kind of guy who keeps on goin' no matter what…. Trying to do his best. Or is be a blamer.

LILY: I told you. He gets up every morning. He goes out and—

DONNY: Yeah. But how. With an attitude?

LILY: What do you mean by attitude. Do you mean, is he mad.

DONNY: Does he go out feeling everything could still turn out all right. Or do you think maybe inside he's basically given up.

LILY: I don't know.

DONNY: Guess.

LILY: Whatya mean, guess?

MAX: He didn't really mean guess. He meant—

LILY: What are you doing. Why are you looking around like that.

MAX: You want me to stop?

LILY: Yes. I do.

DONNY: So. About Henry. Do you think he's got a…hidden attitude, Lil…. Do you think there might be something about him you don't know.

LILY: Well if I don't know…how would I know.

MAX: That's just what I was thinking.

MAX and DONNY exchange a look. A knock at the door.
SANDY is standing there. She is younger than LILY. Wearing a leather jacket, jeans and boots.

SANDY: Hey, am I early.

LILY: No. I was just—

SANDY: Is there some problem. I can meet you later.

LILY: No I'm ready.

LILY begins to gather things. A coat. A purse.

LILY: *(to MAX)* You need anything else? Can I go?

MAX: Sure. Go ahead.

DONNY has moved close to SANDY.

DONNY: Hi.

SANDY: Hi.

DONNY: I'm Donny. Who are you.

SANDY: Sandy. I'm…a friend of Lil's.

DONNY: Me too…. Why are you hanging around the door like that Sandy. Come on in.

LILY has her purse. And starts toward the door.

LILY: No. We're leaving. It was good to see you again, Donny.

DONNY: I'll call you.

LILY: Sure.

DONNY: You need a lift?

LILY: No we're—

DONNY: You taking the van?

LILY: No. We're just—

DONNY: Do you have a car, Sandy.

SANDY: Ah no, we're—

DONNY: I'll drive you.

LILY: We're going downtown.

DONNY: I'll drive you. Come on. So you two are…what. Just going out somewhere? Just for fun or something?

He is escorting the women out.

SANDY: Yeah. Maybe to a movie. Or a club.

DONNY: A club. Ooh. Those are exciting places. People drink and dance there. You gonna drink and dance?

SANDY: Yeah. Maybe.

LILY: I should lock up.

DONNY: Max can do that. He probably wants to wait and talk to Henry anyway. *(to MAX)* Right, Max?

MAX: Yeah.

DONNY: Come on, we better hurry. I hear those clubs are only open 'til four or five a.m.

They are leaving.

DONNY: So, Sandy.... Nice boots.

They are gone. MAX looks around. Takes out a cigarette.

Lights change.

Night.

MAX: ...But you didn't come back.... That night a couple of other cops picked someone up at the bus station. Some whacked-out homeless guy who'd been writing on the bathroom walls. Men's. And women's.

HENRY comes out of the bathroom. Drying his face.

HENRY: What, he wanted the bus company to hire fifty people or he'd blow up the station?

MAX: Yeah. He was on a mission. And fifty was his special number. He was going around to places. Something in the Old Testament set him off. It's usually the Old Testament that gets these guys going. I think it should be banned.... Anyway this was all about revenge and justice on earth. And the only way to achieve this, being to get a lot of places to hire fifty people.

HENRY: So...you don't see him as the guy who's responsible for the bomb in the dumpster.

MAX: No. He was in his pyjamas wandering around the psycho ward by then.... Are you okay..

HENRY: Great.

MAX: Were you sick in there.

HENRY: No. Just freshening up.... So who was this woman Sandy who showed up.

MAX: Beats me. Some friend of your wife.

HENRY: You said she looked kinda...cheap.

MAX: Did I. I don't think so... I said she was wearing high-heeled boots. That's what I remembered.... The boots.

HENRY: And they went out together.

MAX: Somewhere. Yeah. Donny drove them.

HENRY: Your partner. And my wife knows him.... Well...all this is really interesting but what does it have—

MAX: So you don't know this Sandy person. Maybe your wife mentioned her. And with so much on your mind you can't remember.

HENRY: No.... No I don't think so. And even if she did—

MAX: I was thinking maybe she might be some connection to your wife's whereabouts. So you should try hard to remember if your wife ever said anything about her... Okay?

MAX is staring at the cigarette in his hand.

HENRY: Okay.... What's wrong.

MAX: What...ah.... I was wondering where this cigarette came from. I was thinking about—

HENRY: Ah...I don't...understand.... Does this have anything to do with—

MAX: I quit.... I remember.... I mean I quit last week.... Threw them out.... Actually it was here.... Couldn't get the lighter to work so I said fuck it. Threw the lighter in that waste basket.... *(takes object from his pocket)* This is it here.... Found it on the dresser.... Anyway...I quit.

HENRY: Good for you... Listen do you have something else you want to—

MAX: Look I gotta go. I just remembered my kid has a dentist's appointment. I don't think you should go home just yet. I mean...back to your real home.

HENRY: I wasn't planning to. Not with Lily missing. Come on, what kind of man do you think I am.

MAX: I...gotta go.

MAX drops the lighter on the table.

MAX: I'll be in touch...

MAX leaves. HENRY looks through the blinds for awhile. Then goes over to the table. Picks up the lighter. Sits.

HENRY: Fuck.

He lowers his head.

LIGHTS CHANGE.

Very early morning.

HENRY: Fuck. Come on, Lily. I just want you to answer a simple fucking question.

LILY comes out of the bathroom. Wiping makeup off her face.

LILY: I'll talk to you when you calm down. I can't talk to you when you're like this.

HENRY: Like what. Just tell me where this fucking lighter came from. Who's been in this room and left his goddamn lighter!!

LILY: I'm gonna watch some TV.

She turns on the TV.

HENRY: It's three-thirty in the morning for chrissake.

LILY: Maybe there's a movie on.

HENRY: Who left the lighter here! Who!?

LILY: Is that the sound of a man calming down. I don't think so.

LILY is changing the station.

HENRY: Jesus…. Okay…okay listen.

LILY: Why don't you just go to bed. You look beat.

HENRY: No listen! …I'm…calm now. I'm calmly asking you how this lighter got in that waste basket. I'm calmly asking you who it belongs to.

LILY: I don't know.

HENRY: You don't know. Well could you take a guess. Can't you even do that. Take a guess?

LILY: Okay. My guess is the cleaning lady.

HENRY: Why the cleaning lady.

LILY: You don't like that guess? Okay. You guess.

HENRY: Look there's no need to be sarcastic.

LILY: Go to bed. You're too tired to have a conversation.

HENRY: What do you do all day when I'm out there looking for work.

LILY: What do you mean. Is that some kind of criticism. Is there something you think I should be doing. Maybe redecorating our suite here in the Chateau Shit?

HENRY: Look all I'm saying is I…realized I don't know what you do all day.

LILY: You don't know because you don't care.

HENRY: Don't start with that you don't care stuff. I've got lots on my mind. It's like the Grapes of Wrath out there. It's a disaster area. People walking around like they're victims of some huge cataclysm. They've got the eyes of wounded dogs. It's fucking horrible.

LILY: Not for everyone. A lot of people are doing just fine.

HENRY: Well I don't meet those individuals.

LILY: Neither do I. But I hear they're still out there.

HENRY: Is that where you were tonight. Out looking for a better class of people.

LILY: I told you. I went to a movie.

HENRY: What kind of…movie.

LILY: A stupid movie.

HENRY: You went to a fucking movie. We don't have any money and you went to a fucking—

LILY: A stupid fucking movie. Yeah. Now go to sleep before you really piss me off…. I'm doing my best here. I packed the kids off to my sister's because you wanted me with you on this odyssey of doom. You wanted me close at hand so I put my life on hold and I came. I came and parked myself obediently in this room. And now, even though I don't know where the hell you are for hours on end, you feel you've got the right to interrogate me about my activities. Go to sleep.

HENRY: You wanted to come with me.

LILY: I wanted to come because I knew you wanted me to come.

HENRY: You blame me don't you.

LILY: For what.

HENRY: For everything.

LILY: Be more specific.

HENRY: For being unemployed.

LILY: I think there are jobs you could have taken.

HENRY: Well there aren't.

LILY: There are jobs out there.

HENRY: I'm telling you there aren't.

LILY: None up to your standards, you mean.

HENRY: None. Period.

LILY: None…. Really? None.

HENRY: Okay, Lily. Yeah. I could be a janitor somewhere. I was hoping for something better. But I guess I could be a janitor. Is that what you want.

LILY: Maybe you have an attitude. When you go to these interviews maybe you have an attitude that shows you resent being there.

HENRY: I do resent being there.

LILY: Maybe that's something you could work on. Maybe you could consider jobs you wouldn't normally consider and maybe you could work on your attitude.

HENRY: I'll…try. Hey. I know. Maybe if I begged. Cried and begged. *(he cries)* Like this. Please. Please hire me! I'll do anything!! Anything!!

LILY: Henry. Shut up. Listen to me. We'll lose everything we have.

HENRY: No we won't. Don't fucking start with we'll lose everything.

LILY: Well we will.

HENRY: No. We won't.

LILY: If one of us doesn't do something fast, yes we will.

HENRY: One of us? What can you do.

LILY: I don't know.

HENRY: It's up to me.

LILY: Is it.

HENRY: Yes it's up to me. You can't make the kind of money we need to survive. To live the way we lived. I mean really, what can you do. What.

LILY: Now you are truly starting to piss me off. I mean it. Go to sleep.

HENRY: I'm just saying you're not...trained...You know what? You're right. I can't have this discussion. It's too late. I mean really too late. There are bigger things at stake than you and me and our fucking lifestyle here.

LILY: Really.

HENRY: Yeah really. It's hell out there. People's lives are hanging in the balance. And do you want me to tell you why?

LILY: No that's okay. You've told me why plenty of times already.

HENRY: I want to tell you again.... It's because a bunch of greedy pricks can't put any fucking limits on themselves. It's because every asshole who runs a large company can smell these enormous profits, and he knows the only thing between him and these profits is a little human misery. A few...layoffs. A little downsizing. Just a little cutback here and there. A prudent reduction in the labour force. And no one's trying to stop any of this.... Because no one cares, I guess. No one! You don't care do you Lily. All you care about is getting back to your comfort zone. You don't feel the humiliation do you. The humiliation of...filling in all those fucking applications for jobs I could have done blindfolded when I was twenty. And I'm humiliated for all the other poor assholes filling them in too. But you don't care about that at all, do you. Are you a selfish person Lily. Is that what you really are when it comes down to it. A selfish unaware insensitive asshole. But listen, don't feel bad. You're not alone. There's millions of you.

LILY: Get out of here.

LILY goes to door. Opens it.

HENRY: Good idea.

LILY: And don't even think about coming back unless you're ready to apologize for that.

LILY goes into the bathroom. Closes door.

HENRY: Right. I have to apologize. It's my fault. I have to grovel out there and apologize in here. Grovel, apologize, crawl and beg like a fucking dog. That's my life.... That's...my fucking life.

He leaves, slamming the door behind him. LILY comes out of the bath- room. Goes to TV. Turns it off. Sits on the bed. A knock on the door. LILY goes slowly to the door. Opens it. SANDY is standing there. In t- shirt, cut-offs and boots.

SANDY: Hi...

LILY: Ah...hi.

SANDY: Sorry to bother you. Could I use your phone.

LILY: Well I don't— Who are you. I mean are you in trouble or something.

SANDY: No it's okay. I mean don't worry. I'm in the room next door. It's just that my phone is broken. And the office is all locked up and I saw your light and so I knew you were up.... And so can I use your phone please.

LILY: Ah...Okay. Sure.... Go ahead.

SANDY goes to the phone.

SANDY: Also I knew you were up...because I heard you. You know, arguing.

LILY: Oh.... Sorry.

SANDY: Hey. Are you kidding. That was nothing... No physical contact or anything.

SANDY punches in a number.

SANDY: Was that your boyfriend.

LILY: Husband.

SANDY: Really.... You don't find many husbands and wives in this place. I mean together.... Separately, well that's another story.... It's busy. Mind if I wait and try again?

LILY: No.

SANDY: I'm calling a—well you don't care who I'm calling do you. You just want me to make the call and leave. I mean it's late. Even for me it's late. And you look like a woman who goes to bed at a reasonable hour.

LILY: Take your time. I'm not tired.

SANDY holds out a hand.

SANDY: Sandy.

LILY walks to SANDY and shakes her hand.

LILY: Lil. Or...Lily.

SANDY: Still busy.... This could take awhile. He's on the phone a lot. He's my, you know...

LILY: Your...

SANDY: Yeah...

LILY: How does…that work. I hear that can be rough…. Is he rough.

SANDY: No he's a pretty nice guy really…. Well he's not typical. I met him when I was doing some phone sex work. He managed the place with his sister.

LILY: Really.

SANDY: Yeah. Some of these phone sex people are pretty normal…. Anyway I asked him if he could help me, you know manage things…offer some support…. I mean really what it mostly comes down to is taking my messages and arranging bail…. But it's better if you have someone…. Still busy. Do you want me to leave?

LILY: I've seen you go into your room. I've watched you and the men.

SANDY: Yeah I've seen you watching.

LILY: Well I didn't mean anything bad by it. I was…just watching.

SANDY: Yeah you were watching like you were curious.

LILY: Really. You thought I looked curious?

SANDY: Definitely.

LILY: Yeah. Well I am I guess…. A lot of different men. Boy…. I mean…. Do you know any of those men?

SANDY: What do you mean "know" them. From before?

LILY: Yeah. I mean are they all…new.

SANDY: Well some are repeats. A few. But yeah, most are "new"…. You know, just guys you meet.

LILY: On the street?

SANDY: Around.

LILY: But sometimes on the street.

SANDY: I did the street. Just to see if I could. But I didn't ever feel comfortable…. It's…not me…. I'm more comfortable in bars. Hotels. Escort work. You know, meeting people through contacts. It's a more controlled situation…. Okay it's still busy. *(looks at watch)* But I gotta go. I'm meeting a friend downtown. Thanks for letting me in. A lot of people wouldn't.

LILY: Yeah well…

SANDY: Do you wanna come?

LILY: Come downtown?

SANDY: Yeah.... I'm just gonna hang out.

LILY: Hang out downtown. Where. Just downtown? On the street. What, just stand there on the street?

SANDY: No. Look. You've got it wrong. I was just—

LILY: Oh. I'm sorry. You weren't talking about "working" were you.

SANDY: No.

LILY: And even if you were, you wouldn't be doing it on the street. You've already told me that. Sorry. Anyway you were just being friendly. And it's been so long since anyone's invited me anywhere I didn't—

SANDY: I'm going downtown to a club. I thought you might wanna come along.

LILY: There's a club open now? It's about four in the morning, isn't it. I can't go out at four in the morning.

SANDY: Okay.

LILY: Why not.

SANDY: What.

LILY: Why can't I go out at four in the morning. That's stupid. So you really think this club is open?

SANDY: I don't know if it's open or not. Probably. A friend of mind works there. I told her I'd meet her. So.... You wanna come? I've got my friend's car. Or maybe you just wanna stay here and wait for your husband.

LILY: Why would I want to do that.

SANDY: So you can kiss and make up.

LILY: I don't want to kiss him. And I don't want to make up with him because I don't even know who the hell he is.... But I'm not sure I should go downtown.

SANDY: Okay. Whatever. Gotta run. Thanks for the phone.

SANDY starts off.

LILY: No wait. Ah, okay.... I think it's okay if I come downtown. No, you know what? I want to come downtown.

SANDY: Great.

LILY: Do I need anything?

SANDY: Whatya mean.

LILY: I...don't know. Anything.

SANDY: Just grab your coat.

    LILY grabs a sweater.

LILY: Sweater.

SANDY: Great.

    They are leaving.

LILY: I'm a bit nervous. I don't go out much.

SANDY: No kidding.

LILY: Well I've been home with my children.

SANDY: You've got kids?

LILY: Yeah. Two.

SANDY: Me too.

LILY: Really? You've got...two kids?

SANDY: Yeah.

LILY: Oh.

    They leave. Close the door behind them.
    Blackout.

Scene Two

*Lights. Late afternoon. Knocking at the door. Water running in the
bathroom sink. Knocking at the door. LILY comes out of the bathroom.
Drying her face with a hand towel. Her hair is a mess. She looks like she
slept in her clothes. And she is walking very slowly.*

LILY: *(weakly)* Who is it?

DONNY: Donny.

LILY: Who.

DONNY: Lil, it's Donny.... I'm with Max. My partner. We...have to talk to
you.

She opens the door. DONNY is standing there.

DONNY: Hey Lil. You look like shit. No offence.

LILY: I was...out...late...and I was...

DONNY: Drinking a little?

DONNY: Can I come in.

LILY: I...don't know.

DONNY: You still drunk, Lil?

LILY: I think so.

MAX comes to DONNY's side.

DONNY: *(to MAX)* Yeah?

MAX: Maybe.... They'll know in an hour.... What gives. Are we going in or not.

DONNY: Just waiting for permission.

MAX: We need to talk to you, Mrs. Cape. It's about your husband.

LILY: I don't...think he's here.

She turns back. Looks around the room.

MAX: Jesus. *(to DONNY)* What's her problem.

DONNY: She's smashed.

MAX: Is it okay if we talk to you, Mrs. Cape.

LILY: What about.

MAX: *(to DONNY)* I think we'll take that as a yes.

MAX comes into the room.

DONNY: Hey, Lil. How about if I go get you a coffee.

LILY: Yes. A coffee...would be nice.

DONNY: I'll be right back.

DONNY leaves.
MAX looks at LILY for a moment. LILY tries to tidy herself a bit. Then decides not to bother.

MAX: You were out late last night, Mrs. Cape?

LILY: Ah, I was out early. It was early when I left. Late when I got back…. I think that's right.

MAX: Did you see your husband?

LILY: When I was out?

MAX: Wherever. Out… In…

LILY: I saw him…here. He was here…. Before…

MAX: Before when.

LILY: Before I went out.

MAX: Which was when.

LILY: Three or four.

MAX: Yesterday afternoon.

LILY: This morning. I told you.

MAX: I forgot.

DONNY comes in with a coffee in a cardboard cup.

DONNY: It's that crappy stuff from the machine in the office.

He hands it to her. She looks at it.

LILY: Very thoughtful of you. Excuse me. I have to vomit now.

She goes into the bathroom. Closes door.

MAX: She hasn't seen him since early this morning.

DONNY: Did she say where she's been.

MAX: I didn't ask.

DONNY: So we don't care where she's been.

MAX: If she wasn't there with Henry…no we don't.

DONNY: Do you mind if I ask her anyway.

MAX: Sure, if it's important to you, you can ask her what she had for fucking dinner. If you think we've got that kind of time. All I know is we've got two dead people who are in some way connected to her husband. And in an hour when they've finished with that autopsy I'm pretty sure we're gonna have three. But if you—

DONNY: It's not personal. Not really.

MAX: Look. Before you ask her where she's been ask her where she thinks this friend of Henry's, this Al whatshisname lives. Just do that first. Just to humor me.

DONNY: Look I'm telling you it's not personal. Okay now I'm feeling cornered here. Nothing I say to her is gonna sound right to you. Because you think I just want to fuck her.

MAX: Are you saying you don't.

DONNY: I'm saying it's okay to enquire about her whereabouts during the course of our investigation.

MAX: To see if she's fucking anyone else.

DONNY: Well that could be important. It could relate to her husband's state of mind.

MAX: We probably know all we need to know about her husband's state of mind. He's probably got the state of mind of a fucking murderer. Now just ask her about his friend. Okay? ...Well okay or not fucking okay?!

The toilet flushes.

DONNY: Okay! ...Okay.

LILY comes out of the bathroom.

DONNY: How you feeling now.

LILY: I don't drink. That's the problem. I lack...resistance.

MAX: Mrs. Cape, why don't you sit down for a moment.

LILY: Bad news?

MAX: I just want to—

LILY: Bad news about Henry.... Is he dead.

She sits.

MAX: We...think Henry is a—

DONNY: Max and I are homicide detectives Lil. Yesterday when we came here looking for Henry and talked to you...well we were homicide detectives then too. You see what I'm getting at? There had already been a murder. Since then there have been two more.

MAX: All three of the victims were people who your husband had some contact with. At places where he interviewed for jobs.

LILY: Bosses?

MAX: What.

LILY: Bosses. Management. Were they people who interviewed him.

DONNY: No, Lil. They were other men applying for work. Just guys who filled out applications around the same time Henry did.

MAX: We have physical evidence connecting Henry to the first two.

LILY: Henry is killing...guys? Guys who are out of work just like him? No way. If Henry was killing anyone he'd be killing the people in personnel. People in charge. What are you talking about. You're confused.

MAX: No we're—

LILY: Yes you're seriously confused. Try to straighten this out before it gets out of hand. Your thinking about this is all wrong... *(she stands)*

DONNY: Lil...Lil we're just—

LILY: No get out. Go away and get your thoughts straightened out.

DONNY: Lil... Did Henry ever mention a guy named Al... *(to MAX)* Al..?

MAX: Al... Fuck.... Why can't I remember this guy's name.

DONNY: Ah...Mazilli?

MAX: Yeah. Mazilli.

DONNY: Lil.... Al Mazilli. Ever heard of him?

LILY: No.

MAX: He appears as a reference on all of Henry's applications. We've checked the address Henry gave. He's not known there.

LILY: I don't know who he is.

DONNY: So why would Henry use a false reference. Was there no one back home he could use.

LILY: He had good references. I don't know why he'd make one up. I don't know...what's wrong with him. Look you have to think a lot more about this. Henry has his problems. But I just can't see him killing people. Especially if they weren't management.... Excuse me.

LILY goes back into the bathroom.

MAX: What's the problem.

DONNY: She's sick.

MAX: I mean what's going on between her and her husband.

DONNY: Why you asking me.

MAX: I thought you might know. You're an old friend. Maybe you can read her. Also you're a cop so I sometimes expect you to have an opinion about these things.

DONNY: Fuck off.

MAX: I mean professionally. I expect you to be looking at Lil here and trying to figure out what kind of relationship she's got with her husband. Not just looking at her trying to figure out a way to get her in bed.

DONNY: Hey. Didn't I tell you to fuck off.

MAX: Yeah. Right.

MAX starts out of the room.

DONNY: Where you going.

MAX: I'm fucking off.

DONNY: I didn't mean you should leave. God, you're sensitive these days. Everything I say you take offence at...or you question my motives or something.

MAX: Look. I've got work to do. Truth is we're not going to get anything helpful from this one. She's in space somewhere.

DONNY: I'm not so sure. I think she might—

MAX: No. Listen. We've got a serial killer out there who's in a hurry. I mean this guy seems to want to do a lot of damage in record time. So maybe one of us at least should get on his trail.

DONNY: Okay. That can be you. I think I'll stay here because...well...

MAX: Because why.

DONNY: Because I want to?

MAX: You don't care do you. You just don't give a fuck about anything anymore.

DONNY: Harsh. That was harsh.

MAX: Asshole.

MAX leaves. Slams door behind him. DONNY sits in a chair.

LIGHTS CHANGE.

Early morning. SANDY comes in.

SANDY: Ah...hi...

DONNY: Where's Lil.

SANDY: I'm sorry?

DONNY: She was out with you. Where is she.

SANDY: How do you know she was out with me.

DONNY: Because I followed you.

SANDY: You followed us? Really?

DONNY: Really. Yeah.... You went to that club. You left the club with a couple of guys. You went off with one. She went off with the other one. My car stalled.... Where is she.

SANDY: Out. I guess. I mean I thought she'd be back by now. That's why I came over but I guess...she's still...

DONNY: Out. Yeah.... And this guy she's out with, is he a friend of yours.

SANDY: I know the guy a bit.

DONNY: What's going on here. What's your name again.

SANDY: Sandy.

DONNY: Sandy...Sandy, what's happened here. Have you turned Lily on to the pleasures of prostitution.

SANDY: You're a cop, right.

DONNY: Yeah. But don't let that stop you from telling me the truth.

SANDY: I'm just asking because—

DONNY: Come on in. You're standing there like you want to leave. Why don't you just come in and sit down.

SANDY: I'm just asking if you're a cop because I want to know if I've done, you know, something wrong.

DONNY gets up.

DONNY: Wrong? What's "wrong," Sandy. Is fucking men for money wrong. Not to me. I pay for sex all the time. I like paying for it. It makes the situation real clear. I'd gladly pay you for sex.

SANDY: Would you.

DONNY: Yeah, but we'll get back to that in a minute... You were asking about what's wrong. And I'd have to say one thing that might be wrong, I mean in general, but also pertaining to our situation here, would be to place a relatively innocent person in harm's way. Would you agree with that.

SANDY: It depends. Whatya mean by innocent.

DONNY: This woman is not...experienced.

SANDY: No. But she's pretty smart. And she's old enough to make up her own mind about what she wants to do. She told me she wanted to make some money.

DONNY: She did, did she. She just said..."That thing you do. I wanna give it a try."

SANDY: More or less.

DONNY: She told you this...after a few drinks?

SANDY: Yeah. So what. Look take me in for soliciting...anything else related to what I do. But let's drop this bullshit about Lily. What are you, her guardian angel.

DONNY: We were in high school chemistry together. She sat two rows over.

SANDY: That's the most moving story I've ever heard in my life.

DONNY: You've got a smart mouth haven't you Sandy.

SANDY: Some people say that, yeah.

DONNY: Speaking of your mouth. How much for a blow job.

SANDY starts toward the door.

SANDY: I don't do cops.

DONNY: You don't?

SANDY: No. I think it's "wrong." I mean, you know, wrong in a general sense because it always feels like you're being coerced. And also wrong in our specific situation here because I might not be able to stop myself from biting off your prick.

She leaves. DONNY sits.

LIGHTS CHANGE.

Late afternoon. LILY comes out of the bathroom. Wiping her face.

LILY: How long can a person throw up. I mean don't you just have to stop sometime or die.

DONNY: I followed you last night. I'm telling you that straight up because I feel bad about it.

LILY: You thought I might lead you to Henry?

DONNY: Nah. I wasn't functioning professionally. I was…just interested.

LILY: Why.

DONNY: I'm interested in you. I don't know why exactly.

LILY: So when you're interested in someone you follow them.

DONNY: Sometimes.

LILY: That sounds kind of unusual, Donny. Maybe it's just my state of mind. But it doesn't sound like a healthy thing to do.

DONNY: Yeah well…. So…. Are you an experienced hooker now, Lil. Did money change hands between you and that guy.

LILY: Are you're asking me that as a cop.

DONNY: No.

LILY: Then yeah. He paid me. Two hundred dollars.

DONNY: So. Just like that, you're a prostitute.

LILY: How does it usually happen. After years of careful consideration?

DONNY: If you needed money, why didn't you ask me.

LILY: Who the hell are you. Some guy I knew when I was in high school. Some guy I haven't seen in years who's now a police detective who suspects my husband of murder. Oh yeah I was gonna borrow money from you. That would have been the obvious thing to do…. What's wrong with you. You never seemed like a stupid guy, Donny. Has being a cop made you stupid…. Look go away. Why are you here. If you're waiting for Henry, do it in your car.

DONNY: You're mad. I didn't want you to get mad. I'm just trying to help you. You seem to be making some pretty bizarre choices here, Lil.

LILY: I had no money. I had forty dollars. Now I have two hundred and forty dollars. I'd like to have a few hundred more by the end of the week. I choose to have money. I choose to have enough not to worry about it for awhile. So I can send some back for my kids…. Okay?

DONNY: Yeah. Okay but—

LILY: Because I've got a husband who might be nuts. I mean it sounds like he's gone nuts. I don't know for sure. But if he has then where does that leave me.

DONNY: Hey look, there are people out there who can help. You don't have to—

LILY: Please. Shut up. You're talking about a shelter or something? Then what. Welfare? I'm not going into a shelter with my kids. And I'm not doing that humiliating crawl through social service hell. I had a life! I want it back! I need a substantial amount of money to get it back!

DONNY: Yeah but.... Okay. The money might be good, sure if you're lucky, if you make connections. But still hooking is...it has a dangerous side.

LILY: Really. I didn't know that. I guess I'm a fucking idiot. Jesus. Go away. Mind your own business. Get a life.

DONNY: Can't...Can't get a life.... Had one. Lost it. Can't get it back.... Had a wife and a kid. They...don't want to see me because I was a really bad—

LILY: Look stop talking. Why are you telling me this.

DONNY: I knew you...before.... When I was younger. It was different then. It's like we knew each other when we were both...you know...still complete human beings. It's my work. I think it's my work. Anyway I drink and gamble and sleep with...anyone...

LILY sits on the bed.

LILY: What's going on here. What do you want from me Donny.

DONNY: Don't give up.

LILY: I'm not giving up.

DONNY: Don't become a whore. It's...depressing.... When I think back to when we were in school and then I think about us now...it's so fucking sad.

LILY: Henry's going to kill a lot of people. If this is Henry acting out his rage then lots of people are gonna die. Because Henry feels that he has been demeaned and he's very very mad about that. And so he's going to rip everything apart. Including what's left of our lives.... And so okay, that just leaves me to protect the kids.... To, you know, get some money together and get away from here. Far far away. So they don't have to hear about anything their father has done. Ever. So…I'm really just making plans. Getting prepared. And I know I'll need money.

DONNY: I'll give it to you.

LILY: Yeah? Why.

DONNY: How much you need? A few thousand? That's no problem. I can get that…. Remember when we went out that one time.

LILY: We went out?

DONNY: Once. I asked you again. You said no. "Let's just be friends," you said. I kept pushing. "Why won't you go out with me. What's the difference. Come on let's go out again. Please." Finally you looked at me. And said, "Donny, stop begging, have some self respect."

LILY: So what was that. Some kind of pivotal moment in your life or something?

DONNY: Maybe. I don't know.

LILY: Because if you're saying self respect is such a big deal to you, then how come your life is such a mess.

DONNY: I just remember it because…well maybe you were the first person to notice I didn't have any. Yeah maybe that's it.

LILY: So? What you're saying to me now is…what? That I should have some self respect or I'll turn out like you.

DONNY: No I was just…I don't know.

LILY: Fuck you. Go away. Sit in your car, you simple-minded goof. Self respect shit. I had a life!

DONNY: I'm sorry.

LILY: Go away.

DONNY: Ah…. Listen…. Can I stay awhile. I'd just like to stay.

LILY: You know what? I don't care what you do. I need to have a shower.

She goes into the bathroom.

DONNY: I'm having all these weird feelings. It's seeing you again I think…. I'm not sure…. I need to sort out some things I'm feeling…I'm feeling all fucked up for some reason.

LILY: *(from bathroom)* Whatever…

She closes the door. Blackout.

Scene Three

LILY and HENRY. HENRY is messed up. Clothes askew. Hair greasy.
LILY looks nervous. She is dressed in a tight top and short skirt.

HENRY: Oh this is great. This is fantastic stuff. We have a fight.... A mutual disagreement. And you turn into a goddamn street walker. This is all I need. One humiliation after another.... It's a plot. I know it's a plot. It's gotta be.

LILY: What's going on with you, Henry.

HENRY: *(laughs)* What's going on with me?

LILY: I mean are you taking drugs. You look—

HENRY: Hey hey come on. Look at yourself. Don't give me that diversionary crap. I'm past listening to that what's wrong with me shit.... What's wrong with you.

LILY: How'd you get in here anyway. Aren't the police out there.

HENRY: Police? What. No. Why.

LILY: Look, Henry we have to talk.

HENRY: Fucking right we have to talk. You can't do just anything for money, Lil. There are limits. There are limits to what a person can do. There's a certain point at which you have to stop or everything becomes meaningless.

LILY: So what's this thing with Al Mazilli. Isn't he that guy you knew who killed himself.

HENRY: Yeah. After he was laid-off.

LILY: So why are you using a dead guy as a reference.

HENRY: It's a kind of...tribute. My way of keeping his memory alive.

LILY: Have you been killing people out there, Henry.

HENRY: What are you talking about.

LILY: The police are looking for you.

HENRY: No they're looking for you. They know where I am. I'm right here.

LILY: You haven't been here in two days.

HENRY: That's not true. I was here last night.

LILY: No.

HENRY: No?.... Okay yeah that's right. I fell asleep...in the park.... But I called you.

LILY: No you didn't call me.

HENRY: Hey I fucking called you but you weren't in. You were out selling your body.

LILY: I had no money! I didn't know if you were coming back.... I didn't know what you were up to.

HENRY: I was looking for work, Lil. For work!

LILY: Hey. Bombs have been placed at some of those places you applied.

HENRY: Yeah yeah the cops talked to me. I don't know anything about that. Some guy. Some disgruntled guy.... You think everyone's happy out there? Everyone just accepts this shit? Not everyone! Some people get upset. Not enough mind you. Most people just go on, accept whatever degrading thing that occurs. Getting fired after twenty years of loyal service, that's nothing to most people apparently. They just smile, maybe ask for a reference. But some people get upset.

LILY: Are you upset, Henry.

HENRY: You know I'm upset.

LILY: How upset are you .

HENRY: Well I tell you, Lil, I'm just about as upset as anyone can get and still be sane.

LILY: Are you, Henry. Are you sane.

HENRY: Hey, look, I'm as sane as—

LILY: Did you kill those men, Henry.

HENRY: What men.

LILY: The police say you killed three men.

HENRY: Yeah? When? When did they say that.

LILY: They were here. They say they've got evidence linking you to the murders.

HENRY: Bullshit.... What is this. Is this something you've just thought up to take my mind off your behaviour.

LILY: Henry come on it's—

HENRY: Bullshit. Three guys dead and I'm a suspect? Well where are the cops. Why aren't they here. Why aren't they watching this place. How come I'm free. I'll tell you why. It's bullshit. You're fucking with me, aren't you. You really are a piece of work, Lil.... I mean has our whole life together been some kind of bullshit lie. Is this who you really are. Are you just a lying whore, Lil.

He is moving toward her.

LILY: Henry.

HENRY: Is that it Lil. Are you just a lying piece of shit like everyone else I meet.

LILY: Henry. Stop... Stay away from me.

HENRY: Whatya think I'm gonna do, Lil. You think I'm gonna bite you or something? Or kick you? You think I'm gonna kick you, Lil?

LILY: Henry!

HENRY stops. Throws his arms up in the air. Sits on the bed.

HENRY: I just don't know what you're trying to do to me here.... I just...don't know...

LILY looks at him for a long time.

LILY: Did you kill those men, Henry.

Henry turns, looks at her a long time.

HENRY: What men are you talking about, Lil.

LILY: Three men. Three men who applied for some of the same jobs you did.

HENRY: *(leans back on his arms)* Oh those guys. Yeah. I killed them. They were disgusting ass kissers. They had to die.... They were...depressing. Everywhere I went there was a guy or two sucking up in the worst way. Totally desperate. Totally fucking pathetic. Those three were the worst. Desperate and dangerous. It's bad enough when management fucks you over. But when you see your colleagues degenerating like that it's...well demeaning in a way you just can't stand.

LILY: So...you...killed them. Jesus.

HENRY: They were mercy killings in a way.

LILY: Have you been taking things, Henry. Drugs? I know you've had trouble sleeping and maybe if you were on medication at the time

244

there's a chance...I mean aren't you taking something for your.... Oh God...how are we going to...

Lil sits. Puts her head in her hands.

HENRY: *(standing)* I'm chemical free, Lil. There's nothing wrong with me. I just got very annoyed with a certain kind of behaviour. And well let's be honest, life hasn't been all that great lately. So maybe I'm a bit stressed.... Yeah definitely I'm stressed. I mean I totally forgot about killing those guys I've been so stressed by other things. No money. Running out of places I could apply for meaningful work. My wife becoming a prostitute. Stressful stressful things really.... Look I guess I better go turn myself into the police. *(he starts toward the door)* I really don't like you dressed like that.... But you know what? Maybe I understand why you're doing it. Yeah I think I do.... You're stressed too. Stressed, desperate, not thinking clearly.... So you do something outrageous.... Maybe just to...what? See if it helps. Does it help, Lil. Well there's the money I guess. But the rest is...outrageous.... I mean look at yourself. Is that really you, Lil. No. Not even a little. It won't work, Lil. It's too far away from who you really are.

LILY: *(lifts her head)* Yeah?...The guy who kills people. Is that really you, Henry.

HENRY: *(shrugs)* I guess maybe it is.

He leaves. LILY stands. Turns around aimlessly. Sits on the bed. Lowers her head into her lap.
Blackout.

Scene Four

Night. LILY is still on the bed. MAX is standing near her. Hands in pockets. The door to the room is open. LILY looks up.

LILY: Whatya mean he didn't do it.

MAX: He didn't do it.

LILY: He...told me he did it. He told me he killed those people. And why.

MAX: Yeah he told us too. He marched in, sat down and confessed. Gave us a detailed statement about how and why and when. And it all sounded just right. But...apparently he didn't do any of it. The trail of physical evidence took a last minute detour and led us to the door of some other guy. Another out of work guy who'd had contact with all three deceased.

I still can't figure a motive for the guy, but there was a weapon in his car and some other—

LILY: And you told Henry.

MAX: Sure. We brought the guy in. And then we told Henry.... He just shrugged.... He shrugged. Exchanged a few words with Donny. Then he left.

LILY: How long ago was this.

MAX: A few hours.

LILY: He didn't come here.

MAX: Yeah. I know that. He borrowed some money from Donny. Said it was for a bus ticket.

LILY: To where.

MAX: I had a feeling he didn't much care where.

LILY: Did he say anything about me.

MAX: No.

LILY: No "Say goodbye to Lil for me. Tell her I'll be in touch.".…"Tell her tough luck but I need a new start?"

MAX: No. Nothing.

LILY: Nothing.... Who is this guy.... Ah, Jesus...

MAX: Look there's something else we have to talk about.... I'm not sure how to go about this. But I have to know because Donny's my partner. And also...well I just have to know. So...is anything going on between you two.

LILY: Me and Donny? No. No we just... He just— Do you think that's what Henry was thinking.

MAX: I don't know what Henry was thinking. He didn't look like he was thinking anything really. He looked...empty. But maybe Donny said something to him. And maybe that's why he didn't come back here.

LILY: Or maybe he didn't come back for some other reason I wouldn't know anything about. Because I don't really know who the hell he is. Or what he really thinks about anything.

MAX: Listen, we've gotta talk a bit more about you and Donny. Because a couple of things are bothering me. Donny gave your husband a lot of money. I mean Henry asked for a few bucks. And Donny reached in his pocket and pulled out a wad of bills. I asked him why he was carrying so much money around and he gave me some bullshit about having to pay back a loan to some guy at work. Said it was a coincidence he had that much on him. And when I asked him later why he gave it all to your husband he just brushed it off. Said it wasn't that much. But it was. It was maybe three thousand dollars.

LILY: He gave Henry three thousand dollars? Why would he do that.

MAX: Exactly.... And the other thing.... This is dicier. It's about that trail of physical evidence and how it all of a sudden changed direction. I shouldn't be telling you this.... But the guy we've got in custody says he's innocent. And he says it real loud. Says he's been set up. And I've been wondering if that's possible. So...I guess I need to hear your thoughts on that.

LILY: On what exactly.

MAX: If Donny could have done something like that.

LILY: You want to know if I think Donny might have set this other guy up. To save Henry.

MAX: I want to know if Donny would have any reason to do that.

LILY: He's not well. I guess you know that, though. I mean anyone who's spent anytime with Donny could tell he's just not completely mentally healthy. So if I tell you there's nothing between me and him I can't guarantee that's how he sees it.... He could be seeing all sorts of things that aren't there.

MAX: Did you ever ask him for help.

LILY: No.

MAX: Any kind of help. Ask him for anything that he could have interpreted as you wanting him to...get involved.

LILY: No. I didn't ask him for anything. *(stands)* Okay? I didn't ask him to do anything or give anyone anything or blame anyone for anything. So anything he's done, whatever he's done he's done it on his own.... Okay!?

DONNY is at the door. Drunk. Carrying a brown paper bag with something in it.

DONNY: Someone done something? *(he falls against the door)* Well you can only hope it was the decent thing to do.... I mean there's just so much shit going on out there you just hope someone's out there doing a decent thing every once in a while… Max, Maxie… You look like you could use a hug.

He grabs MAX. Hugs him.

MAX: Hey. I'm working here.

DONNY: Hey. Me too. I'm working too. We work together, remember?

MAX: You're hammered.

DONNY: I'm a little hammered, yeah. Look. I brought something to celebrate with. So you guys can get a little hammered too.

He takes a bottle of champagne from the bag.

MAX: What are we celebrating.

DONNY: Well come on. Her dear darling husband isn't a serial murderer. I think that calls for some kind of positive reaction.

MAX: Go home, Donny. I wanna talk to Lil alone.

DONNY: Yeah? About what.

MAX: You.

DONNY: What about me.

MAX: Go home. When I've finished talking to Lil I'll come and talk to you.

DONNY walks a bit unsteadily over to MAX.

DONNY: Talk to me now.

MAX: I can't talk to you now. You're drunk.

DONNY: But I'm always drunk. You know that.

MAX: Go home.

DONNY: Fuck off. Don't tell me what to do…. You think I'm an asshole don't you. A guy tries to do a decent thing and all you can think about him is that he's some kind of fuck up.

MAX: Some kind of fuck up? Hey I think you're the fuck up of all time, Donny. I think you're so fucked up you're doing things you don't understand for reasons you can't even remember. Some half-assed idea comes into your head about someone, maybe taking shit like you think every poor bastard does in this rotten world and you say to yourself… "I know, I think I'll do something extreme now. Some really outrageous extreme action will solve this poor bastard's problem. Maybe I'll frame some other poor bastard and then this poor bastard here can walk away.

And then when poor bastard number one is gone, disappeared forever, I'll plant some more evidence so poor bastard number two is off the hook as well"…So is that it, Donny. With you on the job all the poor bastards in the world are going to get an even break.

DONNY: Something like that.

MAX: Or maybe it was seeing Lil here again. All those warm feelings she aroused. You just wanted to do something for her.

DONNY: Something like that. Yeah. Maybe more that than the other. But both really.

MAX: Three people are dead. Someone killed them.

DONNY: Well the poor bastards of the world are driven to some pretty desperate actions sometime.

MAX: Ah, you fucking psycho. I can't help you with this, Donny. I can't get behind this craziness. Go home. You're finished on this job.

DONNY: Says you.

MAX: Go home.

DONNY: I wanna talk to Lily.

LILY: Me? What have you got to say to me.

DONNY: Stay the course! Hang in there! Henry just needs some time to get himself back on track.

LILY: He killed those men because he thought they were weak, Donny. Because they disgusted him. He's sick. He's probably even sicker than you are.

DONNY: First of all, technically, at the moment, the guy is innocent because technically someone else is under arrest. But okay let's skip that part and assume he is some poor sick murdering bastard. Here's what I have to say about that…. If the fucking world is so fucked up and evil and uncaring and harsh that it creates these poor sick bastards then the fucking world has to suffer the consequences of their actions!!

DONNY looks at LILY. Then MAX. Then LILY again.

DONNY: Right? *(to MAX)* Right?

MAX: Yeah, whatever.

DONNY: Ah don't give me that shit. *(grabs MAX)* Answer my fucking question. I'm your partner for chrissake!

MAX: Let go of me.

DONNY lets go.

DONNY: I'm your friend! Show me some respect!

*DONNY goes to grab MAX again. MAX just moves aside and DONNY
stumbles and falls to the floor.*

MAX: Okay. You won't go home. I'm going home. I'm going home and I'm
going to sleep. Tomorrow you come to work sober and we'll see how
much of this crap we can make right. In the meantime here's something
to consider. I think you need to see a psychiatrist.

DONNY: I know you do.

MAX: So tomorrow you'll tell me everything you did and all the reasons you
think you had for doing it. Then maybe we can maybe get anyone who's
innocent out of jail and anyone who's guilty back in jail. And then
maybe we can get you help.... Is that respectful enough for you.

DONNY: Yes it is. And it's just the kind of thing I'll do for you when you go
over the edge too. And don't think you won't. Because you will. It gets
everyone. The shit in the world gets in the pores of your skin and in
your brain. And it just gets really hard to think in an orderly normal way
when you have shit in your brain, Max. That's my defense. "Your
honour, I have shit in my brain. I'm not responsible for my actions."

MAX: Yeah, that should work.

DONNY: You don't think so? Well I'll blame the job then. "Your honour, I've
seen so many bad things I just snapped. I'm sorry. I'm so—"

MAX: Ah shut the fuck up. I gotta go. *(he starts off, stops)* Oh yeah. We still
don't know who put those bombs in those dumpsters. Maybe it's Henry,
maybe it's another poor bastard. But someone should probably try to
find out who it is and stop him. I mean you can't just throw your arms
up in the air and say it's all shit anyway and here's a little more shit
while we're at it.... So fuck you for doing that, Donny. How does that
help.

MAX leaves.

DONNY: *(trying to get up)* Don't worry, Lil. Everything will be just fine.

LILY: Really. Is that what you think.

DONNY: Definitely. Henry's on the loose. And there's no way I'm gonna
assist them in their efforts to bring him back. I gave him some dollars to

help him get started. And I know with a few breaks the old Henry will re-emerge and begin leading a useful and productive life.

DONNY sits on the bed next to LILY.

LILY: And then maybe the three of us can get together and go camping. Or maybe on a cruise. Yeah. That's what I need. Two lunatics in my life. No thank you. Look Donny. You and I.... Nothing.... Not before. Not now. Not ever. No romance. No friendship. Nothing. Get it?

DONNY: Oh yeah. Definitely.

She is heading for the bathroom. SANDY is at the open door.

SANDY: Ready?

LILY: In a minute. *(to DONNY)* So whatever you did, I don't want you telling anyone not even yourself you did it for me. Get it?

DONNY: I do.

LILY: *(to SANDY)* I just want to freshen up a bit.

LILY goes into the bathroom.

DONNY: She had a normal life. At least that's what she thought. But really you can't hide from the shit of the world forever. It'll find you eventually. Right?

SANDY: Whatever you say.

DONNY: That's what I say. I also say there are two kinds of people basically. There are the purveyors of shit. And the people who get covered in the shit. Which are you.

SANDY: I'm whatever you say I am.

DONNY: Yeah.... So how's business.

SANDY: Great.

DONNY: Would you say this is a good year for whores. Or just average.

SANDY: No. This is a very good year.

DONNY: I'm glad. Because last year wasn't really great was it.

SANDY: Last year was well below average, yes.

DONNY: Do you think that had anything to do with interest rates.

SANDY: Interest rates. Foreign ownership. An unstable currency. All played a part. I think mostly the industry was suffering from lethargy. People weren't dressing for success. This year's fashions are better for business. Boots for example. Boots are back.

DONNY: So...you're a smart whore.

SANDY: I'm pleased you think so.

DONNY: I mean not just smart-mouthed. Actually smart.

SANDY: Yes. I'm an intelligent individual. And compared to you a mentally stable one as well.

DONNY: So how do you think Lily will do as a whore.

SANDY: You're very fond of the word whore.

DONNY: Are you offended by the word whore.

SANDY: No. No I was just commenting on how much you—

DONNY: No. Please. I need you to do me a favour now and shut the fuck up. Just give me your professional assessment of how you think Lil will manage. Don't make me come over there and ask you in a more formal manner. I just need to know if she's going to be...okay.

SANDY: She'll do fine.

DONNY: Because I care.

SANDY: I'm sure you do.

DONNY: I do. I really do.... We were childhood...acquaintances. Happy kids.... She was happy. So was I. We were happy...together.

SANDY: That's nice.

DONNY: You say that like you don't mean it.

SANDY: I do?

LILY comes out. More makeup.

LILY: Okay. Ready.

SANDY: Great. Let's get out of here.

DONNY: You look smashing, Lil. Really.... And so does your friend. *(to SANDY)* What's your name again.

SANDY: Sandy.

DONNY: Both of you. Smashing.

LILY: Thanks.

LILY leaves. SANDY starts off.

DONNY: Sandy.

Sandy stops...turns slowly.

SANDY: What.

DONNY: Remember. I still want that blow job. When would be a good time for that.

SANDY: When hell freezes over?

SANDY leaves. DONNY goes to door.

DONNY: Okay.... *(he yells after her)* I'll call you.... Or you call me.... Whoever is closer to a phone. *(he looks around the room)* What a magical place. So many wonderful things take place here. *(he picks up his champagne bottle. Uncorks it)* To me. *(he drinks)* To this place.... *(he drinks)* Wow.... Lil.... Who are you.... What are you doing.... You came to this magical place a mere housewife and...look at you now.

DONNY drinks his way out of the room. Closing the door behind him.

LIGHTS CHANGE.

Afternoon. Talking. Laughing outside the door. LILY and HENRY come in. Carrying luggage. They are both casually dressed. Neat-looking. They have just arrived.

LILY: I don't know about this place.

HENRY: It'll be fine. It's reasonably priced.

LILY: It smells a little.

HENRY: We'll air it out.

LILY: I'm not sure that's going to help.

HENRY: It's reasonably priced. It's relatively safe. And it's on a bus line. So I can leave the van with you.

LILY: What'll I do with it.

HENRY: I don't know. Get around.

LILY is looking around the room.

LILY: Get around to where.

HENRY: Well.... I thought while I was out looking for work you could visit some of your old friends.

LILY: I don't have any friends here anymore, Henry

HENRY: None at all?

LILY: None that I can think of.

HENRY: So why'd you come along.

LILY: You wanted me here. For support.

HENRY: I meant why'd you agree to it.

LILY: Because I'm...supportive.

They begin to unpack. Put stuff in drawers. Hang things up.

HENRY: You think I'll give up. You do don't you. You think at some point I'll just stop looking and give up.

LILY: Maybe.

HENRY: I won't.

LILY: Why not. Most people would. I probably would.

HENRY: No you wouldn't. And neither will I.

LILY: You've been looking for awhile now. You're getting depressed I can tell.

HENRY: I'm not depressed I'm—

LILY: Mad. You're mad. I know that's what you say. I think you're mad because you're getting...depressed. It's starting to look hopeless.

HENRY: Hopeless? To me? Or to you.

LILY: To you. What do I know about it. I don't know what's going on out there. I've been at home so long I wouldn't even know how to go about it.

HENRY: About what.

LILY: Getting a job.

HENRY: Why are you talking about getting a job.

LILY: I'm not. I'm just saying I don't really know what it's like out there.

HENRY: It's hard. I've told you that. There's a change in how people think about these things. They don't think it's important to have people working.... They don't think that's the most important thing. I'm not sure what they think is important. It can't be...just profit. It'd be totally depressing to think these companies were only thinking of profit.

LILY: What else would they be thinking of.

HENRY: Well some of them used to think about the future.

LILY: Future profit.

HENRY: Well yeah, but that's—

LILY: I think we should have gotten a housekeeping unit.

HENRY: No. Please. I've told you. Cooking in the room is...demeaning. Talk about depressing. Some two-burner stove. Rusty frying pan.

LILY: We'd save a lot of money.

HENRY: Yeah but there's a point.... There's a point at which we have to draw the line.

LILY: Look Henry. I'm not keen on this adventure in have-not land either. But if it comes down to cooking in our motel room versus being able to make the mortgage payment next month—

HENRY: How much will we save. Really.

LILY: Restaurants are expensive. We have to eat.

HENRY: Let's see.

LILY: See what.

HENRY: How we do.... In a week. In a week if it looks like we'll be around here longer, then we'll move to a housekeeping unit.

LILY: Yeah. Okay.... Where's the phone.

HENRY: Over there.... You calling your sister?

LILY: I want to see how the kids are.

HENRY: Wait 'til later. After eleven. It's cheaper.

LILY: They'll be asleep. The kids.

HENRY: The kids? You wanna talk to them?

LILY: Yes, I want to talk to them.

HENRY: You'll just get all upset again. You'll get them upset too. There's really no need. Think about it.

　Pause.

LILY: Okay. I've thought about it and I want to call them.

HENRY: It'll just upset them.

LILY: They're already upset. They've been taken out of their home and dropped in some other home. That's upsetting. It's more upsetting if their parents, who after dropping them off hop in their car and drive away, don't call them and say something like "Hi. We're here. We're fine. We won't be here long. Daddy's going to find work. We'll all be together soon."

HENRY: You're not taking this very well.

LILY: I'm taking this fine. You know someone who could take it better?

HENRY: What's that mean?

LILY: Nothing…. I'm calling. Don't try to stop me.

HENRY: Who's going to try to stop you. Don't talk nonsense. And what was that crack about me knowing someone who could take it better. Was that about Jennifer.

LILY: No.

She punches in a number on the phone.

HENRY: I think it was.

LILY: Well it wasn't.

HENRY: I slept with Jennifer because I was confused. I told you that.

LILY: I wasn't referring to Jennifer. And you slept with Jennifer because you wanted to sleep with Jennifer.

HENRY: Because I was confused.

LILY: Because you thought you could get away with it.

HENRY: Well whatever. It doesn't do any good to make cracks about it. We've got enough problems. I have to know if we're pulling together here.

LILY: There's no answer.

HENRY: Are we pulling together here.

LILY: Maybe she took them out for dinner.

She hangs up.

HENRY: Are we.

LILY: Are we what.

HENRY: Pulling together.

LILY: I'm right behind you Henry. Like I always am.

HENRY: But are we pulling together.

LILY: No, Henry. We're not pulling together. Because I'm right behind you. I can't "pull" from behind you. I can only watch you "pull."

HENRY: What's that mean anyway.

LILY: Exactly. What does it fucking mean. Pulling together. Pulling what. Pulling where.

HENRY: You've got a huge problem. Don't you. Huge.

LILY: Jesus... I'll get the other bags.

HENRY: No wait.

He takes her arm.

LILY: No I need some stuff in one of the other bags—

HENRY: I mean I looked into your eyes just now and...you're really angry aren't you.... You're angry...at me. Aren't you.

LILY: Let me go get the—

HENRY: Why.... Why me. Why not the people who fired me. Why not the people who won't hire me. Why aren't you mad at them.

LILY: Because they didn't feed me a line of bullshit. You did.

HENRY: What bullshit.

LILY: The "it'll be okay" bullshit.

HENRY: I was...trying to— Well maybe it will be okay.

LILY: It's already not okay. All the savings gone. House remortgaged. Kids in someone else's car going out with someone else for dinner. None of that's okay with me.

HENRY: And you blame me.

LILY: Because I could have done something to prevent it if you hadn't fed me the bullshit. If you'd told me the truth. If you'd really wanted to "pull together," I could have maybe gotten a job.

HENRY: Yeah? As what.

LILY: I don't know.

HENRY: As what!?

LILY: I don't know! As something. What's it matter.

HENRY: You think you can just go out and get a job, just like that. So why can't I get one.

LILY: I don't know.

HENRY: You think I'm not trying.

LILY: No I don't.

HENRY: Yes you do.

LILY: No! I know you're trying. But well…why don't you just take something…anything.

HENRY: Whatya mean by anything.

LILY: Anything. Something that pays.

HENRY: I could be a janitor. Clean banks at night. Me and those untrained immigrant women.

LILY: We're going to lose the house.

HENRY: I could mow lawns.

LILY: If we don't pay the mortgage it's gone. Just like that. Gone.

HENRY: Maybe I could wash cars.

LILY: The house is the centre of our life, Henry.

HENRY: Fuck the house! Fuck it. It's not the centre of my life. It's the centre of your fucking life. To me it's just a weight around my neck. My life is work. I'm supposed to get up and go somewhere every day and do a job that people respect me for. That's my life. And if I can't do that then…the hell with it.

LILY: The hell with it?

HENRY: That's right.

LILY: The hell with it as in "I give up"?

HENRY: All the rules of the game are suspended. I went to school. Worked hard. Paid my way as a useful citizen. I made a contract with the world and I obeyed the rules and stipulations of that contract. But if the contract is null and void…if I can just be discarded, thrown away like garbage then okay…okay.

LILY: I still don't see what—

HENRY: Anger! Yeah. I've got anger. You don't know what kind of anger I've got. It's got nothing to do with depression. And you know what, not just anger, contempt. I've got a shitload of contempt for a lot of fucking things, and if the rules are suspended then fuck it.

LILY: Fuck what.

HENRY: Fuck everything. I want...I want revenge.

LILY: Hey look let's just stick to the issue here. We've got a lot of responsibilities.

HENRY: Yeah. You get born. You work. You acquire responsibilities. You die. But before you die, just to give your life a little spice, a whole bunch of people fuck you over. So the hell with it. The rules are suspended. I don't want to demean myself and crawl around begging for work. I want to do something against someone. Against something.

He sits down. Lowers his head. LILY continues to unpack. A moment passes.

HENRY: I'm sorry.

LILY: It's okay.

HENRY: No, you're scared. I'm sorry. I was just.... Sometimes I need to...

LILY: It's okay. You need to.... You need to feel bad...

HENRY: I'm not giving up. Honest. It's impossible for me to believe there isn't something out there for me. I'm qualified. I'm just so...qualified.

LILY: And experienced...

HENRY: So...I'll just keep trying.

LILY: I know.

HENRY: I didn't mean that about the house just being your life...

LILY: I didn't think you did.... I mean it sounded like you did at the time but—

HENRY: I've been sitting on a lot of rage.

LILY: It's good to let it out then... Did you bring that navy blue cardigan.

HENRY: I don't know.

LILY: I can't find it.

HENRY: Maybe I didn't bring it. I brought that...maroon pullover I think.

LILY: Yeah I've seen that.

She continues to unpack. Pause.

HENRY: What would you do.

LILY: What do you mean.

HENRY: If we needed you to.... I mean if we needed some money short term.

LILY: I don't know. Office work. Waitress. Anything.

HENRY: Waitress?

LILY: Whatever.

HENRY: Whatever? ...You just don't get it do you. It's been...how long since you had a...job outside the house.

LILY: So that must be a rhetorical question right.

HENRY: I mean...jobs...all of them...they can be hard to find.

LILY: So I hear.

HENRY: Have you ever been a waitress.

LILY: No.

HENRY: But they'll hire you though. Even when there are hundreds of waitresses out there looking for work...they'll...hire you.

LILY: So basically what you're saying is forget it. And I should just rely on you.

HENRY: I'll get something.

LILY: And if you don't we're all screwed. Because there's just no way I can help. Oh I can be supportive. I can "pull" along with you. But basically it's your rope we're pulling on. And if there's nothing on the end of the rope worth anything then well that's it... We might as well gather up the kids, go home, lock the doors, make up some Kool-Aid with arsenic in it and have our own little Jonestown. Are you saying that.

HENRY: Is that what you think I'm saying, Lil.

LILY: It sounds like that's what you're saying. If you think about what you're saying. I mean instead of just opening your stupid mouth and letting words tumble out you might stop every once in awhile and consider the impact you're having.

Pause.

HENRY: Yeah…well…

LILY: You didn't pack any underwear. What's wrong with you.

HENRY: I had a lot on my mind. Don't worry about it.

LILY: Well what are you going to do. Are you going to wear mine?

HENRY: I'll buy some.

LILY: We can't afford it.

HENRY: We can't afford for me to buy new underwear.

LILY: That's right.

HENRY: Get serious.

LILY: Sure. Okay. Buy underwear. We'll eat in restaurants. Spend our last few hundred dollars. You can wear your new underwear. Everything will be fine.

HENRY: Get ahold of yourself.

LILY: What kind of an idiot doesn't pack any underwear.

HENRY: I wasn't paying too much attention. I thought you'd check.

LILY: What.

HENRY: You usually check. You usually go through my suitcase. Put in anything I've forgotten.

LILY: I do?

HENRY: Yeah…

LILY: How long have I been doing that.

HENRY: I don't know. A long time.

LILY: Yeah, long enough that I'm not even aware anymore that I do it…. Pathetic. I'm pathetic.

HENRY: Well I wouldn't worry about it. I mean you didn't do it this time, Lil. So I wouldn't be worried about a habit you've already broken…. I mean it's okay.

LILY: What's okay.

HENRY: The underwear. It's okay that you didn't pack some for me.

LILY: Oh…thanks.

She sits.

Pause.

LILY: I think I'll just buy the paper. Look through the want ads.... Maybe it'll make me feel better.

HENRY: Sure.... Or maybe it'll depress you.

LILY: I can't...just...not do anything.

HENRY: The want ads are depressing. They're a horror story. They're worse than reading about war atrocities. They suck your soul out.

LILY: I'll just...browse.

HENRY: Okay but...

He gestures.

LILY: I won't lose that house. I won't...

HENRY: I'm going to try my best. I am. But you know what I think?

LILY: I won't lose it.

HENRY: I think we need something drastic to happen. A wakeup call for the whole society. Because maybe...it hasn't occurred to people that once the rules...the rules of responsibility are suspended they're...suspended maybe forever... I've got a headache.

LILY: Take a couple of Advil.

HENRY stands.

HENRY: No. I got this prescription filled before I left.

He takes a bottle out of his pocket.

LILY: What's that.

HENRY: Something the doctor gave me.

LILY: For headaches?

HENRY: Headaches, depression, whatever. He thought they were all the same thing.... All tied together in some way. He explained. But I can't remember.

LILY: What exactly are they...the pills.

HENRY: Something...whatever...I need to take them with some water.

He goes into the bathroom.

LILY: I'm going to try the kids again.

LILY goes to phone. Punches in the number. Waits. No answer.

HENRY: *(from bathroom)* I'm gonna have a shower. That okay?

LILY: Sure.

Still no answer. LILY hangs up. Water running in bathroom.
LILY goes to the bed. Sits. Looks around the room. Stares off. Lost in
thought. Sits there. For about two minutes before...

Blackout.

The End

RISK EVERYTHING

PERSONS
CAROL
DENISE
R.J.
MICHAEL

PLACE
A slightly run-down motel on the outskirts of a large city.

Risk Everything was first produced by Rattlestick Productions at Theatre Off Park in New York City on June 15, 1997 with the following cast:

R.J. ....Christopner Burns*
DENISE ....Tasha Lawrence*
CAROL ....Patricia Mauceri*
MICHAEL...Christopher Hurt*

Director ....Daniel De Raey
Set Design...Van Santvoord
Lighting Design ....Chad McArver
Costume Design...............................Rachel Gruer
Sound Design....................................Laura Grace Brown
Production Manager ....Vicoletta Arlia
Casting...Liz Woodman Casting
Stage Manager..................................Federica Lippi

* Member of Actors Equity Association

Scene One

The room is empty. The door opens. DENISE comes in. Carrying a small suitcase. And a garbage bag full of stuff. Tosses the suitcase and the garbage bag on the bed. Turns and leaves the room. A moment passes. DENISE comes back in supporting her mother, CAROL who is limping and using a cane. CAROL also has a black eye. And several facial cuts.

CAROL: You're moving a bit too fast, honey.

DENISE: I want to get you over to the bed.

CAROL: Yeah but slow down. I'm really unsteady on my feet.

DENISE: Okay we'll just head for that chair.

CAROL: Yeah but slow, okay.

DENISE: Mom, you're pinching my arm.

CAROL: I'm in pain. It hurts to walk.

They are at the chair. DENISE is helping CAROL sit.

CAROL: Be careful.

DENISE: I am.

CAROL: Be careful. *(groans)* Shit...

DENISE: I'm sorry.

CAROL: That hurt. You bumped my knee.

DENISE: I said I was sorry!

CAROL: Hey don't get testy. It's me who got her knee bumped.

DENISE: I gotta go pay the cab driver.

CAROL: You need money?

DENISE: No.

CAROL: There's some in my purse. Where's my purse.

DENISE: I put it in the suitcase.

CAROL: Can you get it for me.

DENISE: It's okay. I've got money.

CAROL: I don't want you paying for the cab. Get my purse.

DENISE: It's okay. I'll be right back.

CAROL: Just get me my purse.

DENISE: It's...okay.

DENISE leaves.

CAROL: It's not...okay!

CAROL struggles up. Limps to bed. Gets suitcase. Opens it. Grabs purse. Turns and starts toward the door. Falls. DENISE comes in.

DENISE: Jesus, Mom. Whatya doin'?

CAROL: I told you not to pay. Did you pay.

DENISE: Yeah, but it's—

CAROL: I told you not to. Why won't you ever listen to me. Ever. Not even now. Why. How come.

DENISE: Let me help you up.

CAROL: Is it a thing with you. How come you won't take money from me. Is that a thing too.

DENISE is helping CAROL stand. And get into a chair.

DENISE: Is it a thing with you that you wanna give me money.

CAROL: I'm just paying my way. It's not you that needed to come here. It's me. So I should've paid the cab. How much was it. Fifteen dollars?

DENISE: Yeah.

CAROL: Fifteen.

DENISE: Yeah.

CAROL: I bet it was more. I'm gonna give you twenty.

DENISE: Sure. Whatever.

CAROL: Here's the purse. Open it. Take a twenty.

DENISE: Okay.

She does. Holds up a twenty dollar bill.

DENISE: Okay. Here it is. Satisfied? Look I'm putting in my pocket. It's in my pocket. Now can we stop talking about it for chrissake.

CAROL: Come on. Calm down. I'm just trying to pay my way. I don't want money to become a thing between us. That's what happens when you're not well-off. Money becomes a thing.

DENISE: Christ.

CAROL: What.

DENISE: You're bleeding. You've opened up that cut over your eye.

CAROL: Is it bad.

DENISE: You might have torn a stitch.

CAROL: Look. I don't care. I'm not going back to that hospital…. It's depressing, that place. All that crap in that emergency ward. Did you see that crap.

DENISE: Yeah. What crap.

CAROL: People crap. People who…looked like crap.

DENISE: Yeah, right.

CAROL: Don't look at me like that. I didn't look as bad as most of those people.

DENISE: Yes you did. To me you did.

CAROL: Why are you saying that. Do you think that's gonna make me feel better about going back there. Well it doesn't.

DENISE: I'll get a cold cloth. I'll put pressure on the eye. *(heads to bathroom)* If it stops bleeding we don't have to—

CAROL: Well whether it stops bleeding or not I'm not going back there. I'd rather bleed to death right here.

DENISE is in the bathroom.

DENISE: Sure you would.

CAROL: What, you don't believe me?

DENISE: Yeah I believe you, Mom.

CAROL: If you don't believe me come out here and look into my eyes. Like you used to when you were little. Look into my eyes and you'll see that I mean business.

DENISE comes out of the bathroom.

DENISE: I'm not gonna look in your eyes, Mom. I haven't got time for that shit anymore. I'm gonna try to stop the bleeding with this cloth. That's what I'm gonna do. After that we'll see.

CAROL: We'll see what

DENISE: What happens.

CAROL: I'm not going to the hospital. That's one thing that's not gonna happen.

DENISE: Okay then. Stay here and die.

CAROL: What's wrong with you.

DENISE: Nothing.

CAROL: What's this attitude you've got.

DENISE: Right. I'm the one with the attitude.

CAROL: You're mad. You're mad at me aren't you. It's like you think this is all my fault. I didn't do this to myself. Ray did this, Denise.

DENISE: I told you to get away from that asshole.

CAROL: You do think it's my fault.

DENISE: Last month when he pushed you down the stairs—

CAROL: That was an accident. I told you at the time.

DENISE: Yeah. And I told you he was going to put you in the hospital. Do you remember me saying that.

CAROL: No.

DENISE: Yes you do.

CAROL: What is this. What are you trying to prove.

DENISE: I told you. You heard me.

CAROL: Well you never liked him. I thought you were just being pissy about him because of that.

DENISE: He pushed you down the fucking stairs.

CAROL: That was an accident!

DENISE: Was this an accident.

CAROL: No this was a beating. I know the difference, Denise.

DENISE: Ah you're...you're a—

CAROL: A what.

DENISE: I gotta get some air. I'll go across the street and get us a couple of coffees, okay.

CAROL: I don't want a coffee.

DENISE: Whatever. I still need some air.

DENISE leaves. R.J. meets her at the door.

R.J.: Where you goin'?

DENISE: I need to just—

CAROL: She needs to get away from me.

R.J.: Hi Carol…. Ah man, look at you. Look what he did to you.

DENISE: Can you stay with her awhile.

R.J.: Sure. But where are you—

DENISE: Out. Just out. I'll be back.

DENISE leaves. R.J. is staring at CAROL.

CAROL: I haven't looked at myself in the mirror yet.

R.J.: Maybe you shouldn't.

CAROL: That bad, eh.

R.J.: Well it might…upset you. I dunno. You ever had your face punched in before.

CAROL: Well I've had a shiner, yeah.

R.J.: Well maybe you could look…tomorrow. Maybe after the swelling goes down or something.

CAROL: Can you close the door. I'm getting a little nervous with it open.

R.J.: What. You worried about Ray?

CAROL: Did you see any sign of him out there.

R.J.: He wouldn't have followed you here would he.

CAROL: He wants to kill me.

R.J.: He said that?

CAROL: Yeah.

R.J.: But that's just something he said, right?

CAROL: He said it because he meant it. He's not the kind of guy who says something like that just to make a point…. Look now that we're talking about him I'm getting pretty nervous. Look out the window for me. See if there's a red Olds Cutlass out there anywhere.

R.J.: Ray drives a Chevy van, doesn't he.

CAROL: Please. Just go to the window and look for a red Olds Cutlass.

R.J.: Sure.

CAROL: A red Olds Cutlass convertible with a black top. I'm not sure what year.

R.J. is at the window.

R.J.: I don't see anything like that.... Shouldn't I be looking for the Chevy Van too.

CAROL: Forget the Chevy Van. Concentrate on the Cutlass.... So?

R.J.: No.... Nothing.

CAROL: Okay.... That's good.... Okay I feel better.

R.J.: Yeah you look better too.

CAROL: I do?

R.J.: Not really.

CAROL: So what the hell are you talking about.

R.J.: Well you said you felt better. And I was just trying—

CAROL: I meant I felt more at ease. Look I have to go to the bathroom. Do you think you could help me.

R.J.: I'm...not sure what you mean.

CAROL: I mean help me into the bathroom.

R.J.: Oh yeah I could do that.

He goes over. Helps her up.

R.J.: So you mean just take you in there...and...then leave.... You don't need me to stay or anything.

CAROL: What's wrong with you. Why are you talking like an idiot.

They are going to the bathroom. She is leaning on him.

R.J.: I heard one of the doctors say you might have a bruised kidney.... I didn't know if you might need me to...massage it or something.

CAROL: The stuff that comes out of your mouth R.J.... Where do you get that stuff.

R.J.: I think I saw a medical show. On one of those life stations. I remember something about massaging a kidney.

CAROL: Well you don't have to massage mine. I mean even if my kidney did need massaging it's not likely I'd ask you to do it. You're my son-in-law for chrissake.

They are in the bathroom.

R.J.: Are you okay now?

CAROL: Yeah.

R.J.: I can leave now?

CAROL: Please.

R.J. comes out.

CAROL: R.J.?... It's Denise isn't it. She's told you so many bad things about me it just makes you really nervous to be around me.

R.J.: She hasn't told me anything bad about you, Carol. I mean she some-times talks about your life.... Things that happened to you both.... But I don't think she blames you...not really...not for everything.

CAROL: Yeah right.

R.J.: No...I mean, you know Denise. She's got attitude. About everything... About you and me... About everything really so—

CAROL: R.J.?

R.J.: Yeah?

CAROL: Can you close the door?

R.J.: Sure.

He turns. Leans in to get door handle. Stops.

CAROL: What are you staring at.

R.J.: That...bruise on your...thigh.

CAROL: Close the door.

R.J.: Okay.

R.J. is closing the door.

CAROL: And take another look for that Olds Cutlass.

R.J.: Okay.

> *R.J. Closes the door. DENISE comes in. Carrying three take-out coffees.*

R.J.: Hi.

DENISE: Where is she.

R.J.: In the bathroom… Wait I gotta do something before I forget.

> *R.J. goes to window. Looks out.*

DENISE: Whatya doing.

R.J.: Your mom's worried Ray might have followed her here.

DENISE: You looking for his van?

R.J.: No. She wanted me to look for an Olds Cutlass.

> *DENISE puts the coffees down. Fast. Turns on R.J.*

DENISE: A red Olds Cutlass convertible?

R.J.: Yeah.

DENISE: Shit…. Fucking shit!

> *She bangs on the bathroom door.*

DENISE: Mom! Mom, get out here! Mom you get out here now or I'm gonna kick this fucking door down!…Mom!

R.J.: Denise, just—

DENISE: Be quiet! …Mom! I mean it!

R.J.: She might be having trouble…. She's got a bruised kidney, Denise.

DENISE: I told you to be quiet! Mom! Come on out!

> *The door opens. CAROL is standing there. In her underwear. Her skirt around her ankles. There is an enormous bruise on one of her legs.*

CAROL: It wasn't locked. You could have just opened it and come in. And we could have talked in a normal way. But that's not your style is it.

DENISE: Pull up your skirt.

CAROL: I was getting ready to have a shower.

DENISE: Yeah. But for now can you pull up your skirt. Jesus.

> *CAROL pulls up her skirt.*

DENISE: Why is R.J. looking for a red Cutlass, Mom. Doesn't Steamboat Jeffries drive a red Cutlass.

CAROL: I think maybe...he used to.

DENISE: Used to?

CAROL: Well it's been a long time since I had anything to do with Steamboat Jeffries, honey.

DENISE: You fucking liar.

CAROL: Who are you calling a fucking liar, Denise. I'm your mother. There's no way you should be talking to me like that. Especially when I'm in pain. What's wrong with you. There must be something wrong with you.

DENISE: Ray didn't beat you up, did he.

CAROL: Help me into that chair.

DENISE: Help yourself.

R.J.: Denise.

DENISE: Stay out of this.

CAROL: He's just being nice.

DENISE: Answer my question. Why won't you answer my question.

CAROL: I didn't hear you ask a question.

R.J. looks at his watch. Makes his way over to the TV.

DENISE: I'm asking you, now that we have this information about a red Cutlass out in the open if you still want to stick to your original story about Ray beating you up.

CAROL: If it's good enough for the police Denise, it should be good enough for you.

DENISE: You told the police Ray beat you up. You actually named him to the police?

CAROL: Well the hospital called them, and I had to tell them something.

R.J. turns on the TV.

DENISE: Turn that off.

R.J.: In a minute.

CAROL: I mean I didn't actually name him. I gave a general description of a guy who I said I met in a bar. Because well I still have some feelings for Ray and—

R.J. is slowing turning up the volume.

DENISE: You fucking liar.

CAROL: *(to R.J.)* There she goes again with that fucking liar comment. There's something wrong with her. Really. Denise, why are you talking to me like this.

DENISE: Steamboat Jeffries had you beat up because you screwed him somehow. You were doing a job for him and you…. What…. What did you do. What was the job. Were you carrying something for him. Were you meeting someone to hand something over! What!

CAROL: I'm denying any connection to Steamboat Jeffries.

DENISE: Don't give me that crap. You're not talking to your lawyer.

CAROL: I might as well be with all the warmth and understanding I'm getting from you.

DENISE: I just want you to tell me the truth…. R.J. turn the fucking television off.

R.J.: Yeah in a minute.

DENISE: *(to CAROL)* You got in deep with that slimehole again. You screwed up bad, and he had you mauled. And we both know what that guy starts he's gonna want to finish. So you better level with me. Because this affects us all. We're all in danger here.

CAROL: You can leave.

DENISE: I will leave, Mom. I'll take R.J. and get the hell out of here unless you're honest with me. We'll just go back to our life. You know, the one we were trying to straighten out. I mean that's basically what we were doing when you called from the emergency room. Trying to live. Trying to leave all the shit behind us.

CAROL: You can't leave the shit behind. It's an ocean of shit. It's all around you.

DENISE: Same old mom. Always an encouraging word…. Come on, I need you to tell me the truth here!

CAROL: Okay! Okay. Believe it or not the reason I didn't tell you is because I knew you'd get upset. But here you are upset just the same. So I give up. I mean what's the point of me even trying to protect your emotional well-being if you're gonna go around in a constant state of anger and suspicion anyway.

DENISE: Constant? Please. You think I'm like this when I'm not with you?

CAROL: Well anyway, you're right. Good for you. Steamboat had one of his associates pay me a visit because he's convinced I set him up on a deal involving—

DENISE: Hold on for a second... R.J. R.J.! Turn it off!!

R.J.: I've been waiting all week for this. It's National Geographic's "Lions of the Serengeti." It tells the story of one particular lion and the difficulties of her life.

DENISE: Turn it off.

R.J.: You see there's this pack of hyenas. One hyena has this thing for Lyla. That's the lion. Anyway the hyena hates Lyla in an almost personal way. And that's a really weird thing for a hyena. So—

CAROL: You've seen it before?

R.J.: Part One. This is Part Two.

CAROL: Let him watch it. We can talk later. So R.J. you watch a lot of TV?

R.J.: Quite a bit, yeah. Well I started in prison.

CAROL: Really.... (to DENISE) Some guys learn a trade in prison.

DENISE: All prison did for R.J. was get him addicted to television.

R.J.: I'm not addicted.

DENISE: So turn it off.

R.J.: No.

DENISE: I need to talk to my mother about this mess she's in. It's a pretty heavy thing R.J. It could be the end of everything. It could mean that we get killed.

R.J.: I'll turn down the sound a bit.

He does.

DENISE: Jesus.

CAROL: Who said anything about getting killed.... Okay. Sure we could get killed. But maybe it won't turn out that way. Maybe with your help I can find a way out of this mess.

DENISE leans against a wall.

DENISE: This is my life. Basically this is it. You and him. The two of you. That's basically my life right now. I mean, what I'm getting at is...is it even worth the effort.

CAROL: Nice talk. *(to R.J.)* Did you hear what she just said R.J.?

R.J.: Ah. Look at that. She's had a litter.

DENISE slides down the wall onto the floor.
Blackout.

Scene Two

CAROL is sitting at the table. Eating a bowl of takeout soup. Smoking a cigarette. R.J. is flicking the TV's remote. The sound is down and R.J. is explaining a few things to CAROL. There is another bowl of soup on the table.

R.J.: I think the biggest problem you have to solve is the depressing feeling that hits you when the program is interrupted by commercials. I mean if you're really into the show it's like life has just stopped. It's that bad. It's that depressing. It's like God has all of a sudden stopped everything and what are you supposed to do. Just wait? Because that thirty seconds, that minute, that minute and a half is just like forever. And you hate them. The commercials. If you're really into the show you hate them a lot and promise yourself you'll never buy that product. In fact, fuck it, you don't even pay attention. You don't even wanna know what the product is. You feel that intense about it.... It was the sit-com that solved that problem for me. It was when the networks started programming a whole evening of funny shows together. I mean how strung out can you get watching lighthearted family entertainment. It's like taking a pill. They make you feel nice. I even started liking some of the commercials. Cats in commercials were very big at this time. I mean let's not kid ourselves. This wasn't any golden age of television comedy. There were no Barney Millers here. No Rhodas. I've seen those shows on late-night re-runs. And I'm impressed. No. These ones were mostly about families and everybody talked too loud and only a few of the jokes ever worked. But it was enough to chill me out. The detective show, that's something else. I feel nothing for them. Nothing. Anyway, everything after Colombo is crap. Colombo, McCloud, Hart to Hart, Cagney and Lacey. Shows around that time, they had...class. I've got a friend who has copies of Hart to Hart that he's been watching for ten years. That's five years in prison and five on the outside and he's still a loyal fan…My thing is reality. I turned into a reality fan with the talk shows. But I got hooked…. All those people with all those problems. It was too much. I got too emotional. Sometimes I couldn't sleep, thinking about those people. So I moved off the talk shows into cooking and maintenance shows. This was with the coming of age of cable, in the last couple of years. You know, the "life" channels. How to Do Everything basically. I love those. On Sundays on one of those channels there are nine cooking shows in a row. Chinese, Thai, Italian, French, Indian, Mexican, Ethiopian, Vietnamese, Dutch…. It's a great time for me. Totally relaxing. And you know how I feel about wildlife shows. They're the best…. I saw one once about a snake. A fucking snake. And by the end of it I felt like I knew this snake personally. I mean, sure I knew where it lived, and what it ate, how much venom it could inject into its victims, but really I think I knew how it felt, what made it tick. That show was awesome. It changed my life. I'm sure it did. I don't know how. But I feel better than I did before I saw that show…. I mean a snake.. A snake…

CAROL: Your soup's getting cold…

R.J.: Yeah… That soup's good cold though. I can eat it cold.

CAROL: Sit down.

R.J.: I'm thinking about that snake.

CAROL: I know. Sit down and eat your soup.

R.J.: Sure. *(he sits)*

CAROL: So basically television is your life?

R.J.: No way…. It's important. But it's not my life. It's part of my life… Do you understand that. The difference, I mean?

CAROL: Sure. It's like I feel about gambling…. I could live without it. But why bother.

R.J.: No no. That's different. Gambling has gotten you into a lot of trouble.

CAROL: Trouble? You call this trouble?

R.J.: Yeah I do. You're beat up. Someone is maybe gonna kill you.

CAROL: No! Trouble is when you have no reason to live. Don't you get it.

R.J.: You live to gamble?

CAROL: When I'm living, I'm gambling. Listen maybe you don't understand it because you haven't seen it on TV. Denise told me that about you once. "If he hasn't seen some guy on TV doing it he doesn't really get it."

R.J.: That's bullshit... That's just Denise giving me the gears.

CAROL: Wait a minute. How about those shows you like.... Someone's out there with those animals. That's a gamble.

R.J.: Who's out there. No one's out there. The whole point of these shows is not to disturb the animals in their natural world.

CAROL: Well someone is working the camera.

R.J.: Maybe.

CAROL: Whatya mean maybe.

R.J.: It could be a remote.

CAROL: Jesus. Look, all I'm saying is feeling like you're taking a risk can make life...okay.... That's all I'm saying. Because life isn't really okay at all. So it's good if you can feel that it is...sometimes.

R.J.: Are you saying I'm not taking enough risks.

CAROL: You used to be wild. When Denise first met you, you were wild.

R.J.: I was fucked up, Carol.

CAROL: Yeah but interesting.

R.J.: You hated me, remember?

CAROL: I'm not saying I didn't.

R.J.: Twice I almost got killed. I spent three years inside. Two on probation. That was a bad time.

CAROL: Yeah, but that's also when Denise fell for you.

R.J.: Yeah well she was fucked up too.

CAROL: I'm not saying she wasn't. Yeah. She was messed up. And wild herself. I'm just saying she saw something in you.... You might want to stay in touch with that guy a little is all I'm saying.... Just keep a little of the old R.J. in your mind. Just remember what he was like in case you need to...resurrect him. Just in case Denise gets bored. Because Denise can get bored.... Sure she can get pissed off, we all know that. But she can also get bored.

R.J.: Bored.... Bored with me?

CAROL: Why not.... I mean you do watch an awful lot of television. How interesting can that be for her.

R.J.: So whatya saying.... I should go commit a crime or something.

CAROL: I'm definitely not saying that.

R.J.: I'm glad you're not saying that. Because you would be misreading the situation if you think that would go down good with Denise. If I fuck up again she'll kill me.

CAROL: All I'm saying is the old R.J. would be sympathetic to someone in my position.

R.J.: I'm sympathetic.

CAROL: Enough to help?

R.J.: I'm helping... I went out for soup.

CAROL: But if I were to ask for a favour. Something maybe involving risk...something the old R.J. would have done...but something maybe we should keep from Denise—

R.J.: Wait. You want me to do something for you without telling Denise.

CAROL: Basically. Yes.

R.J.: Something involving risk?

CAROL: There would be risk.

R.J.: So...if I'm supposed to be doing this so Denise doesn't think I'm boring...how come I can't tell her.

CAROL: Because what Denise needs to know and what she wants to know and also what she secretly admires as opposed to what she says she hates is not always clear.... Get it?

R.J.: No.

CAROL: Think about it.

R.J.: I don't want to think about it.

CAROL: Why not.

R.J.: Because I don't understand it. And when I think about things I don't understand I get depressed.... Maybe that's why I like shows about birds and snakes.

CAROL: All I'm saying is Denise is complicated. There are a few Denises really. Never bet on one Denise when you could bet on them all.

Including the Denise who gets bored with someone even when she doesn't want to.

R.J.: Just so I know…. In case I want to, you know, think about it, what would you want me to do.

CAROL: Once you're told, you're told. You'd have to do it then.

R.J.: Why.

CAROL: I can't tell you without telling you. Do you want me to tell you.

R.J.: No…. Not yet.

   DENISE comes in. Carrying a grocery bag.

R.J.: Hi.

DENISE: Hi. How are we doing.

CAROL: He brought me soup.

DENISE: Yeah, he's a sweetie. *(she pinches his cheek)* See anything good on TV today?

R.J.: Whatya mean by that.

DENISE: Just asking…

R.J.: I took the day off work to be with your mother. To watch over her.

DENISE: Yeah. I know that.

R.J.: I didn't do that so I could watch TV.

DENISE: So are you saying you didn't watch any TV.

R.J.: That's not…the point, is it

DENISE: What's your problem, R.J.

R.J.: Nothing…. I need some air.

DENISE: Sure.

R.J.: Is that okay. You're here now. I just need some air.

DENISE: Go ahead.

R.J.: Thanks.

   He grabs his coat. Leaves.

DENISE: What did you say to him.

CAROL: Nothing.

DENISE: Sure you did. You messed with his head somehow. Whatever you're doing to him, stop it. We don't have time for me to undo any damage you cause by confusing him.

CAROL: You talk about him like you think he's a child.

DENISE: Do I? Do you have some advice to give me about that. Will you be giving it to me now or should we wait until I tell you what I found out about Steamboat Jeffries.

CAROL: You saw him?

DENISE: I talked to him on the phone.

CAROL: What lies did he tell you about me.

DENISE: What lies do you think he told me.

CAROL: I could only guess.

DENISE: Well if your guess is anything less than thirty-five thousand dollars you're wrong.

CAROL: He said I stole that much from him. He's lying.

DENISE: I know.

CAROL: You believe me?

DENISE: About what.

CAROL: That he's lying. That I didn't steal any money from him.

DENISE: No. I think he's lying. I think you're lying too. I think I'm stuck in the middle between two lowlife liars. And to keep myself from going nuts until I figure a way out, all I'm gonna do is deliver messages. His message to you is he wants his thirty-five thousand in twelve hours or he finds you and kills you. Now what's your message to him. I have to call him back in... (*looks at her watch*) five minutes.

CAROL: Tell him to fuck off and die.

DENISE: That's it? Nothing else.

CAROL: Tell him Murray Lawson has his money. Tell him Murray Lawson left on a bus this morning going...south. Also tell him I want compensation for the beating he had inflicted on me. I think five thousand will do the trick.

DENISE: You're a piece of work.

CAROL: I think you should get behind your mother on this, Denise. I don't think being neutral is a good choice.

DENISE: So let me see if I've got this straight. Fuck off and die. Murray Lawson. Bus heading south. Five thousand for pain and suffering.

CAROL: Or I'll go to the police.

DENISE: Oh here's a new wrinkle. Our family hasn't gone to the police in, what, three generations?

CAROL: I'm willing to break the tradition for what that fat fuck did to me.

DENISE: You'll go to the police and do what?

CAROL: Tell them stuff. Stuff about Steamboat and all his…business activities.

DENISE: So you wanna go that route. You wanna threaten him. You think that's our best chance here.

CAROL: Call him. Tell him.

DENISE: I will.

DENISE goes to phone.

DENISE: Look Mom. I'm picking up the phone. I'm about to dial a number and threaten a guy who could have us all blown away by sundown. Here I go…. You're sure about this?

CAROL: Definitely.

DENISE: Okay.

DENISE punches in a number.

DENISE: *(into phone)* Hi…It's Denise. Can I talk to Steamboat.

CAROL: Hold on a second.

DENISE covers the receiver.

DENISE: Having second thoughts?

CAROL: Hang up…. I need time to think.

DENISE: About what.

CAROL: Hang up!

DENISE: The truth? Are you considering telling me the truth here. That would be worth hanging up for. Otherwise I think I'll just go ahead with that threat thing.

CAROL: Okay! The truth. I'll give you the truth if you hang up.

DENISE: Give me a taste now. Just to see if you can actually tell the truth. I mean it's been a long time, mom. Maybe you've lost the knack.

CAROL: It's not thirty-five thousand. It's actually sixty-eight thousand. He just hasn't found out about the rest yet.

DENISE: Great.

She hangs up.

DENISE: Great…. You stole sixty-eight thousand dollars from fucking Steamboat Jeffries.

CAROL: It was Murray Lawson's idea. I'll tell you about it.

DENISE: Go ahead.

CAROL: I need to pee.

DENISE: Go ahead.

CAROL: I need help.

DENISE helps her up.

DENISE: You didn't need help earlier. You were moving around okay.

CAROL: I've stiffened up since then. I can…barely move.

They are going into the bathroom.

DENISE: How did you meet up with Murray Lawson again. I thought he was training horses in the Bahamas or someplace.

CAROL: No. He's back. I'll tell you everything after I pee. Promise.

They are in the bathroom. R.J. comes in.

R.J.: Are you in the bathroom.

DENISE: *(from bathroom)* She needed a little help.

R.J. looks around. Goes over to TV. Stares at it. DENISE comes out of the bathroom.

DENISE: Feeling better?

R.J.: I love television.

DENISE: I know.

R.J.: I love it… .But I'd give it up for you.

DENISE: Why would you have to give it up for me.

R.J.: If you wanted me to.

DENISE: Why would I want you to.

R.J.: If you ever wanted me to...do something else. Be the kind of guy who...does something else.

DENISE: I'm not getting what you're—

CAROL: *(from bathroom)* There's no toilet paper in here!

DENISE: *(to R.J.)* Would you go to the office and get more toilet paper.

R.J.: Sure. *(he starts off)*

DENISE: You're a sweetie.

R.J.: When did you start calling me sweetie.

DENISE: I...don't know.

R.J.: I just noticed you doing that.

DENISE: I think I've done it for awhile.... You don't like it?

R.J.: I just noticed it.

DENISE: Did my mom say anything to you before.

R.J.: About what.

DENISE: Anything.... Did she say something that...confused you.

R.J.: Hey... Hey. I watch television, okay. That doesn't mean I'm soft-headed.... Jesus.

   R.J. leaves.

DENISE: Mom. I should call Steamboat back. If you're gonna tell me the story you should tell me so maybe we can figure a way out of this.... If I don't call him back he'll have his guys start looking for us.... Mom?

CAROL: *(from bathroom)* There's blood in my urine.

DENISE: Really?

CAROL: Should I be concerned?

DENISE: Yes! God! We should probably get you to the—

CAROL: No no it's okay! I just remembered. It's all those beets in that borscht soup stuff. I had two bowls... I had one earlier. Then I sent R.J.

out for another one. It's okay. It's just the soup.... Sorry to worry you. Do you forgive me, honey! Do you!?

DENISE sits.

DENISE: Yeah. Sure.

Blackout.

Scene Three

Later. CAROL is in bed with MICHAEL. Foreplay.

CAROL: Ah.... Be careful honey. I've got sore points all over my body.

MICHAEL: Okay.... Should I not touch you?

CAROL: What's the point if you don't touch me? Just be careful.

MICHAEL: Okay...okay...yeah. Is this okay.

CAROL: Oh yeah...that's fine.... Oh be careful.... I'm bruised. Very near there is where I've got a bruise.

MICHAEL: I'm sorry.

CAROL: I'm just letting you know. It's okay where you are...but a little further is a big bruise.... Okay?

MICHAEL: Listen. Maybe we should stop.

CAROL: We just started.

MICHAEL: Yeah but...you've got a lot of...bruises.

CAROL: You're nervous aren't you. I've made you nervous.

MICHAEL: I don't wanna hurt you.

CAROL: Ah you're sweet.... That's nice.... I tell you what. Let's forget the bruises. Let's just go for it.

MICHAEL: Really? You're sure.

CAROL: Yeah. Let's get going. If we get going really good then I'm not gonna feel the pain anyway because...well because... So let's just go for it. Okay?

MICHAEL: Okay. Yeah okay...

They kiss. They move around a bit.

CAROL: Ah. Jesus.

MICHAEL: What.

CAROL: Nothing.

More movement.

CAROL: Ah Jesus.

MICHAEL: Is it okay.

CAROL: It's getting…better.

More movement.

CAROL: Oh fuck! Oh Jesus!

MICHAEL sits up.

MICHAEL: I have to stop.

CAROL: Why.

MICHAEL: You're screaming in pain…. I can't get into it when you're in pain.

CAROL: Ah what a sweet guy. Really…. But let me worry about that, okay…. Okay?

MICHAEL: I don't know…

CAROL: Sure you do. Come here.

She pulls him down.

CAROL: Ah shit. You landed on my fucking ribs!

DENISE comes in. Carrying a bag of groceries.

DENISE: Oh look. Mommy's in bed with a total stranger…. Now there's a blast from the past.

CAROL and MICHAEL stop moving.

CAROL: Hi, honey.

DENISE puts the bag down on the table.

DENISE: I bought groceries. Lots of canned items. Tuna. Devilled ham. Spaghettios. All your favourites. So when you're in here hiding and afraid for your life you'll at least have the comfort of food.

CAROL: Denise, this is Michael.

MICHAEL: Hi.

DENISE: You like Spaghettios, Michael?

MICHAEL: Well I'm not sure I've ever—

DENISE: Tuna? Do you like tuna.

MICHAEL: Yeah. I like tuna a lot.

DENISE: You hear that Mom. He likes tuna. A lot. But you must have sensed that. That must be what brought the two of you together. So. What happened? You come in here to repair something Michael? You walked in to look at the plumbing and my mother picked up that really strong tuna lover's vibe you send out, ripped off your clothes and threw you on the bed.

CAROL: You seem a little hyper, honey.

DENISE: Do I. I wonder why.

CAROL: Michael and I were merely sharing an adult moment here. Aren't I entitled to that.

DENISE: No, Mom. You're not.

CAROL: Really. Since when, Denise. Since when do you tell me what I can do.

DENISE: Hey it's not me. It's the rules of...you know...society.... It's basic behaviour stuff.... When you've screwed up so bad that your life and the lives of your family members are in serious danger—no fucking!

MICHAEL: I think I should leave.

DENISE: So do I.

CAROL: Why should he leave. He's not hurting anyone. He just lying here beside me. Showing me some affection.

DENISE: Well maybe I'm weird Mom. But I don't want him showing you affection in front of me.

CAROL: Well he's not showing me affection at this very moment, Denise. I meant he was just—

DENISE: Michael. Have you got anything on.

MICHAEL: You mean am I wearing a condom?

DENISE: No. I mean are you wearing anything.

MICHAEL: Ah. Yeah.... Underwear.

DENISE: Good. So… You can get up and—

MICHAEL: Yeah I'll just get up and—

CAROL: Stay put if you want to Michael.

DENISE: Either he goes or I go. Him or me. Make a decision. Right now.

CAROL: You better go, Michael. There's no point arguing with her when she's like this. She's hyper. And she doesn't care about anyone else's feelings.

DENISE: Jesus.

MICHAEL: *(getting up)* I'll just grab my stuff and… Is it okay if I get dressed in the bathroom.

MICHAEL is gathering his clothes.

DENISE: Yeah.

MICHAEL: Thanks.

MICHAEL goes into the bathroom. Closes door.

CAROL: He could help. I detect abilities in him. He seems able and reasonably smart. And I can tell he's already devoted to me…. So…. He can help.

DENISE: Help with what.

CAROL: Our problem with Steamboat.

DENISE: I don't think we should get anyone else involved.

CAROL: I think we should get anyone involved who can help. We are talking about my life here.

DENISE: Who is he.

CAROL: He's…Michael.

DENISE: How'd you meet him.

CAROL: He was making a movie next door. There was too much noise. I couldn't sleep. I banged on the wall. He came over to apologize. The rest is just the occurrence of a natural event.

DENISE: Yeah…. A movie? What kind of movie.

CAROL: What kind of movie gets made in a motel room.

DENISE: Jesus. So he's a porn director.

CAROL: Yeah.

DENISE: You were having sex with a porn director.

CAROL: You say that like it's a bad thing, honey. Why is that. He has to make a living doesn't he.... As I remember you were once involved in the sex trade. Or have you forgotten.

DENISE: No, Mom. I can vaguely remember.

CAROL: I didn't say that to make you feel bad.

DENISE: You didn't?

CAROL: I'm just reminding you that people shouldn't be judged for what they do for a living necessarily.

DENISE: Are you just going to lie there, Mom. You don't want to get up or anything? Brush your hair? Wash the saliva off your face?

CAROL: I'm not feeling that well. In the heat of the moment I think I might have aggravated some of my injuries. Do we have any painkillers left.

DENISE: I don't know.

CAROL: Could you look.

DENISE: Look where.

CAROL: In the bathroom.

DENISE knocks on the door.

DENISE: How you doin' in there, Michael.

MICHAEL: *(from bathroom)* Almost finished.... I heard what you said.... I'm looking for those pain killers.

CAROL: Isn't he sweet.

DENISE: Yeah he's delightful.... By the way, Mom. Where's R.J.

CAROL: R.J.? I don't know where R.J. is. Why should I know that.

DENISE: Well when I left he was here. Is he still here. No. So he must have gone somewhere. Are you with me so far.

CAROL: Well.... Maybe he followed you.

DENISE: What are you talking about. Why would he follow me.

CAROL: You were going to the track. Maybe he thinks a racetrack is a dangerous place.

DENISE: Why would he think that.

CAROL: I don't know what goes on in R.J.'s head Denise. Maybe he saw something on TV about a race track or something. The point is, maybe going to that track to nose around had consequences you didn't think about.

DENISE: Really.... Well I didn't have much choice. You hardly tell me anything. And anything you do tell me I'm not sure I can believe.

CAROL: Don't worry so much about believing me, Denise. And just concentrate more on getting on my side.

DENISE: What? What's that mean.

CAROL: Well did you find out anything at the track. No. And I said you wouldn't. So maybe you should stop running around all hyper and distrustful and let me handle this in my own way. And if R.J. has, you know, disappeared...don't blame me.

The bathroom door opens. MICHAEL comes out.

MICHAEL: Hi.

DENISE: Hi. *(to Carol)* Whatya mean if he's disappeared.

MICHAEL: Ah...I couldn't help overhearing—

DENISE: Sure you could. All you had to do was not listen.

MICHAEL: I mean I'd like to help. Your mother filled me in. Before.

DENISE: She what?

MICHAEL: I mean I'm up to scratch on your predicament. And I'm—

DENISE: You told him?

CAROL: I thought he could be trusted.

MICHAEL: She's right. I can be trusted. I've had a bit of experience with Steamboat Jeffries myself. So I know what you're dealing with here.

DENISE: Really. Did you steal sixty-eight thousand dollars from him.

MICHAEL: No but I've done him some favours. I've hustled up girls for a few of his clubs and—

DENISE: Ah man I'm not going to want to hear this shit.

MICHAEL: No I never procured. I mean I just cut costs for him in a few instances. All I'm saying is maybe I could intervene...in this instance.

DENISE: Do you have sixty-eight thousand dollars to give him.

MICHAEL: No.

DENISE: Well there goes that idea.... Nice to meet you anyway. *(she goes to door, opens it)* If you're ever making another skin flick in the area just drop by. If we're not dead we'll be glad to see you.

CAROL: I think you should take something, Denise. When you were young and you got hyper like this I always gave you something.

DENISE: *(to MICHAEL)* A shot of vodka. She gave me a shot of vodka.

CAROL: Well it worked.

DENISE: *(to MICHAEL)* She gave me vodka when I was nine, ten years old.

CAROL: I was advised to do that.

DENISE: *(to MICHAEL)* By a vet. She had a friend who took care of horses. A horse doctor advised her to liquor me up.

CAROL: I was desperate. You got hyper and it was scary. Hyper just like you are now. If I had any vodka don't think I wouldn't try to give it to you either. It worked then. It'd work now.

DENISE: Well, Michael. Now that you've heard a little of the family history I'm sure you're eager to be on your way.

MICHAEL: Well the truth is—

DENISE: Ah shit!

DENISE has seen something coming.

DENISE: Ah my God.

And R.J. appears. He has been beaten. Not too bad, but he has a cut on his nose. And his shirt is ripped.

DENISE: What happened to you. Where have you been.

R.J.: Didn't your mother tell you.

R.J. comes in.

DENISE: She said she didn't know.

CAROL: I didn't want to worry you.

R.J.: I went on an...errand for her. *(to MICHAEL)* Who are you. Haven't I seen you before.

MICHAEL: This morning. I asked you for change for the Coke machine.

R.J.: Yeah. And you were with those two hookers.

MICHAEL: Well actually they're ac—

DENISE: *(to MICHAEL)* Excuse me. You have to leave now.

MICHAEL: Sure. But maybe I can help.

DENISE: If we need help you'll be the first one we'll call.

CAROL: You better leave Michael. There's no arguing with her when she's like this.

DENISE: She's right Michael. When I'm like this I'm a total asshole.

MICHAEL: It's okay. No need to apologize.

DENISE: Jesus.

MICHAEL: See ya, Carol.

CAROL: You were great, sweetie. Strong. Considerate. The best.

DENISE: Jesus.

She pushes MICHAEL out the door. Closes it.

DENISE: *(to R.J.)* What kind of errand. What happened.

CAROL: Now is probably not a good time to tell you, Denise. With you being so hyper I mean.

R.J.: Are you hyper, Denise.

DENISE: A bit. What happened.

R.J.: I went to— Are you all right, Carol. Why are you in bed.

DENISE grabs R.J.

DENISE: She's sick! She's very sick. She was screwing Michael's brains out and she reinjured herself. Okay? Now what the fuck happened?!

R.J.: Murray Lawson didn't go south on a bus. He's hiding in a hotel downtown.

DENISE: How do you know that.

R.J.: *(points to CAROL)* She told me.

DENISE: She told you. And you believed her?

R.J.: She said he'd be in this particular hotel. And he was.

DENISE: You saw him.

R.J.: Not exactly…. But he's registered there.

DENISE: *(to CAROL)* Didn't you tell us he was heading south on a bus.

CAROL: No. I told you that's what I wanted you to tell Steamboat Jeffries.

DENISE: *(to R.J.)* Is that true. I don't think that's true. I think she lied to us about that.

R.J.: What's it matter.

DENISE: Whatya mean what's it matter.

R.J.: I mean we're beyond that. We're beyond who was lying and when. Or if they were lying and why. We're somewhere else now.

DENISE: Yeah? Where are we.

R.J.: We're in the shit.

DENISE: You mean deeper in the shit?

R.J.: Definitely deeper. I went to see Murray Lawson like Carol asked me and—

DENISE: *(to CAROL)* Like you asked him. Jesus, Mom. What's wrong with you. You have no right asking him to do something like that.

R.J.: Forget blaming her. We don't have time for that. We're beyond blame.

CAROL: Did you hear that, Denise. We're beyond blame. Maybe that could be your motto from now on. What good is blame anyway. Especially in a family. It just poisons the—

DENISE: Be quiet. *(to R.J.)* Go ahead.

R.J.: I go to his room. I go to his room to make a simple request. I'm planning to tell him I just want the original thirty-five thousand they "borrowed" from Steamboat back. He can keep the other thirty-three thousand they made by betting Steamboat's money. *(to CAROL)* That's what you wanted me to tell him, right.

CAROL: Well actually I wanted you to suggest he pay me a commission on that thirty-three thousand if you remember.

R.J.: But I told you I wouldn't do that.

CAROL: But I thought you would.

R.J.: Why would you think I would when I told you I wouldn't.

CAROL: Because that's the way you are. You…change your mind sometimes.

R.J.: You mean I'm weak.

CAROL: I didn't say that.

R.J.: *(to DENISE)* She thinks I'm weak. She thinks you think I'm weak too. She thinks I watch too much television and I don't take enough risks.

DENISE: Don't worry about what she thinks.

R.J.: It's too late for that now. If I wasn't worried about what she thought I wouldn't have gone on the errand. *(to CAROL)* Which I did by the way, never intending to ask Murray Lawson for a fucking commission on that thirty thousand. I had only one intention. And that was to get Steamboat's money back to him. So we could get you out of this mess and go back to our normal lives.

DENISE: But that didn't work out.

R.J.: You could say that.

DENISE: Murray wasn't agreeable. You had...a conflict with Murray.

R.J.: Murray wasn't there. I knocked on the door and Steamboat Jeffries answered.

DENISE: Really? Ah shit. So Steamboat Jeffries did that to your face.

R.J.: Yeah. I think so. Maybe.

DENISE: You think so, maybe.

R.J.: Yeah well he could have done something to my face. Or I could have done it when I—I mean I'm not sure. Because I saw him there and...I passed out.

CAROL: Ah for chrissake.

R.J.: Hey. He's a big guy. He's huge. And he was mad. Very mad...an —I bet a lot of guys would have passed out.

CAROL: Yeah. Right.

DENISE: Mom. Back off.

CAROL: Don't get me wrong. There are certain things I like about the way R.J. is now.... But I gotta be honest. I miss the old R.J. That guy could kick a little ass if he had to. There's no way the old R.J. would have passed out. No way at all. The old R.J. would have stood his ground. And made a deal with Steamboat based on a mutually advantageous...you know...outcome.

R.J.: *(to CAROL)* He...was...mad. I thought he was going to kill me. He...lunged at me.

DENISE: So what happened then.

R.J.: I told you. I passed out. Why are you making me repeat it. Are you trying to humiliate me.

DENISE: I meant after...after you passed out. I mean you woke up at some point, didn't you.

R.J.: Yeah. In a park.

DENISE: In a park? By yourself?

R.J.: Yeah...

DENISE: And that's it? You woke up in a park.

R.J.: No that's not it. There was this note in my pocket..

He hands DENISE the note.

CAROL: What's it say.

DENISE: *(reading)* "The money by midnight. All sixty-eight thousand. And Murray Lawson too."

CAROL: No way.

DENISE: Mom.

CAROL: No way. I object to those terms. I'm not handing Murray Lawson over to them. I wouldn't do that even if I could. He's an old friend. A decent guy. And also why the hell should Steamboat get all sixty-eight thousand. All we did was borrow his thirty-five to make a bet. The winnings are ours. Murray's and mine. I strenuously object to the terms of this settlement.

R.J.: You can't.

CAROL: Whatya mean I can't.

R.J.: You can't. You can't object to anything.

CAROL: You can always negotiate, R.J. Always. It just takes backbone.

R.J.: There's something else.

DENISE: What.

R.J.: This.

He opens his jacket. Takes it off. He is wired with explosives.

DENISE: Oh...no...

R.J.: It's on a timer.

DENISE: Oh...my God...

R.J.: I think it might be controlled by a remote.

CAROL: Maybe it's not real. We should check it closely to see if it's real.

DENISE: No we're not going to do that Mom. We're not going to touch it.

CAROL: How are we going to tell if it's real.

DENISE: We're going to assume it's real.

R.J.: Yeah. That's what I'm assuming. I mean I'm not an expert but it seems real. So I don't think we should touch it or anything like that.... Okay? Okay!? *(he cries)*

DENISE: Okay, honey.... It's okay. We won't touch it. I promise!

CAROL: Come on. Let's pull ourselves together here.

She wraps herself in a sheet. And gets out of bed.

CAROL: We can't just let that fat prick dictate to us like this. We have to—

R.J.: Denise. Denise don't let her near me.

DENISE: Mom, stop.

CAROL: I was just going to—

R.J.: Please keep her away from me.

CAROL: Oh come on. I was just going to look at it more closely.

R.J.: She'll yank on it or something. I know it. She'll get close and pull a wire. Or move something. And then...I'll be dead.

CAROL: Well it's better to be dead than have that big piece of shit dictate the terms.

R.J.: *(to DENISE)* See?

DENISE: Mom. R.J. and I have a different position on this. You're going to have to respect our position. And just back off a bit. I mean it is his fucking body their fucking explosives are tied to.

CAROL: No, think about it. It's worth the risk. Let's just take a little closer look is all I'm saying. A little fiddling. A little nudge.

R.J.: Stay away from me.

DENISE: Mom. I'm asking you for the last time. Just...stop.

CAROL: Okay look, the worst is we could all get blown up. And yes, that's a lose lose situation. But suppose it's just a big pile of nothing. A cheap trick. Then we'll have an immediate advantage over that big fat evil asshole. I think it's worth the gamble. We've got good odds here. Based on my knowledge of Steamboat I'd say there's a fifty-fifty chance that device isn't real. And even if it is real, there's only about a one-in-three chance we could set it off by messing with it a bit.... So right away we're dealing with odds that are less than half of what you've got in getting a terminal illness.

R.J.: *(to DENISE)* What's wrong with her. What's she talking about. Where does she get all those odds from.

DENISE: She makes them up. That's what she does. She decides what she wants to do then she makes up odds that tell her it's okay to do it.

CAROL: I just feel good about this. That's all. I think it's the way to go. I think if we just stand up straight say, "Screw you Steamboat Jeffries" and just take that thing right off then we'll—

R.J.: Take it off? Now she's talking about taking it off.

DENISE: We're not taking it off, Mom.

CAROL: But suppose it's not real.

DENISE: We think it's real.

CAROL: The odds are better that it isn't.

R.J.: Says you.

CAROL: Well who's the gambler here.

DENISE: It's not going to happen Mom.

CAROL: Just let me take a closer look.

CAROL steps closer.

R.J.: Keep her away, Denise.

DENISE: Mom.

DENISE gets in front of R.J.

CAROL: I just think it's better for us to take some kind of action. It's been my experience that life really only pays off when you bet to win.

DENISE: Mom. Look at yourself.... Are you winning.

CAROL: Well honey. It's not over yet. I mean I'm still alive.... You know, I'm thinking if we could determine if Steamboat is bluffing we could probably find a way not only to hold on to that sixty-eight thousand but to maybe double it.

R.J.: What's she talking about.

DENISE: I don't know.

R.J.: She's edging nearer.

DENISE: Mom, we can see you getting closer. Don't think we can't see you.

CAROL: Steamboat is every rotten thing short of a killer. But he doesn't have the stomach for the big deed. I think what happened is, Murray saw that tub of lard coming, got out of his hotel room and took the money with him. Then Steamboat was presented with an opportunity to attach this phony device to R.J. because R.J. obliged him by passing out. I mean real explosives have to be handled in a certain way and a conscious guy could tell that these—

R.J.: *(to DENISE)* She seems to be blaming me for this. I mean if you listen to her it sounds like this whole mess comes down to me passing out. Not her stealing the guy's money to make a fucking bet on a fucking horse. But me passing out. Jesus.

CAROL: R.J.... Remember. It doesn't matter who's to blame. We're beyond blame, remember. If we can turn this around on Steamboat we can—

DENISE: I saw that, Mom. That little step. If you take another little step, I'm gonna take action. I'm gonna have to stop you even if it means hurting you.

CAROL: But I could be right, Denise. I—

DENISE: I mean it!

CAROL: Okay!.Okay okay. *(she sits on the bed)* But...but what is the purpose of life....

R.J. and DENISE look at each other.

CAROL: Well?

DENISE: Well what Mom.

CAROL: What is the purpose of life.

DENISE: All life?

CAROL: No. Just...your life. I ask that seriously, Denise. I mean I know you and R.J. are trying to be useful careful citizens. Hold down jobs. Put all your sins behind you. But what's in that for you really. You'll never get your kid back from social services. Never. I'm sorry, Denise. But it's not going to happen. You can go to that stupid clothing store where you work for the next five years, without missing a single day, and it still won't make those social workers trust you enough to give you back your daughter. Because to them you're a bad girl who's just pretending to be a good girl, and it's just a matter of time until you stop pretending and lead the life you have to lead.

DENISE: Really.... And what life is that.

CAROL: Well...I think you're the most unpredictable person I've ever met. You think I'm unpredictable. But really I just like to gamble. You're genuinely unpredictable, Denise. And eventually you'll have to —

DENISE: Okay Mom. Just get to it.

CAROL: This is your chance! We could turn this thing back on Steamboat and make a lot of money. You could take a chunk of that money. And you and R.J. could just grab your kid from that foster home, and the three of you could take off and start a new life together.

R.J.: You're not listening to any of this are you, Denise. I mean I know it's hard not to listen to her. But I listened to her and look at me. So Denise, don't—

DENISE: I'm not buying this Mom. I want you to understand that. I mean.... I have a question to ask you. But I want you to know I don't really believe a word you're saying. Okay?

CAROL: Sure, honey. Ask away.

DENISE: In what way does this being a fake explosive device give us the means to make a lot of money off Steamboat Jeffries.

CAROL: If I tell you will you consider letting me fiddle with it.

R.J.: No. She won't.

CAROL: If I tell you, Denise. And if it makes sense to you. I mean to the real you, Denise, the dangerous adventurous Denise, not the scared suspicious Denise—

R.J.: None of the Denises are going to listen to a word you say about this, Carol.

CAROL: I'm just asking for a chance to get us all free here. That's all I'm asking.... A chance to get us all free to...explore new directions in our lives.... So?

DENISE: Go ahead. Explain.

R.J.: Ah man.

DENISE: *(to R.J.)* Don't worry. I won't let her trick me. Go ahead, Mom. Explain.

CAROL: Okay, okay.... *(she gets up, begins to pace)* It's complicated... Well complicated isn't really right. It's unusual.... It requires some unusual thinking.... So let me just...let me just work it out in my mind a bit first...

She continues to pace.

R.J.: *(whispering)* She'll say anything. She's just itching to get her hands on this thing... I don't know why really.

DENISE: *(whispers)* It's a challenge. She can't help it.

R.J.: *(whispering)* She'll say anything.... Don't let her fool you. Listen carefully. Make sure what she says makes sense.

DENISE: *(whispering)* Okay. You too.

R.J.: *(whispering)* Me? I can't listen. I'm too scared. I'm scared...of this thing. I'm scared she's going to make a grab for it. I'm scared of passing out again and humiliating myself in front of you.

DENISE: Don't worry about that. You can pass out if you have to.

R.J.: I didn't say I had to pass out. I said I was afraid of passing out.

DENISE: Don't be afraid, sweetie.

R.J.: I'm not afraid. I'm afraid of passing out. Ah forget it. Don't call me sweetie, okay.

DENISE: Sure...

DENISE looks at her watch.

DENISE: It's ten after six.

R.J.: Yeah. So? It's okay. There's still plenty of time. The note said we had until midnight.

DENISE: Jeopardy is on. It's the first time in a year you haven't turned the TV on at six o'clock. I mean it really is like clockwork... You turn on the

TV, I check my watch to make sure it's keeping time. But just now...well something didn't feel right and I just checked my watch for some reason I didn't understand...and then it hit me...you know...Jeopardy.

R.J.: So what's your point.

DENISE: I'm just saying—

R.J.: What, is that the old Denise talking. Is the old Denise saying it sure is more exciting and unfucking-predictable that instead of watching Jeopardy every night I'm now out getting explosives tied to my body.

CAROL: Okay. I think I've got it.

R.J.: Great. Count me in!

DENISE: R.J., come on.

R.J.: No. No matter what, I'm in. Let's go for it. Let's poke away at this thing and fuck the consequences.

CAROL: Is he serious.

DENISE: No.

CAROL: He sounds serious.

DENISE: I hurt his feelings.

R.J.: You didn't hurt my feelings. You make me sound like a little kid.... Jesus.

DENISE: Go ahead, Mom. Speak, explain...

CAROL: Okay it's—

R.J.: All right. I've heard enough. I'm in.

DENISE: Be quiet, R.J. I mean it. We need to hear her out. There's no way I'm gonna proceed with anything until I hear what she has to say. Okay?.. Well okay or not okay?!

R.J.: Whatever you say.

DENISE: Go ahead, Mom.

CAROL: I...ah...lost...my train of thought. I had it...then I lost it.... *(she begins to pace)* Okay okay it's coming back...

R.J.: *(whispering)* Denise...Denise?

DENISE holds a finger to her lips.

DENISE: Shush.

R.J.: But...something's wrong.... It's making a noise...

CAROL stops pacing. She and DENISE are both looking at R.J.

DENISE: What...kind of noise.

R.J.: Ah...I'm not sure.... Ticking? Hissing? ...A kind of hissing ticking noise.... So?

DENISE: I...don't know.

CAROL sits on the bed.

CAROL: Just because it's making a noise doesn't mean it's real.

R.J.: Maybe something's gone wrong with it.... Or...maybe it was set to go at midnight.... But maybe it's been re-set to go...sooner...

DENISE comes over to R.J. Bends over near his chest.

R.J.: Can you hear it.

DENISE: Yeah. Yeah I can.

CAROL: Can I listen.

R.J.: No.

DENISE starts to pace.

R.J.: Well?

DENISE: I'm thinking.

R.J.: I'm getting a little worried.... Maybe we should do something.

CAROL: Do you want to know what I think we should do.

DENISE and R.J. look at CAROL. Long pause.

CAROL: Well do you or don't you.

Long pause.

CAROL: Come on. Let's not fall apart here. Do you want a solution to this or not.

Long pause.

CAROL: Jesus. Okay.... Let me know when you're ready.

She leans back on her arms. Blackout

Scene Four

DENISE is leaning against a wall. Staring at MICHAEL and R.J. who are sitting side by side on the bed. MICHAEL is wearing the same explosive device as R.J.

DENISE: *(to MICHAEL)* This is what you get for sticking your nose in other people's business.

MICHAEL: I thought I could help.

DENISE: Well...I guess you were wrong.

MICHAEL: Yeah. But at the time it seemed like a good idea. I know Steamboat from before, so I thought I could intervene. You know...for Carol's sake. I guess going to the police is out of the question.

DENISE: Absolutely. We don't go to the police about anything in my family.

MICHAEL: Not even something...life threatening?

DENISE: Especially not something life threatening. It's better to die than let them get into a position where you owe them a favour. *(to R.J.)* Right?

R.J.: Definitely.

MICHAEL: Is that how your mother feels.

DENISE: In spades. It might be the only thing we agree about.

MICHAEL: Okay then.... Okay. No police. What ever...ah...happens.

DENISE: Did she ask you to go to Steamboat.

MICHAEL: No I took the initiative. I'm...I'm very fond of your mother. She's struck a cord in me. It's a very strong thing I'm feeling for her. It's not just sexual.

DENISE: Really.

MICHAEL: Well it's...mostly sexual, I guess. The joy and the freedom she expresses during intercourse is a really remarkable—

DENISE: Please. I don't need to hear this. Really.

MICHAEL: I'm sorry.... It's just that it's been a long time since I've experienced such—Well I make pornography so the sexual climate I'm used to isn't always happy and spontaneous.

DENISE: That's too bad...

MICHAEL: Yeah well—

DENISE: Listen, Michael no offence but could you shut up for a minute. You're giving me a headache.

R.J.: *(to MICHAEL)* She's worried.

MICHAEL: Yeah well I'm a bit worried myself. How about you?

R.J.: Listen, I'm not saying you get used to it or anything but I've had mine on for a few hours now and—

MICHAEL: What's that noise.

Silence.

R.J.: *(to DENISE)* He's hissing.

DENISE: Yeah well... *(she shrugs)*

R.J.: *(to MICHAEL)* I was hissing before. I stopped. I guess you'll stop too. I mean Carol wanted to fiddle with it. But we decided that was too risky.

MICHAEL: So it...just stopped on its own.

R.J.: Yeah.

MICHAEL: So it...doesn't mean anything then.

R.J.: I don't know if it means anything or not. All I'm saying is I stopped. Maybe you'll stop too.... Whether that's good in the long run who knows. Is it better to hiss then stop. Or is it better to keep hissing. Or is it better to have, you know...never hissed in the first place.

DENISE: Jesus.

R.J.: What.

DENISE: What are you talking about. Be quiet. You're talking like a fucking idiot.

R.J.: *(to MICHAEL)* She's worried. She loves me very much. She's only talking like that because she's worried.... I mean here we are in this dilemma. And it's outta her control. And when things get outta her control she doesn't know how to act.... She worries. And worrying isn't her thing really. Doing something is her thing. But in this situation what can you do? Not a hell of a lot. *(to DENISE)* Right?... *(to MICHAEL)* So she worries...and she gets, you know...insulting.

DENISE: Listen. Here's an idea. Let's see what's on the television.

R.J.: I don't want to watch television.

DENISE: Sure you do. You'd rather watch TV than talk like a fucking idiot. I know you would.

She turns it on.

DENISE: Sports?

R.J.: I told you I don't want to watch television.

DENISE: Sure you do.

She flicks.

DENISE: News?... Weather?...

She flicks.

R.J.: *(to MICHAEL)* As if I ever watched the fucking weather network.

DENISE: *(to MICHAEL)* He watches the fucking weather network all the time.

R.J.: I sometimes watch a weather *special.* I guess that makes me weak. I guess watching television to see what damage a particular hurricane has done to some poor little island somewhere is a weak boring thing to do.

DENISE: Hey. Look. A Lucy re-run.

R.J.: Not interested.

MICHAEL: You don't like Lucy?

R.J.: She's the best. No one can touch her.... I mean that's comedy with a capital C.... But I can't. She won't respect me if I do.

DENISE: Did I ever say that.

R.J.: I got the message.

DENISE: Did I ever say "Stop watching Lucy, it's not manly."

R.J.: I picked up on your attitude. I could feel you being down on me every time I laughed.... *(to MICHAEL)* You know, Lucy and Ethel would really get on a roll, the cookie dough would be all over the place, or everyone would be covered in wallpaper paste and I'd be roaring with laughter. And I could see her in the kitchen, frowning and shaking her head...Probably thinking to herself "What a goof".

DENISE: My mother did this, didn't she. All of it. She planted these seeds of doubt in your head. Just because I never got into situation comedy the way you did doesn't mean—

R.J.: It's something we could have shared!

DENISE: Ah Jesus.

R.J.: They're funny! We could have shared a lot of comic moments. Or we could have watched a lot of miniseries together and shared in the longing and the fears of a lot of really interesting characters.

DENISE: Please, what's wrong with you.

R.J.: And all those nature shows. There was never anyone sitting beside me to go…"ahh"…or "wow"…or "amazing" or anything. I felt deep…feelings for those animals, and I felt them alone.

DENISE: It's fucking television!

R.J.: It's fucking…better.

DENISE: Better than what!?

R.J.: Better than this!

DENISE: This is life!

R.J.: Life sucks!!

> *CAROL comes in. She looks a little better. Makeup is partially obscuring the bruises. She is dressed in a leather jacket, jeans, and sneakers.*

CAROL: Hey, what's with all the yelling…. You're attracting a crowd out there.

DENISE: It's…nothing.

CAROL: Going a little stir-crazy are we?

DENISE: No we're okay. We're great.

CAROL: R.J. for chrissake turn that thing off. What's wrong with you, watching TV at a time like this.

> *R.J. looks at DENISE. Goes to TV.*

R.J.: I'll turn down the volume.

CAROL: *(to MICHAEL)* How are you doing, Michael.

MICHAEL: Hanging' in.

CAROL: You sweet courageous man. *(to DENISE)* Do you believe the thing he did for us, Denise.

DENISE: For you, Mom. He did it for you.

CAROL: Whoever he did it for, it was an act of pure balls. A woman can usually only dream about balls like that.... Michael, I'm going to do something very special for you later. In repayment. Very special.

MICHAEL: Really?

CAROL: Oh yes.

DENISE: Mom. What about Murray Lawson. Did you meet him.

CAROL: I have some news to tell you about Murray. But there's something I'm not sure about. Were you close to him. I remember when you were young you were very fond of either Murray Lawson or his brother Eddie. I remember one of them used to let you ride the horses around the paddock. Who was that.

DENISE: That was Eddie.

CAROL: So you weren't particularly close to Murray.

DENISE: No.

CAROL: Okay then. He's dead. Steamboat Jeffries had him killed in a really brutal fashion. And I'm so upset that when I think about it I could almost go out of my goddamn mind with grief. Because…even though he apparently didn't mean shit to you, Murray Lawson was a dear friend of mine.

She sits.

DENISE: Where's the money.

CAROL: You're asking me about money at a time like this. What's wrong with you. Is that all you're going to ask me about. The money? Nothing else? Not how I'm feeling? Or how can you help me feel better?

DENISE: Did Steamboat get the money from Murray before he killed him or did Murray put the money someplace you might know about. Was the whereabouts of the money known only to Murray. Is the money gone. Can we get the money. Do you have the money on you. Can you send someone to pickup the money. Is there anyone who might know where the money is. Is there anyone we can ask for money. Is money the only thing we can give to Steamboat. If we can't give him the money now can we give him the money later. If we can't give him all the money can we give him some of the money. If he doesn't get the money, all the money, the money you and Murray stole from him, plus the money you made on the money you stole from him, will he blow us all up at midnight. Are we gonna die for money. Is money gonna kill us. Because you like to gamble money and fuck around with other people's money are we all gonna die. And if we die, if we all die, in a horrible explosion, will that be the only reason we ever lived, so that we could die because of money.... So? Well?...So!? Well!?

CAROL: I'm grieving here. I'm in pain here... You have to give me some space.

DENISE: So I guess you don't have the money.... Could you just take the time, put your grief on hold for just a minute, to confirm that.

CAROL: All right. I don't have the money.

DENISE: And you don't know where it is?

CAROL: No.

DENISE: But Steamboat doesn't have it. He didn't get it back.

CAROL: I called Steamboat, the murdering asshole, I gave him a piece of my mind. Yes I did. I expressed my emotions to him very clearly.

DENISE: And what did he say...about the money.

CAROL: The money is still an issue.

DENISE: Which means he doesn't have it.

CAROL: Well I don't know if he has it or not.... He said it's still an issue. I said what the fuck do you mean you fat puke. And he just laughed and hung up. So either he doesn't have it and it's still an issue, or he does have it and it's still an issue. Because maybe he doesn't think it's enough or maybe he wants to make examples of us or...I don't know.... Now can I return to my grief here.

DENISE: No. No you can't. We have to do something. We can't just wait around to get blown to bits. We have to devise a plan.... R.J. turn off that fucking television.

R.J.: You don't have to talk like that, Denise. I didn't turn it on in the first place.

DENISE: But you watched it didn't you. Oh you resisted at first. But eventually it sucked you in.

R.J.: Hey, Denise. I'm wired with explosives. A little diversion isn't a bad thing under the circumstances.

MICHAEL: It helped me.

DENISE: Turn it off.

R.J.: I'm going to turn it off.

DENISE: Turn it off now.

R.J.: I wanna wait 'til the commercial.

DENISE: Turn it off. It's driving me nuts.

R.J.: Really. Well don't blame me. You turned it on.

DENISE: And now I want it off!

R.J.: At the commercial!

DENISE: Now!

MICHAEL: Ah come on. Let him watch 'til the commercial. What's it hurting.

CAROL: Really, Denise. If you turned it on, the least you can do is let them watch until the friggin' commercial comes on.

DENISE: Stay out of this.

CAROL: I mean especially if it keeps them calm.

DENISE: I want it off!

CAROL: Because I've been thinking maybe those explosives are real. I didn't think Steamboat could kill. But he can. He can kill in horrible ways. So maybe we should rethink our opinion about those explosives. Maybe the odds have changed.... Maybe these guys really are gonna get blown up at midnight. And yeah maybe we're gonna die too.... All of us dead because of that vicious slob Steamboat Jeffries.... So maybe letting people watch the television until a commercial comes on is a small thing to agree to under the circumstances.

DENISE: Are you finished.

CAROL: Finished what.

DENISE: Finished talking.

CAROL: I don't know. What a thing to ask. Do I ever ask you that. You're allowed to talk when you want. Why not me.

DENISE: But...are you finished...for now.

CAROL: For now?...Yeah, I guess.

DENISE: Good. *(to R.J.)* How long to the commercial.

R.J.: I don't know.

MICHAEL: A few minutes?

R.J.: Yeah, maybe. But we don't know for sure. Because they sometimes schedule a—

DENISE: What I'm asking is how long until we can all get to work finding a way out of this rotten horrible terrifying mess we're in. I'm not really asking about the commercial, you know? Do you understand what I'm really asking. I guess what I'm really asking is how come that fucking television program is more important to you than your fucking life!

R.J.: Okay. Fuck it. You want it off.... *(he turns it off)* It's off.

Long pause.

R.J.: Okay so.... What now.

CAROL: I still think we should do something outrageous.... Some really ballsy outrageous thing and somehow stick it right in Steamboat Jeffries' big fat piggish face!

R.J.: Maybe the thing to do is for me to go and explode all over him. Just pop over to his place at three seconds to midnight and take him with me in the blast.... How about that Denise? Is that strong enough for you. Is that "manly" enough for you?

DENISE: *(to CAROL)* You're responsible for this, aren't you. This shit he's talking about me thinking he's too predictable and...boring or something.

CAROL: It's an old can of worms.

DENISE: What's that mean.

CAROL: You had concerns. Don't deny it.

DENISE: I thought he watched too much television for chrissake. Big deal.

CAROL: It goes deeper. Much deeper. It goes into the place where you really are who you are.

DENISE: Please. Shut up. Wait a minute. What did you just say.

CAROL: Me? I said that you—

DENISE: Not you. *(she points at R.J.)* You.

MICHAEL: Me?

DENISE: No not you. Him.

R.J.: Me?

DENISE: Yes yes! You! Yes!

R.J.: Ah...ah I—

DENISE: You said you wanted to explode on Steamboat Jeffries.

R.J.: I think I said something like you'd probably like me more if I exploded on him.

DENISE: Whatever. It was a good idea. Get up. Come on.... Come on. We're going.

R.J.: I'm not going anywhere with you until you apologize.

DENISE: Apologize for what?

R.J.: For the way you've been.

DENISE: For the way I've been about what.

R.J.: Things.

DENISE: What things.

R.J.: Forget it.

DENISE: Okay I'm...sorry.

R.J.: Sorry for what.

DENISE: Jesus.... Everything. I'm sorry. For everything. I'm sorry I insulted your television...habit. I'm sorry I haven't shared enough classic comedy moments with you. I'm sorry I don't know much about Lyla, that lion you love.... I'm sorry that you think that I think you're boring.... I'm sorry for all that but mostly I'm sorry that you tried to help get my mother out of a jam and you wound up as a human bomb. And that's the thing I'd sort of like to concentrate on at the moment.

R.J.: You didn't have to apologize for getting me to help your mother. I did that on my own. I like your mother. In spite of everything. You know that.

CAROL: That's what I always thought. I always figured we'd gotten pretty tight.... I don't know why the hell she had to apologize for helping me.... I mean forget the fact that I'm her friggin' mother.

DENISE: We gotta go.

CAROL: Who.

DENISE: We. Me and him.

CAROL: Not me?

DENISE: No! Not you. Me! And him!

CAROL: Okay. Calm down. I'm just asking.

DENISE: Stop asking. We gotta go! Come on.

R.J.: Okay. *(he stands)* Where.

DENISE: To Steamboat Jeffries' place. You're gonna explode on him.

R.J.: Yeah right. Is that your plan.

DENISE: Yeah. Come on.

R.J.: Are you kidding or what.

DENISE: Come on! We're running out of time.

> *She grabs him.*

R.J.: So. What. You're not kidding.

DENISE: Come on.

CAROL: Good luck.

DENISE: Thanks.

CAROL: I'd come too if I wasn't feeling so bad.

DENISE: Whatya mean. Is it your kidney. Are you in pain.

CAROL: No! I told you! I'm grieving. I'm grieving over the loss of my good friend Murray Lawson. Why the hell don't you ever listen to me!?

DENISE: See ya.

R.J.: Yeah. Here's hoping.

> *She grabs R.J. and they leave. Pause.*

CAROL: She's got a plan.

MICHAEL: You think so?

CAROL: Oh definitely. She's got a plan and the determination it requires to carry it out. She's amazing. Once she sets her mind to a task she goes full out.

MICHAEL: So you think everything's going to be okay.

> *CAROL shrugs.*

CAROL: I haven't got a clue…. *(she looks at her watch)* So…I forget. Did Steamboat tell you you were set to go off at midnight too.

MICHAEL: Yeah.

CAROL: That's a little over two hours from now.... In case you were wondering.

MICHAEL: Thanks.

CAROL: You look worried.... Listen. I still think there's a chance that thing is just a bluff.

MICHAEL: How good a chance.

CAROL: Well...he did kill Murray Lawson. I mean I didn't think the big prick had it in him. Really I didn't. But life is complex. Even at its darkest. Especially at its darkest. It's always full of surprises.

MICHAEL: Do you mind if I turn on the TV.

CAROL: Go ahead.

MICHAEL: It helps keep my mind off...you know...

He turns on the TV.

CAROL: Remember now. You've got a special thing coming to you.... I just have to finish my grieving process. It shouldn't take long. I'm just reliving a few special moments Murray and I shared. It's my way of making a tribute to him.

MICHAEL: Sure.... Ah listen. The police might be able to help us with this situation but your daughter wasn't too keen and I was just wondering—

CAROL: *(stands)* The kind of man I thought you were could never involve the police. He'd take the consequences of his actions anyway they were dished out. But he'd never go to the police.

MICHAEL: So you really do...think asking for help from the police is...bad.

CAROL: It fucking sucks! Going back years. Many many years. No one in my family has gone to the police about anything. We solve it ourselves. Or we die trying.... Are you losing that thing you have, honey. That special mixture of courage and sweetness. Is it deserting you.

MICHAEL: I...guess. A little.

CAROL: Maybe you just need a little re-edification.

She is running her fingers through his hair.

MICHAEL: Yeah. Maybe I do.

MICHAEL smiles. CAROL turns off the television. CAROL moves her body up against him.

CAROL: It's very very important to me that you stay brave. It gives me hope in a way.

MICHAEL: I'm...glad.

CAROL: I mean there you are possibly wrapped in high explosives. And yet you remain sweet-natured and courageous. If that isn't a victory over all the negative shit that goes on in this world, what is.... In some way, I take how you are and what we're about to do as a tribute to Murray Lawson. And a kick in the crotch to Steamboat Jeffries. When you and I crawl into bed and begin to have free wild uninhibited sexual intercourse while we both face imminent destruction it will be a blow for our side.... That's funny. A blow. I said a blow for our side... *(smiles)* Would you like a blow for our side, Michael.

MICHAEL: Yeah. I would.

CAROL: Okay then.

She pushes him back on the bed. Drops to her knees. Unbuckles his pants. Looks up to...heaven.

CAROL: This one's for you, Murray.

She unzips his fly. DENISE bursts into the room.

DENISE: Grieving? Grieving?... I must be outta my mind. I let you get away with that shit. "I'm grieving. I'm in grief"... Grief. Grieving. Gimme a fucking break. You've never grieved for anyone. You never grieved for your own mother.

CAROL: My mother was a callous slut. Murray Lawson was a dear devoted—

DENISE: You fucking liar.

CAROL: There she goes again with that fucking liar stuff.

DENISE: Look do me a favour. Zip that guy up and get off your knees. I'm trying to have a serious discussion with you here.

CAROL: *(zipping up MICHAEL)* Where's R.J.?

DENISE: He's out in the parking lot. Sitting in Steamboat Jeffries' Olds Cutlass.

CAROL: Holy shit. We better get outta here.... Michael. Pull up your pants.

MICHAEL: Okay.

DENISE: Michael stay where you are.

MICHAEL: Okay.

DENISE: Yeah ol' Steamboat grabbed us when we were leaving. At first I was in shock. I was scared. I was you know...very very scared. Then it hit me. Why is this guy here. Does he wanna be anywhere near this place if these explosives go off. Then I think, only if there's something he wants here, would he be here. And then something else hit me. The "grief" shit. So then I thought, she's pretending to grieve so that I'll believe Murray Lawson's really dead and that all that money's gone too. So I ask Steamboat "What part did Murray Lawson play in this?" And guess what Steamboat says. He says "Fuck all. Your mother did it on her own. I just found out Murray Lawson's been living down south for two years. And he hasn't been back, not once." So. Here I am. So do you have anything to tell me.

CAROL: I was just trying to—

DENISE: Why were you using Murray Lawson as a front for this thing. You even got a room in his name in that hotel. Why go to all that trouble.

CAROL: I was trying to—

DENISE: Why. For protection in some way? So they'd take you more seriously? Tell me!

CAROL: I'm trying to tell you for chrissake.... I was just trying to keep his memory alive. Murray *is* dead. Last year one of his horses had a heart attack and fell on him. So I used his name in one last scam, as a show of respect. And also as a reminder to myself that you gotta keep putting your life on the line because eventually some friggin' horse or something is gonna fall on you anyway. And then what. It's just you and the horse lying on the ground. And the horse is on top. Get it?

DENISE: No. Just give me the money.

CAROL: What money.

DENISE: Give me the money.

CAROL: What money.

DENISE: Give me the money. Go get your purse. Or your coat. Or whatever it is and get the money and give it to me.

CAROL: I don't have any money.

DENISE: Give it to me.

CAROL: No.

DENISE: Give it to me.

CAROL: No...I...can't.

DENISE: Give me the money now. Give me the money. Give it to me. Give it to me! Give it to me!! I want it. I want it now. Now fucking give it to me!!

CAROL: Okay, okay! Calm down. For chrissake. It's only money.

CAROL is getting her purse.

DENISE: You were willing to risk all our lives for sixty-eight thousand dollars.

CAROL: I figured it was a risk worth taking.

DENISE: It's only...sixty-eight thousand dollars.

CAROL: I could quadruple that at the track. I could turn that into half a million in a crap game.

DENISE: Hand it over.

CAROL: All of it.

DENISE: Yes.

CAROL: How about if I keep a little back.

DENISE: Steamboat has R.J. He wants all his money before he'll let him go. Hand it over.

CAROL: I hate doing this. Wait a minute. Think fast. Maybe there's some other course of action.

DENISE: Hand it over.

CAROL gives DENISE the money.

DENISE: Thanks, Mom. You're a pal. *(she holds it out to MICHAEL)* Here. Go out there and give this to Steamboat and he'll take that thing off you.

MICHAEL: I'm a bit embarrassed to stand up.... I have...an erection.... Your mother...is an incredibly exciting woman. I'm still hard.

DENISE: Did I need to know that. I don't think so!

MICHAEL: You would have noticed.

DENISE: No. I wouldn't. Now take the money out there to Steamboat. Come on.

MICHAEL: Okay...okay.

MICHAEL stands. His hands in front of his crotch. MICHAEL is leaving.

CAROL: Look at him. Isn't he sweet.

DENISE: Yeah. He's a peach.

MICHAEL leaves.

CAROL: I'm mad at you.

DENISE: You're mad at me? You scam us, me and R.J....just like we were a couple of assholes you met at the track. But you're mad at me.

CAROL: If you knew I had the money you would have made me give it back. Right?

DENISE: Yeah.

CAROL: I mean I understand your position. Your husband had explosives on him.

DENISE: Yeah. They're real by the way. Steamboat told me.

CAROL: I knew they were real.

DENISE: You did.

CAROL: Hey, was I born yesterday.

DENISE: You knew but you were willing to hold back the money anyway. I mean R.J. could have been blown to bits! Jesus!

CAROL: See? That's why I couldn't tell you. You get too emotional! Okay I understand. Faults and all you love the guy. But you gotta admit the two of you have gone a bit soft and timid. I mean really, don't you think that's true. Be honest.

DENISE: And you let us go off. You knew I was planning to do something desperate to Steamboat. Maybe threaten to let R.J. blow up in his face or something. But you let us go anyway.

CAROL: I thought it was a risk worth taking.

DENISE: Really? You really did? You really...think that way about life. Really.

CAROL: Yes. I do. If you don't take risks it's not worth shit. If you're not willing to—

DENISE: What, risk the life of someone you're supposed to love? Even that?

CAROL: Especially that. That's the real test.

DENISE: You're nuts. You're deceitful and you're nuts.

CAROL: Ah don't start. None of this would have happened if I felt I could level with you about the money. If I thought you still had...guts, I would have levelled with you. And together we could have found a way out that allowed us to keep the money. All of it. Every friggin' cent!...But hey, why hold a grudge. What good is that.

DENISE: That's big of you.

R.J. comes in. The explosives are gone.

DENISE: You okay?

R.J.: Yeah.... But he laughed. He was taking them off and he was laughing and saying shit like "I hope I know what I'm doing. We could both get blown up here. I'm new at this stuff... .You look scared. Are you gonna shit. You look like you're gonna shit...." What a rotten prick he is...

CAROL: The worst. He's the lowest of the low.

R.J.: You should talk. Putting us through this just for money.

CAROL: Hey what is this new-found contempt you two have for money. Seems to me there was a time you'd both do anything for money.

R.J.: Not anything.

CAROL: Anything.

R.J.: Not anything.

DENISE: He's right.

CAROL: Well that's not how I remember it.

DENISE: Well you remember it wrong.

R.J.: And you wonder why I watch shows about lions and snakes. Lions, snakes, crocodiles. The long-horned sheep.... None of them treat each other like this.... I mean I was wired to explode.... Imagine a long-horned sheep doing something like that to another...long-horned sheep... I need a shower.

He starts toward the bathroom.

DENISE: No let's get outta here. You can have one later.

R.J.: Can't wait.... And...Carol...ah...do you have any underwear I can borrow... Yes that's right. Steamboat was right... He was taking off those explosives and he was laughing and shaking and...I shit myself.... Okay? *(to DENISE)* I'm sorry.

DENISE: Sorry? For what.

R.J.: Hey. I shit myself.

DENISE: Big deal.

R.J.: You mean that?

DENISE: Yeah. So what. Who wouldn't under those circumstances. Go have your shower…. *(to CAROL)* Do you have any underwear for him.

CAROL: What makes you think my underwear will fit him.

R.J.: Well it's better than nothing.

CAROL: Why not just go without.

R.J.: Yeah…I could do that I guess.

He goes to the bathroom. Closes door.

CAROL: Don't you think it's weird that he wants to wear my underwear…. I mean….think about it.

DENISE: Don't start.

CAROL: Okay…. But don't try to convince me you're not just a bit put out by the fact that he messed his pants.

DENISE: Well I'm not.

CAROL: Oh it doesn't bother you at all. You don't just wonder a bit about his…his capacity to deal with difficult—

DENISE: Look. I mean it. Let it drop.

CAROL: Sure… I wonder how Michael's getting on.

She goes to the open door.

CAROL: Oh here he comes. He's fine. Hey look he's walking like he still has that erection…. I tell you. I've made a real impression on this guy.

DENISE sits on the bed. Puts her head in her hands.

DENISE: Great.

CAROL: I think I could make something with this guy. Some kind of relationship or something…. What do you think. Do you think just the fact that he adores me is enough to start a relationship with.

DENISE: Sure.

CAROL: Hey. What's wrong with you. Cheer up. I'm the one that lost the money. Cheer up.

DENISE: I don't wanna cheer up.

CAROL: Cheer up.

DENISE: No.

CAROL: Come on. Cheer up…. We're still pals, aren't we. Aren't we still pals.

DENISE: No. We're not.

CAROL: Yes we are.

DENISE: No we're not.

CAROL: I think we are.

DENISE lies back on the bed. Her arm over her eyes.

DENISE: Well we're not.

CAROL: Oh yes we are… Oh yes…we are.

DENISE groans. The shower gets turned on. MICHAEL appears at the door. Without explosives. One hand casually over his crotch. CAROL looks at his crotch. Smiles.

CAROL: *(to Denise)* Hey!

DENISE gets up on her elbows. CAROL gestures proudly to MICHAEL's crotch. DENISE groans. Collapses back down on the bed.
Blackout.

The End